THE
ONLY GUIDE
TO A
WINNING
INVESTMENT
STRATEGY
YOU'LL EVER NEED

Also by Larry E. Swedroe

The Successful Investor Today
Rational Investing in Irrational Times
What Wall Street Doesn't Want You to Know

THE
ONLY GUIDE
TO A
WINNING
INVESTMENT
STRATEGY
YOU'LL EVER NEED

THE NEW 2005 EDITION

◆

LARRY E. SWEDROE

◆

T·T

TRUMAN TALLEY BOOKS
ST. MARTIN'S PRESS
NEW YORK

www.stmartins.com

Library of Congress Cataloging-in-Publication Data

Swedroe, Larry E.
  The only guide to a winning investment strategy you'll ever need : index funds and
  beyond—the way smart money invests today / Larry E. Swedroe.
     p. cm.
  Originally published: New York : Truman Talley Books/Dutton, c1998.
  Includes bibliographical references (p. 311) and index (p. 315).
  ISBN 0-312-33987-9
  EAN 978-0312-33987-6
  1. Mutual funds. I. Title: Index funds and beyond. II. Title.

  HG4530.S894 2005
  332.63'27—dc22

                                                                         2004055369

First Revised and Updated Edition: January 2005

10 9 8 7 6 5 4 3 2 1

*This book is dedicated to
the memories of the greatest man I ever knew, my father,
Jerome David Swedroe,
and my beloved sister, Jayne Swedroe.*

Contents

Preface

Prior to 1996 I had spent my entire career either managing various types of financial risk, including interest rate, foreign exchange, and credit, or advising corporations on how to manage the same types of risk. In 1996 I joined Buckingham Asset Management (a registered investment advisor) and its affiliate BAM Advisor Services (a provider of asset management services that helps over one hundred advisory firms across the country serve their clients) as both a principal of the firm and its director of research because the firm's investment philosophy is based on what I strongly believed to be the winning investment strategy. Also important to me is that Buckingham is a fee-only advisor and therefore does not present the conflicts of interests with which commission-based advisors must deal.

My main role as director of research is to communicate to our clients (investors and other advisors) the principles of modern portfolio theory (MPT) and the efficient market hypothesis (EMH) upon which our investment philosophy is based. It is also my role to keep our clients advised of the latest academic research. However, my most important role is to help investors understand how to apply the principles of MPT and the EMH to their own unique circumstances and personalities so that they have the greatest chance of reaching their financial and life objectives.

Upon joining Buckingham, one of my first tasks was to find a book that would explain the principles of MPT in a simple way so that investors could find answers to these important questions:

- How do investors generally believe markets work?
- How do markets really work?
- How can you apply the knowledge of how markets really work to develop a winning game plan tailored to your unique situation?

Despite a thorough search, I could not find a book that fully addressed these three important issues. Most investment books promise spectacular results with easy-to-follow formulas. Unfortunately, none of those types of books stands up to scrutiny. I was searching for a book that did not promise instant wealth but instead provided the road map to a long-term winning investment strategy.

Since my search proved unsuccessful, in mid-1996 I set out to write such a book, one that would appeal not only to sophisticated investors, but also to intelligent investors with little or no knowledge of financial markets. The result of my efforts was the publication in May 1998 of *The Only Guide to a Winning Investment Strategy You'll Ever Need.* While explaining the principles of modern portfolio theory, it clearly laid out the case *against* active management and *for* passive management, and it explained why diversification is the winning strategy. The book also attempted to destroy many of the sacred cows of investing—the myths in which Wall Street and the media need you to believe in order for them to maximize their profits (at your expense). And, finally, it showed how to use this information to help you construct a portfolio unique to your personal circumstances. The book received very favorable reviews, including a strong endorsement from the *Wall Street Journal,* which included it among three 1998 books that, uncharacteristically, were "worth the paper they are printed on, and then some."[1]

In January 2001 my second book, *What Wall Street Doesn't Want You to Know,* was published. Like its predecessor, this book attempted to present the evidence on how markets have worked and the logic of why they should continue to operate in a similar manner in the future. It built on and extended the evidence in my first book, presenting the results of the latest academic research on financial markets as well as much of what I had learned since my first book was completed.

During my time as an investment advisor I have seen investors and advisors alike make a wide variety of mistakes in their investment decisions. I decided that I could help investors greatly improve the likelihood of achieving their financial objectives by writing a third book that would:

- Describe the many mistakes I have witnessed.
- Explain why they are mistakes.
- Explain why investors make them.
- Explain how to avoid them.

Rational Investing in Irrational Times was published in June 2002. As Oscar Wilde said: "Experience is the name everyone gives their mistakes." My hope was that investors would benefit from my experiences and thus avoid the many common mistakes investors make.

In September 2003 my fourth book, *The Successful Investor Today: 14 Simple Truths You Must Know When You Invest,* was published. It was written during the period of the greatest bear market of the post–World War II era. Millions of investors unnecessarily incurred trillions of dollars of losses because:

- They believed the investment myths of Wall Street, including, "This time it's different," and, "The price you pay for a great company doesn't matter."
- They were bamboozled by Wall Street's many conflicts of interest, such as between the investment banking arms of brokerage firms and the recommendations of their security analysts, ultimately leading to the destruction of their financial health.
- They were caught up in the hype and exuberance created by the media, particularly TV, which only wants to excite investors to grab their attention, not educate them.
- They wanted to believe there was easy money to be made.
- And, perhaps most important, most investors did not have the knowledge about how markets really work that would have allowed them to defend themselves against the heavily armed propaganda forces of the investment community.

My hope was that after reading this book investors would learn that if they had been armed with the knowledge of the *14 Simple Truths You Must Know When You Invest* and followed the commonsense advice contained within those truths, they would have been able to avoid the disastrous results that have devastated millions of investors.

Eight years have now passed since I sat down to write my first book. I have learned a great deal from my experiences as a financial advisor and director of research. In addition, since 1996 there has been a tremendous amount of new research on capital markets. There have also been financial innovations, providing investors with new passive investment vehicles that provide lower cost and more tax-efficient ways to play a winner's game. And there have also been major changes in the tax law that should be considered. With this in mind I felt it was time to update my original manuscript. While this updated edition provides a wealth of new material, one thing that has not changed is its basic message: While active investing (stock picking and market timing) provides the small hope of outperformance, the odds of success are so low that the prudent approach is to be a passive investor. It is the surest way to enable you to achieve your financial goals.

In summary, this revised and updated edition is about making you an informed and, therefore, better investor. In order to accomplish this objective, as well as to make it as entertaining as possible, the book is filled with analogies to cooking, gardening, sports, histories, movies, etc.—analogies that make difficult concepts easy to understand. I believe that this is why this book was so well received when it was first published.

Finally, I have greatly enjoyed the hundreds of e-mails and letters I have received over the years from readers of my books. If you have any questions about the book or how to implement the strategies recommended, please feel free to contact me at Buckingham Asset Management, 8182 Maryland Avenue, Suite 900, Clayton, Missouri 63105, or e-mail me at lswedroe@bamstl.com.

Introduction

On January 20, 1891, the first official game of basketball was played at the International YMCA in Springfield, Massachusetts. Each time a basket was scored, play was stopped while someone climbed a ladder to retrieve the basketball from the bottom of the peach basket. It was not until 1905, fourteen years later, that someone was smart enough to remove the bottom of the peach basket.

For decades individual investors have been trying to beat the market by either actively managing their own portfolios (picking individual stocks and/or timing the market) or investing in actively managed mutual funds. The vast majority have done so with about the same disappointing results that the Brooklyn Dodgers had when they faced their archrivals, the New York Yankees, in the World Series. The rallying cry of the Dodger fans, "Wait until next year," has been adopted by active managers who fail to outperform their benchmarks because "it wasn't a stock picker's kind of year." The problem for both the Dodger fans and active managers is that "next year" has rarely delivered their hearts' desire.

In 1990 the Nobel Prize in economics was awarded to three economists for their contributions to the body of work known as MPT. This theory presented every investor with a way to win the investment game without really trying. In fact MPT has demonstrated that efforts to beat the market are not only nonproductive, they are highly likely to prove counterproductive because of the expenses and taxes that are generated by the practice of active management. The only likely winners in the game of active management are the Wall Street firms that generate commissions, the publications that offer "expert" advice, and Uncle Sam, who collects more taxes. MPT demonstrated that all investors can have a positive investment experience if they adopt the strategy known as passive asset-class investing.

Unfortunately, the media in America have a great effect on the behavior of individuals. While you rarely find in the press or hear over the airwaves a story on the death of a single individual in an automobile accident, every form of media will cover, as a lead, or as a front page story, a plane crash that kills hundreds. This phenomenon may be the main reason so many people are afraid to fly when all the statistics show that it is far safer to fly than to drive. Similarly, the media are often filled with warnings from so-called financial experts that the market is overvalued. These warnings often cause investors to panic and sell or delay investing available funds despite the overwhelming evidence that market timing is far more dangerous to your financial health than is a buy, hold, and rebalance strategy. While investing in equities is *always* risky, even if your investment horizon is a very long one, the longer the investment horizon, the more likely it is that stocks will earn what is called a risk premium—they will outperform riskless instruments such as Treasury bills.

It has now been fourteen years since the awarding of that Nobel Prize in economics, and many investors are still climbing the ladder to retrieve the ball from the peach basket. While many sophisticated institutional investors have adopted passive asset-class investing, the vast majority of individual investors are still trying to beat the market through active management strategies. However, as the financial press continues to report on the failure of active management strategies, the tide is starting to turn. As recently as 1994 only 3 percent of individual investors inflows into mutual funds went into index funds.[1] By 1999 almost 40 percent of net new investments were going into index funds.[2] Investors had obviously noticed the poor performance of active managers relative to their benchmarks. By 2002 an S&P survey found that there was over $900 billion in assets placed in S&P Index–linked products alone (this does not include assets indexed to other benchmarks such as the Wilshire, Russell, and MSCI [Morgan Stanley Capital International] Indices). And while this was down 15 percent from the prior year, the falloff was less than the 23 percent drop in the market—indicating that there was a net inflow into these index-related securities.[3]

This book provides you with a road map that will hopefully shorten the fourteen-year journey (the time it took before they removed the bottom of the peach basket) to the winning strategy that is staring investors right in the face. Following this road map will make you a better informed and therefore more effective investor. Part 1 describes how and why individuals invest in active strategies. It also provides the evidence on why those strategies are called the loser's game. Part 2 describes the foundation of MPT, in other words, how markets really work. The remainder of the book is our "TripTik®" to implementing the winning strategy in a way that will meet your ability, willingness, and, perhaps most important, need to take risk. The choice is yours. You can invest according to theories that led to a Nobel Prize in economics and been deemed as the prudent approach by the American Law Institute, or you can continue to climb the ladder to the top of the peach basket by actively managing your portfolio and/or investing in actively managed mutual funds.

Having described the contents of the book, the following analogy will provide you with an easy way to relate to some of its concepts and help you find the way to the winning strategy.

At a tennis clinic I learned something that not only dramatically improved my tennis game but also provided me with an insight about games in general.

After making what I thought was a great shot, a forehand that landed right in the backhand corner of my opponent, my teaching pro said, "That shot will be your worst enemy." While it was an exceptional shot, he explained, it was not a high-percentage shot for a good "weekend player." Remembering how good that shot felt, I would try to repeat it. Unfortunately, I would be successful on a very infrequent basis. The pro asked me if I wanted to make great shots or would I rather win matches? (I thought that one was the cause of the other.)

The pro explained that in the game played by weekend warriors such as myself, most points are not determined by successfully hitting the rare, low-percentage shot. Instead, the vast majority of points are lost when balls are hit into the net, long, or beyond the lines, in a failed attempt to hit those exceptional winning shots. That is why this type of strategy produces what is called a loser's game. It is important to note that it is not the *people* who play the game who are losers; instead it is the *strategy* they are following that is a losing one.

In order to improve my results, the teaching pro told me that all I had to do was to understand the game I was playing. Since, unlike professional tennis players, I am certainly not capable of consistently hitting winning shots, I was playing a loser's game. Instead of trying to hit winners (and end up hitting the ball long, wide, or into the net), I should just try to hit the ball safely back, with a bit of pace, and utilize the middle of the court. Let the opponent play the loser's game. Recognizing the brilliance of his insight, I immediately put his advice to work, with astonishingly good results. I was now regularly beating players with whom I had previously experienced difficulty.

What does tennis have to do with investing? Simply this: Like any game, consistently successful investing requires a successful strategy. The vast majority of individual investors (and unfortunately even most professionals) try to beat the market. They do so by attempting to uncover individual securities they believe the rest of the market has somehow mispriced (the price is too high or too low). They also try to time their investment decisions so that they are buying when the market is "undervalued" and selling when it is "overvalued." Such a strategy is known as active portfolio management. Occasionally, with the same infrequent timing of my great tennis shots, these active portfolio managers will make the proverbial killing. On the other hand, over the long run, the great likelihood is that they will lose more often than they will win. Just as in loser's tennis, the only way to be a successful investor is not to play the loser's game. If you begin with an open mind, you will conclude that active management is the loser's game. If you decide to play the loser's game, the only people you will likely be enriching are your broker; the manager of the actively managed mutual fund or portfolio in which you are investing; and the publisher of the newsletter, magazine, or ratings service to which you are subscribing.

In this book you will see that there is an alternative strategy to the loser's game, one that the most sophisticated investors use—it is estimated that as much as 40 percent of institutional funds are invested passively, by 2003 exceeding over $3 trillion.[4] It is based on over fifty years of research by the world's leading financial economists, which culminated in the awarding of the Nobel Prize in economics in 1990 to Harry Markowitz, Merton Miller, and William Sharpe.

This book will provide the skills necessary for you to play the winner's game. Applying this strategy will require three commitments on your part:

- You must be willing to be patient with your portfolio. The financial markets are volatile. The longer the time horizon, however, the more confident you can be that the expected outcome will occur (of course, the opposite is also true).

- You must have confidence in your strategy so that you will have the discipline to stick with the approach throughout the inevitable bad days. A well-thought-out investment plan is only a necessary condition for successful investing. The sufficient condition is the discipline to stay the course. All too often emotions cause even the best of plans to end up in the trash heap.

- You will need the courage to ignore what I call the investment pandering put out by Wall Street firms, trade publications, and market gurus. Investment manager and author Nassim Nicholas Taleb put it this way: "Prominent media journalism is a thoughtless process of providing the noise that can capture people's attention."[5]

Much of what you will read in this book directly contradicts conventional wisdom—ideas that have become so ingrained that very few question them. I am confident, however, that if you keep an open mind you will find the evidence presented here so overwhelming that you will be convinced of its accuracy. Remember, "The earth is flat" was once conventional wisdom. Legends do die hard—especially when there is an establishment in whose interest it is to perpetuate the legend.

I am also confident that you will acquire the essential knowledge you need to win the investment game, beat the vast majority of professional money managers, and sleep well while achieving your financial objectives.

Thanks for coming along, and I hope you enjoy the ride.

THE
ONLY GUIDE
TO A
WINNING
INVESTMENT
STRATEGY
YOU'LL EVER NEED

PART ONE

◆

The Loser's Game:
The Game Wall Street Wants and Needs You to Play

Like everybody else in this industry I have an ego large enough to believe I'm going to be one of the select few that will outperform. —George Sauter, Vanguard Group

The investment business is, by definition, a business of hope. Everyone hopes that he can beat the market, even if few people actually can. —Avi Nachmany

A fool and his money are soon parted. —Arthur Zeikel

It must be apparent to intelligent investors that if anyone possessed the ability to do so [forecast the immediate trend of stock prices] consistently and accurately he would become a billionaire so quickly he would not find it necessary to sell his stock market guesses to the general public.
—Weekly staff letter, August 27, 1951, David L. Babson & Company, quoted in Charles Ellis, *The Investor's Anthology*

Every reasonable effort should be made to disabuse the public of the unwarranted and erroneous yet widespread belief that competent investment management is largely a matter of anticipating stock-market movements.
—Henry Dunn, Scudder, Stevens and Clark

One of the funny things about the stock market, every time one is buying another is selling, and both think they are astute.
—William Feather

The people on Wall Street simply can't imagine how they would make a living if they weren't trying to beat the market. But that's their problem, not yours. It's not your responsibility to provide livelihoods for stock analysts. What's rational on Wall Street isn't usually aligned with the best interests of you as an investor.
—Paul Samuelson

CHAPTER 1

♦

Why Individual Investors Play the Loser's Game

The most costly of all follies is to believe in the palpably not true. —H.L. Mencken

It is undesirable to believe a proposition when there is no ground whatever for supposing it true. —Bertrand Russell

For of all sad words of tongue or pen / The saddest are these: "It might have been." —Whittier, "Maud Muller"

Galileo was an Italian astronomer who lived in the sixteenth and seventeenth centuries. He spent the last eight years of his life under house arrest, ordered by the church for committing the "crime" of believing in and teaching the doctrines of Copernicus. Galileo's conflict with the church arose because he was fighting the accepted church doctrine that the Earth was the center of the universe. Ptolemy, a Greek astronomer, had proposed this theory in the second century. It went unchallenged until 1530 when Copernicus published his major work, *On the Revolution of Celestial Spheres,* which stated that the Earth rotated around the Sun rather than the other way around.

History is filled with people clinging to the infallibility of an idea even when there is an overwhelming body of evidence to suggest that the idea has no basis in reality—particularly when a powerful establishment finds it in its interest to resist change. In Galileo's case, the establishment was the church. In the case of the belief in active management, the establishment is comprised of Wall Street, most of the mutual-fund industry, and the publications that cover the financial markets. All of them would make far less money if investors were fully aware of the failure of active management.

Most investors, investment advisors, and portfolio managers engage in active management of their investment portfolios. They try to select individual stocks they believe will outperform the market. They also try to time their investment decisions by increasing their stock investments when they believe the market will rise and decreasing them when they believe the market will fall. These investors, advisors, and portfolio managers attempt to beat the market through active management strategies despite an overwhelming body of academic evidence that has demonstrated that the vast majority of returns of a diversified portfolio of securities is explained by investment policy (asset allocation). The evidence is that only a very small percent of returns is explained by active management—individual stock selection (attempts to find mispriced securities) and timing the market decisions (shifting assets into and out of the market or between asset classes). For example, a study of the ten-year performance (period ending March 31, 1998) of ninety-four balanced mutual funds and the five-year performance of fifty-nine pension plans found that about 100 percent of the level of returns is explained by asset allocation. The conclusion was that, on average, active management added no value above the level of return that could be expected from passive management.[1]

Asset allocation is the process of determining what percentage of your assets are allocated, or dedicated, to various specific asset classes. An asset class is a group of assets with similar risk characteristics. Asset classes can be as broad as fixed income or equities. Alternatively, they can be more narrowly defined. Fixed income

4

can be divided into short term and long term. Equities can be divided into such categories as small companies and large companies. They can also be split into categories such as growth companies or value companies (a term we will fully explore later). They can even be more narrowly defined into such categories as small-value and large-value companies. Adding the broad category of domestic versus international, one ends up with such categories as U.S. small value and international large value. As was stated earlier, academic research has determined that investor decisions about the allocation of assets among available asset classes (what is referred to as investment policy) are by far the major determinant of the risk and the returns of a diversified portfolio of securities.

Considering that one academic study after another has demonstrated that well over 90 percent of returns are determined by asset-allocation decisions, one has to wonder exactly why individual investors and the majority of professional money managers spend virtually all of their time trying to pick stocks and time the market. We will shortly examine the causes of this peculiar behavior.

If you had a heart condition and your doctor offered you a choice between two drugs, an old drug with say a 5 percent chance of success or a new drug with a 95 percent chance of success, which would you choose? What would you say if I told you that you can get the 95 percent solution for your investments, and that this solution is the result of over fifty years of academic research, which culminated in the awarding of the 1990 Nobel Prize in economics to three of the main contributors to the body of work known as MPT? What would you say if I told you that you could increase returns and reduce risk at the same time? Would you be surprised if I told you that the solution did not require a degree in financial economics and that it was based on a commonsense approach that every investor could understand? However, given the availability of the 95 percent solution, we are confronted with the enigma that the majority of investors choose the 5 percent solution, active portfolio management. I believe that there are several cultural phenomena contributing to this peculiar behavior.

The Black Hole of Knowledge

Most Americans, having taken a biology course in high school, know more about amoebas than they do about investing. Despite its obvious importance to every individual, our education system almost totally ignores the field of finance and investments. This is true unless you go to an undergraduate business school or pursue an M.B.A. in finance. My daughter is a senior in an excellent high school, and she is graduating very close to the top of her class. Having taken a biology course, she can tell you all you would ever need to know about amoebas. She could not, however, tell you the first thing about how financial markets work.

Just as nature abhors a vacuum, Wall Street rushes in to fill the void. Investors, lacking the protection of knowledge, are susceptible to all the advertising, hype, and sales pressure that the investment establishment is capable of putting out. The problem with this hype is that, in general, the only people who are actually enriched are part of the investment establishment itself. As you will discover, the vast majority of investment firms, mutual funds, and individual investors consistently underperform the Standard & Poor (S&P) 500 Index. This index is made up of the stocks of five hundred of the largest U.S. companies (hence the name "S&P 500"). It is often considered a proxy for the market itself. It is, therefore, the most often used benchmark against which the performance of active managers is judged.

One well-known Wall Street advisor, Robert Stovall, when asked about Wall Street's underperformance, responded: "It's just not true that you can't beat the market. Every year about one-third of the fund managers do it." He then quickly added, "Of course, each year it is a different group."[2] Amazing! How is the average investor to know which group of fund managers will succeed? The lack of persistence of outperformance is one reason why mutual funds have been created to mimic the performance of the S&P 500 Index and other indices as well. For obvious reasons, such funds are called index funds.

Hard Work *Should* Produce Superior Results

A second factor in this behavioral dilemma is the great faith in the Protestant work ethic. To quote my ex-boss, an otherwise intelligent and rational man: "Diligence, hard work, research, and intelligence just have to pay off in superior results. How can no management be better than professional management?" The problem with this thought process is that while these statements are correct generalizations, efforts to beat the market are an exception to the rule. If hard work and diligence always produce superior results, how do you account for the failure of the vast majority of professional money managers (in all likelihood all bright, intelligent, capable, hard-working individuals) to beat the market year in and year out? In the face of all this evidence, they continue to give it the old college try. The lesson: Never confuse efforts with results. As you will see, hard work is unlikely to produce superior results because the markets are efficient.

Behavioral Finance

When the vast majority of active managers underperform their respective indexes, why do individual investors continue to place the vast majority of their funds with active managers? Richard Thaler, an economist at the University of Chicago, an advocate of "behavioral finance," attributed this behavior to overconfidence. "If you ask people a question like, How do you rate your ability to get along with people? Ninety percent think they're above average. Ninety percent of all investors also think that they're above average at picking money managers."[3]

Prof. Richard Thaler and Robert J. Shiller, an economics professor at Yale, noted that "individual investors and money managers persist in their belief that they are endowed with more and better information than others and that they can profit by picking stocks. While sobering experiences sometimes help those who delude themselves, the tendency to overconfidence is apparently just one of the limitations of the human mind."[4] This insight helps explain why individual investors think they can identify the few active managers who will beat their respective benchmarks.

There are other behavioral reasons why investors choose active managers. For example, many investors feel that by not selecting an actively managed fund they give up the chance of being above average, and the vast majority think they can at least do better than that. When asked whether fund managers were also overconfident, Thaler responded: "All fund managers think they're above-average money managers. Active fund managers can't believe that markets are efficient. Otherwise they would have no reason for existing."[5]

Individuals also like to be able to blame active managers when they underperform yet be able to take credit for choosing the active managers who happen to outperform the market. Another explanation for choosing actively managed funds is that people often feel a sense of loss of control if they invest in passive investment vehicles. Individuals fail to understand that passive investors have total control over the most important determinant of risk and returns—the asset-allocation decision. Once an investor turns over control to an active manager, they actually lose control as the active manager is now at the helm, making decisions on market timing and asset selection.

Playing the Market

Another reason Americans choose the 5 percent solution, curiously almost in opposition to the work ethic reason, is that they love to gamble. Americans love lotteries, Las Vegas, wagering on sporting events, and so on. That is why you hear the term "play the market." Serious investors never play the market; they invest in the market. Serious investors do not care that a passive strategy (buy and hold the market) is boring. They do not look for markets to provide them with excitement. Instead, they look for markets to produce returns commensurate with the amount of risk taken. Serious investors follow the advice of Girolamo Cardano, a sixteenth-century physician, mathematician, and quintessential Renaissance man, who said: "The greatest advantage from gambling comes from not playing at all."[6]

The Gambler's Fallacy

Investors also fall prey to what is known as the gambler's fallacy, the idea that winners ride "hot streaks." Of course, there is no proof of that idea, either in gambling or investing. As proof that selecting mutual funds that beat the market is not the winner's game, Mark Hulbert, publisher of the *Hulbert Financial Digest,* a newsletter that tracks the performance of investment newsletters, put together a portfolio of "market beaters." He chose managers who had managed to beat the market in the preceding year. That portfolio earned a 99 percent return over the next fifteen years. Not a bad return, except for the fact that a portfolio of "market losers," those funds that lagged the market in the previous year, returned 350 percent over the same period. In contrast to these seemingly impressive returns, the stock market as a whole rose about 600 percent over the same period.[7] Belief in "hot streaks" leads to the mistake of confusing *luck* and *skill.*

The Cocktail Party Syndrome

Finally, many investors choose the 5 percent solution so that they will have a great cocktail party story to tell, boasting about their great investments. Of course, you never hear about investments that did not turn out well.

There is a winning strategy to outfox the loser's game of trying to select individual "undervalued" securities or trying to time the market. It is the same strategy that is the winner's game in tennis: choose not to play the loser's game.

10

CHAPTER 2

◆

Active Portfolio Management
Is a Loser's Game

*The value of an idea has nothing to do with the sincerity of
the person expressing it.*   —Oscar Wilde

An idea is not responsible for the people who believe in it.
                                          —Don Marquis

All great ideas are controversial, or have been at one time.
                                          —George Seldes

No matter how thin you slice it, it's still baloney.
                                          —Alfred E. Smith

*For better or worse, then, the US economy probably has to
regard the death of equities as a near-permanent condition.*
                    —*BusinessWeek,* August 13, 1979, with the
                    Dow Jones Industrial Average (DJIA) at 875.26

In building their investment portfolios most investors pursue
one or more of the following alternative strategies:

- They select individual stocks based on their own research,
  advice from a broker, or on a "hot tip" from a friend.
- They choose mutual funds based upon their past performance, particularly chasing the hot money managers.
- They rely on the recommendations of trade publications
  such as *Forbes, Money, SmartMoney, Worth,* and the *Wall
  Street Journal.*

- They rely on the advice gleaned from newsletters to which they subscribe or "market gurus" who appear on CNBC and elsewhere, including the Internet.
- They rely on fund ratings by such services as Morningstar, which rates funds using a star system similar to the one used by film critics.

We will explore each of these strategies in this chapter, plus some additional insights regarding the weaknesses inherent in an active management approach.

Individual Stock Selection

Bull market: An upward movement in prices causing an investor to mistake himself for a financial genius.
—Anonymous

Investors attribute successes to their own brilliance, and they attribute failures to bad luck. If you keep doing that, at the end of the day you think you're a genius. —Nicholas Barberis

Brad Barber, Professor of finance at the University of California, Davis, and Terrance Odean, Associate Professor of finance at the University of California, Davis, studied the performance of individual investors by examining over one hundred thousand trades covering the period 1987–93. Their conclusion: Individual investors aren't as bad at stock picking as many people think. They're worse! The study found that stocks individual investors buy *trail* the overall market and stocks they sell *beat* the market after the sale. The longer the time span the study covered, the more their performance trailed the market. Investors shot themselves in the foot with their trades even before taking into account the transaction fees and taxes they paid for the privilege of "playing the market." These costs would further depress trading performance. The authors concluded: Individuals shouldn't be trying to pick stocks. They further stated that investors probably don't realize just how badly they are doing. Since they were trading in a rising market, their portfolios generally showed gains. Unfortunately, the time and money they spent trying to pick stocks cut into their profits instead of enhancing them.[1]

In another study Barber and Odean found that the more investors traded, the worse the results (except, of course, for the wallets of their brokers). The conclusion we can draw is that there is an inverse correlation between confidence and performance—the more confident one is in his/her ability to either identify mispriced securities or time the market, the worse the results.[2] In studying men versus women, they found that although the stock selections of women do not outperform those of men, women produce higher net returns due to lower turnover (lower trading costs). Also, married men outperform single men.[3] The obvious explanation is that single men do not have the benefit of their spouse's sage counsel to temper their own overconfidence. It appears that a common characteristic of human behavior is that, on average, men have confidence in skills they don't have while women simply know better.

Barber and Odean also studied the performance of investment clubs. The study, "Too Many Cooks Spoil the Profit: The Performance of Investment Clubs," covered 166 investment clubs using data from a large brokerage house, from February 1991 to January 1997.[4] They found that the average club lagged a broad market index by 3.8 percent per annum, returning 14.1 percent versus 17.9 percent. After adjusting for the fact that the clubs tended to buy riskier stocks, the underperformance on a risk-adjusted basis increased to 4.4 percent per annum.

Relying on Past Performance

Even if you identify the managers who have good past performance, there's no guarantee that they'll have good future performance. —George Sauter, Vanguard Group

Yesterday's masters of the universe are today's cosmic dust.
—Alan Abelson and Rhonda Brammer,
Barron's, October 5, 1998

I own last year's top performing funds. Unfortunately, I bought them this year. —Anonymous

If picking stocks is a random walk down Wall Street, as Princeton economist Burton Malkiel famously put it, then picking mutual funds is an obstacle course through Hell's Kitchen. —Robert Barker, reporter for *BusinessWeek*

One of the strongest pieces of conventional wisdom about investment performance is that the past performance of investment managers is prologue to future performance. The logic is sound enough. For example, when a business seeks to hire a new executive, it will look at candidates who have clearly demonstrated the skills necessary to do the job. Unfortunately, as we have seen, just because something is conventional wisdom doesn't make it correct. In addition, what works in one paradigm might not work in another. The following is a powerful example of the fallacy of relying on past performance of active fund managers.

Relying on the Micropal database, Dimensional Fund Advisors (DFA) studied the performance of the top thirty funds for successive five-year periods beginning in 1971 and then compared their performance against that of the S&P 500 Index through 2002. Here is what they found:[5]

- The top thirty funds from 1971 through 1975 did manage to outperform the index by 0.67 percent per annum.

- The top thirty funds from 1976 through 1980 went on to underperform by 2.37 percent per annum.

- The top thirty funds from 1981 through 1985 went on to underperform by 1.79 percent per annum.

- The top thirty funds from 1986 through 1990 went on to underperform by 0.68 percent per annum.

- The top thirty funds from 1991 through 1995 went on to underperform by 4.84 percent per annum.

- The top thirty funds from 1996 through 2000 went on to underperform by 5.68 percent per annum.

In only one case did the top performers from one five-year period continue to outperform, and the outperformance was less than 1 percent per annum. In the five other cases, underperformance of the top funds averaged in excess of 3 percent per annum and in one case approached 6 percent per annum.

As *Fortune* magazine put it: "Despite the solemn import that fund companies attribute to past performance, there's no evidence that the 4 percent who beat the index owe their record to anything other than random statistical variation. The whole industry is built up around a certain degree of black magic." *Fortune* concluded: "Despite volumes of research attesting to the meaninglessness of past returns, most investors (and personal finance magazines) seek tomorrow's winners among yesterday's. Forget it. The truth is, much as you wish you could know which funds will be hot, you can't—and neither can the legions of advisers and publications that claim they can."[6] Despite being the very same magazine that glorifies the latest hot-fund manager, they added in another issue: "We have learned that past investment records make lousy crystal balls."[7]

Even Salomon Smith Barney, which heavily advertises performance when a fund of theirs has done well in the recent past, had this to say: "One of the most common investor mistakes is choosing an investment management firm or mutual fund based on recent top performance." Their own study on past performance, covering the full spectrum of investment styles, from large cap to small cap, value to growth, and domestic to international, found: "The investment returns of top quintile managers tended to plunge precipitously while the returns of bottom quintile managers tended to rise dramatically."[8]

Listen carefully to the following words of wisdom on using past performance of money managers to predict their future performance.

- Charles Ellis, who has served as president of the Institute of Chartered Financial Analysts for over twenty years and has taught finance at Harvard Business School, Yale, and several other institutions. "In investment performance, the past is not prologue."[9]

- John Bogle, founder of Vanguard: "No matter where we look, the message of history is clear. Selecting funds that will significantly exceed market returns, a search in which hope springs eternal and in which past performance has proven of virtually no predictive value, is a loser's game."[10]

It seems that Wall Street has something in common with Hollywood—sequels are rarely as good as the originals. Thus relying on the past performance of actively managed funds has proven to be an unreliable indicator of their future performance. You might as well flip a coin or consult your horoscope.

Chasing the Hot-Fund Manager

The following is one of my favorite stories about investors believing in both past performance predicting future results and "riding the hot hand." On January 1, 1996, the Van Wagoner Emerging Growth Fund opened its doors to new investors. By late May the net asset value of the fund had risen an incredible 61 percent for any investor lucky enough to have invested on day one.

Unfortunately, most investors in this fund were not so fortunate. Having posted such impressive returns, the fund received a tidal wave of new money. By July 24 the fund's asset base had grown dramatically, but the net asset value of the fund was now only 23 percent above where it had started. Because the fund was so much larger, the May–July decline "not only burned through $90 million in net profits that shareholders had accumulated in the first five months, it also added $80 million in losses. Not surprisingly, investors headed for the exits."[11]

Admittedly, the above tale is based on results of chasing a fund that had a very short track record of outperformance. To demonstrate that even very long periods of superior results cannot be relied on as predictors of future performance, the following two examples are presented. For each of the eleven years from 1974 through 1984 the Lindner Large-Cap Fund outperformed the S&P 500 Index.[12] How were investors rewarded if they waited eleven years to be sure that they had found a true genius and then invested in the fund? Over the next eighteen years, the S&P 500 Index returned 12.6 percent. Believers in past performance as a prologue to future performance were rewarded by their faith in the Lindner Large-Cap Fund with returns of just 4.1 percent, an underperformance of over 8 percent per annum for eighteen years. After outperforming for eleven years in a row, the Lindner

Large-Cap Fund managed to beat the S&P 500 Index in just four of the next eighteen years, and none of the last nine—quite a price to pay for belief in a discredited theory.

Next we consider the case of David Baker and the 44 Wall Street Fund. Baker even outperformed the legendary Magellan Fund over the entire decade of the 1970s and was the top-performing diversified U.S. stock fund of the decade. Unfortunately, 44 Wall Street ranked as the single worst-performing fund of the 1980s, losing 73 percent.[13] During the same period, the S&P 500 Index grew at 17.5 percent per annum. Each dollar invested in Baker's fund fell in value to just twenty-seven cents. On the other hand, each dollar invested in the S&P 500 Index would have grown to just over $5. The fund did so poorly that in 1993 it was merged into the 44 Wall Street Equity Fund, which was then merged into the Matterhorn Growth Fund Income in 1996.

Relying on Trade Publications

I call much of the output of Wall Street and the trade publications that cover the financial markets "investment pandering." You may be wondering what pandering has to do with the world of investments. A panderer caters to or profits from the weakness or vices of others. The panderer titillates, stimulates, and excites people into action. The roller-coaster swing of opinions that come from Wall Street, the media, and the trade publications covering the industry reflects attempts to do just that. Pandering is also exploitative; the investment community is exploiting the individual investor's lack of knowledge. That is why I find "investment pandering" an accurate as well as descriptive term for much of what passes as expert advice. Jane Bryant Quinn, the highly regarded, nationally syndicated columnist goes even further than I do. She writes: "Americans are indulging themselves in investment porn. Shameless stories about performance tickle our prurient financial interest." Then she writes: "Mainline magazines (like *Money, SmartMoney,* and *Worth*) . . . rarely descend to hard-core porn. That is what you get from the greedy gurus on cable TV, or the cruising shysters on the Internet. Senator James Exon is wasting his talents trying to vaporize Internet sex. Let him go after the schmucks who molest your pocketbook by hyping stocks online."

Quinn adds: "We in the quality-media crowd specialize in soft-core porn. . . . *The porn test isn't the headline, but whether the story is anchored in reality.* [Emphasis mine]" And she concludes: "In this tough and competitive marketplace (of personal finance magazines) publications that merely dispense information will see their readers melt away. Investors want action . . . they want to peep."[14]

Merton Miller, a Nobel Laureate, in an interview with *Barron's* was asked: "What advice would you give the average investor?" His response: "Don't quote me on this, but I'd say don't read *Barron's*." He continued, ". . . because it will only tease you about investment opportunities that you'd best avoid."[15]

Let's examine why much of the output of Wall Street and the media deserves the term investment pandering.

Money Talks, Investors Walk

Many investors get their investment advice from popular trade magazines. They believe that these publications somehow can provide them with the secret to outperforming the market. While the data is a bit old, the story is so compelling that it must be told.

Salomon Smith Barney Consulting Group studied the performance of *Money*'s buy and sell recommendations for the period 1990–94. For the period their buy recommendations produced a cumulative return of minus 4 percent. *Money*'s buy recommendations managed to underperform the S&P 500 Index by a cumulative 55 percent. As sad a story as that is, if an investor had purchased their sell recommendations instead of their buy recommendations he/she would have earned a cumulative 95 percent. The sells recommendations outperformed the buy recommendations by a cumulative 99 percent over the five-year period and even outperformed the market by a cumulative 44 percent.[16]

While trade publications know that editions that tout the "10 Best Stocks" or the "10 Best Funds" to buy generate greater sales than any other headline, you virtually never hear of a publication holding itself accountable by publishing the results of those recommendations. The woeful tale of *Money*'s selections is just one example of why you rarely see after-the-fact reporting of results.

The following tale is one of the rare exceptions of a publication holding itself accountable.

The Class of 2001

Each year *BusinessWeek* selects the one hundred *best* small companies, its self-proclaimed "Hot Growth" list. Unfortunately, an investor believing in *BusinessWeek*'s skill in stock selection would be tempted to build a portfolio of these one hundred great companies. *BusinessWeek* reported on the results of such a strategy in this way: "For the Class of '01, a Run In with Reality." For the two-year period ending April 30, 2003, an investor buying one share in each of the one hundred companies would have lost

22.4 percent of their investment. That is, of course, before any commissions or other trading costs. As a comparison we can look at the returns of two passive asset-class funds that invest in the same asset class of small-cap stocks, the Dimensional Fund Advisors (DFA) Small Cap Fund and the DFA Micro Cap Fund. For the same two-year period, the DFA Small Cap Fund lost a cumulative 8.6 percent, outperforming the Class of '01 by 13.8 percent. The DFA Micro Cap Fund actually gained a cumulative 3.3 percent, outperforming the Class of '01 by 25.8 percent.

Where did *BusinessWeek* go wrong? In searching for the best companies they certainly seemed to look in all the right places. Their screening process ranked companies by such metrics as sales and earnings growth and return on capital over the prior three-year period. They also required companies to have a net worth of at least $25 million and a stock price of at least $5. They then eliminated companies with recent earnings declines or ones whose stock price had underperformed the S&P Industrial Composite Index. The companies that survived this rigorous screening process had produced annual sales growth of over 25 percent per annum and average earnings growth of over 44 percent per annum over the prior three years. That compared with sales growth of just 5.8 percent and a 24 percent drop in profits for the S&P industrials. In addition, the average return on capital of the Hot Growth 100 was almost 15 percent versus just over 5 percent for the S&P industrials.[17]

This example is not meant to single out *BusinessWeek*. In fact, they should be congratulated for at least holding themselves accountable and providing the results of their prior recommendations. Accountability is very rare in the financial press because the track record of such prognostications as the "Hot Growth Companies" or the "Ten Hot Mutual Funds to Buy Now" is so poor that it would ruin the game.

21

Does this failure of process deter *BusinessWeek*? Certainly not. The June 9, 2003, issue contained its new list. Articles like "The Hot Growth Companies of 2003" sell magazines to investors searching for the next Microsoft. Articles that recommend boring investments like index funds simply don't excite investors. In addition, each year *BusinessWeek* gets to publish its new list. On the other hand, while passive investing is the winning strategy for investors, it would not sell magazines. After all, passive investing is boring, and you can only say buy and hold index funds so many times in so many ways before people would stop buying your magazine.

The Honor Roll

The Yanni-Bilkey Investment Consulting Company provided further evidence against relying on trade magazines in a 1991 study. Each year *Forbes* recommends its now infamous "Honor Roll" list of mutual funds that individuals should buy. For the seven five-year periods beginning in 1980, only once, and by the smallest of margins, did the group beat the S&P 500 Index. However, the "Honor Roll" list never once beat the average equity fund. Another study on this famous list covered the period 1983–90 and found that a portfolio of the Honor Roll funds would have returned 10.5 percent versus 16.4 percent for the S&P 500 Index.[18]

Here is another interesting point. If past performance had predictive value, then *Forbes'* Honor Roll would list the same group of funds year after year. Investors should be asking themselves: Why don't the same funds repeat their appearance on the "Best Buy" list? If the same funds don't repeat, how valuable is the list?

Keep this insight in mind the next time a broker, or any other investment advisor, shows you a list of their recommended funds and how well they have performed. It is very simple to search a database and come up with such a list. However, that list, as we have seen, almost certainly has no predictive value. My recommendation is that whenever presented with such a list you should request the list that was given to investors five years ago. If the names are the same, perhaps there is value. However, it is my experience that this is virtually never the case. And if the names are not the same, the question is what will the advisor be doing differently to avoid making the same mistake and having to replace one of their recommendations?

Relying on Market Newsletters

There are newsletters that tout their ability to help individual investors choose mutual funds that will outperform the market. In addition, there are newsletters that tout their ability to time the market. Let's examine the evidence, beginning with a study on the performance of newsletters that tout their ability to identify the future outperforming funds.

Mark Hulbert, editor of the *Hulbert Financial Digest*, examined the performance of twenty-seven mutual fund portfolios for which he had ten years of data. During that time, only one (3.7 percent) was able to beat the market as measured by the Wilshire 5000 Index. When he studied 106 newsletter portfolios with at least five years of data, he found that just 12 (11.3 percent) had managed to outperform the Wilshire 5000 Index. Not surprisingly, the longer the time frame covered by Hulbert's study, the lower the percentage of newsletters that were able to beat a market benchmark.[19] What is surprising is that despite this poor performance, these mutual-fund newsletters continue to proliferate in number, providing Hulbert with a marketplace for his product, which ranks their performance. Investors should wake up to the fact that newsletters that tout their ability to predict which mutual funds will outperform the market are no more valuable than tout sheets gamblers purchase at the racetrack. While I admire Mr. Hulbert for his integrity, one has to wonder why anyone would buy even his newsletter in the face of his own evidence that mutual-fund newsletters are the equivalent of such tout sheets. The tout sheet analogy is appropriate as it supports one of the theses of this book: one of the reasons that investors choose the path of active management is that they love to gamble.

Let's now examine the evidence from two studies on newsletters that tout their ability to time the market.

Two researchers, from Duke University and the University of Utah, collaborated on a study examining the performance of the stock selections of 237 market-timing newsletters over the period June 1980–December 1992. An investor holding an equally weighted portfolio of all the newsletters would have earned an 11.3 percent rate of return. This compared to the rate of return of 15.6 percent earned by the Vanguard S&P 500 Index Fund. If the costs associated with the trading recommendations of these financial tout sheets were considered, the results would look even worse as transaction costs would have to be subtracted; the negative impact of the taxes generated by all of the trading activity would have to be considered; and, adding insult to injury, the cost of the newsletters themselves would have to be subtracted from returns. Perhaps most telling is that only 5.5 percent (13 of 237) of the newsletters survived the entire period. How would an investor, at the start of the period, have known which thirteen would survive?[20]

Mark Hulbert studied the performance of thirty-two of the portfolios of market-timing newsletters for the ten years ending in 1997. During this period, the S&P 500 Index was up over 18 percent per annum. He found that the timers' annual average returns ranged from 5.84 percent to 16.9 percent, that the average return was 10.09 percent, and that *none of the market timers beat the market.*[21]

Relying on Rating Services

Almost certainly the most common approach to selecting mutual funds is to rely on the very popular rating service provided by Morningstar. They rate funds using a star system similar to the one used by film critics. Ads touting four- and five-star ratings are found everywhere. As evidence that investors believe the stars have predictive value, a study covering the period January—August 1995 found that an amazing 97 percent of fund inflows went into four- and five-star funds, while three-star funds experienced outflows.[22] Unfortunately, investors who followed that approach achieved about as much success as the Grinch had in his attempt to steal Christmas. Let's look at the evidence.

Morningstar gives the coveted five-star rating to the funds it believes are among the top 10 percent of all funds and a one-star rating to the bottom 10 percent. *The Hulbert Financial Digest* tracked the performance of the five-star funds for the period 1993–2000. For that eight-year period the total return (pretax) on Morningstar's top-rated U.S. funds averaged +106 percent. This compared to a total return of +222 percent for the total stock market, as measured by the Wilshire 5000 Equity Index. Hulbert also found that the top-rated funds, while achieving less than 50 percent of the market's return, carried a relative risk (measured by standard deviation) that was 26 percent greater than that of the market. If the performance had been measured on an after-tax basis, the tax inefficiency of actively managed funds relative to a passive index fund would have made the comparison significantly worse.[23] In another study, Hulbert found that a portfolio that was always fully invested in the fifty-five funds that Morningstar rates highest in a twice-a-month newsletter, buying when they climb into this elite group and selling when they drop out, from January 1991 through March 2002 trailed the market by 5.9 percent per annum, after paying sales charges, redemption fees, and other transaction costs.[24]

Only the Grinch would be pleased with the following tale of woe. For the period 1995–2001, funds rated one star outperformed funds rated five star by 45 percent.[25]

John Rekenthaler, editor of *Morningstar Mutual Funds,* has stated clearly that "the connection between past and future performance has not been firmly established by stars, historic star ratings, or any raw data."[26] In the December 8, 1995, issue of *Morningstar Mutual Funds* he stated: "We never intended to suggest that the stars could be used to predict short-term returns or to time fund purchases. They were just a way to sort funds according to past success." He also stated: "[Our] five-star bond funds have posted lower aggregate returns than their peers." Don Phillips, *Morningstar*'s president, was asked: "How should the star system be used by investors?" His response: "*As a way of identifying funds that have had past success.* The stars take into consideration performance, all costs, and risk. And *performance is probably the weakest of the three factors in terms of projecting from the past into the future*" (emphasis mine).[27]

Relying on the Experts

We have two classes of forecasters: those who don't know—
and those who don't know they don't know.
—John Kenneth Galbraith

It may seem a bit harsh to call the prognostications of such market experts investment pandering. However, these "experts" are dangerous because individual investors take their advice seriously.

Consider the following headlines that appeared in late 1994 and early 1995, just as the U.S. markets were about to soar to record heights. These quotations, from market gurus and widely read publications, all warn investors about the dangers ahead in the coming months. Such forecasts and headlines are dangerous because they cause investors to veer from the academically proven winner's game of buy and hold.

Followers of Dow Theory Say Something Has to Give

What I don't understand is why nobody is willing to talk openly about the fact that we're already in a bear market. (Richard Russell, *Dow Theory Letters*)

—Wall Street Journal, December 12, 1994,
Dow Jones Industrial Average 3691.11

One can only conclude that Mr. Russell must have thought a conspiracy existed among investors to only talk in whispers and behind closed doors about the "fact" that we were in a bear market. The bear market that he was talking about proceeded to rally over **7,000** points over the next five years before peaking in early 2000. Russell managed to cause the subscribers to his *Dow Theory Letters* to miss out on the greatest bull market in history.

27

From the same article:

Every time you've had this kind of drop in the Transports you've always had a significant decline in the Industrials. (Tim Hayes, market analyst, Ned Davis Research)

Calvert Strategic Growth Prepares for the Worst

Every time all five of our indicators turned negative, we had at least a 20% decline. Over the last 40 years, it would have worked every time. (Cedd Moses, portfolio manager, Calvert Strategic Growth Fund)

—*Barron's,* Dow Jones Industrial
Average 4208.18 (April 17, 1995)

The last two quotations are particularly dangerous examples of investment pandering. At first glance, both Mr. Hayes and Mr. Moses seem to make legitimate claims as reliable predictors. It certainly sounds pretty scary: *"every time."* The problem is that investors are generally not aware that if you look hard enough you can always find some correlation that seems to explain, or predict, past behavior. The availability of today's high-speed computers makes this process, called data mining, an easy one. Unfortunately, identifying patterns that worked in the past does not necessarily provide you with any useful information about stock price movements in the future. As Andrew Lo, a finance professor at MIT, points out: "Given enough time, enough attempts, and enough imagination, almost any pattern can be teased out of any data set."[28]

The stock and bond markets are filled with wrongheaded data mining. David Leinweber, of First Quadrant Corp., illustrates this point with what he calls "stupid data-miner tricks." Leinweber

28

sifted through a United Nations CD-ROM and discovered that, historically, the single best predictor of the S&P 500 Index was butter production in Bangladesh.[29] His example is a perfect illustration of the fact that the mere existence of a correlation does not necessarily give it predictive value. Some logical reason for the correlation to exist is required for it to have credibility. For example, there is a strong and logical correlation between the level of economic activity and the level of interest rates. As economic activity increases, the demand for money, and therefore its price (interest rates), also increases. Investors who were scared off by the types of alarms set off by Mr. Hayes and Mr. Moses missed out on the largest bull market in history.

Stock Gains Fly in the Face of Convention

There is great risk in the stock market. I just don't think investors are paying attention. (Geraldine Weiss, editor, *Investment Quality Trends*)

> —*USA TODAY,* May 2, 1995, Dow Jones
> Industrial Average 4316.08

Did Ms. Weiss think that all investors had gone to sleep? If you read such stories in the right light, you can find them entertaining; just don't rely on these market gurus for your financial advice.

A valuable lesson can also be learned from Michael Berry, manager of Heartland Mid-Cap Value Fund, who ruefully claimed credit for calling the bottom of the February–April 1997 market tumble. In an April 25, 1997, speech, he declared that a bear market had begun. Mr. Berry then watched with chagrin as the market immediately began one of its greatest bull runs ever.[30]

Possibly the most dramatic and humorous example of the danger of heeding the forecasts of experts is the relating of an interview by

Joe Kernen of CNBC with Michael Metz of Oppenheimer, at the time a highly regarded Wall Street veteran. When Mr. Metz spoke, people (unfortunately) listened—because he is highly intelligent and what he says appears to make sense. Even I frequently have to remind myself to ignore what appears on the surface to be intelligent advice. On Friday, June 20, 1997, the Dow Jones Industrial Average (DJIA) set an all-time high closing at 7,796. On Monday the DJIA experienced one of its worst days ever, dropping almost 200 points. When asked by Mr. Kernen for his view given the preceding day's debacle, Mr. Metz responded: "I'm bearish." Mr. Kernen then reminded Mr. Metz that he had been bearish for several years (and about 4,000 points). Mr. Metz then responded: "I'm even more bearish now." Mr. Kernen's response was perfect, and went something like this: "I guess if you were bearish at 3,800 you should be more bearish at 7,800. Eventually you'll get it right." (Postscript: By July 3 the DJIA had already made a new all-time high and then proceeded to rise over 3,000 more points.) Maybe the type of forecast made by "experts" such as Mr. Metz should be required to carry a warning from the surgeon general: "This forecast may be dangerous to your financial well-being." Investment advisor John Merrill suggests the following alternatives:

The views expressed are the views of our guest and not of this network. They may be unfounded, biased, self-serving and completely at odds with your long-term investment success. No due diligence on all past recommendations has been attempted.

or

Warning!! The following market analysis will likely be hazardous to your long-term investment strategy if acted upon. It is designed to motivate you to be a short-term trader (most of whom eventually fail) instead of a long-term investor (most of whom succeed).[31]

Investors who follow the dire warnings of the so-called experts are heeding the adage, Better safe than sorry. Unfortunately, they usually end up safe and sorry. Peter Lynch put it this way: "Far more money has been lost by investors in preparing for corrections, or anticipating corrections, than has been lost in the corrections themselves."[32] As supporting evidence the following is presented. A Goldman Sachs study examined mutual-fund cash holdings from 1970 to 1989. In their efforts to time the market, fund managers raise their cash holdings when they believe the market will decline and lower their cash holdings when they become bullish. The study found that mutual-fund managers miscalled *all* nine major turning points.[33]

You will become a much better investor if you understand the following basic principle:

It cannot be possible to make reliable predictions about when the market will rise or fall. If it were possible, the market would respond in advance and it could not then rise and fall in the way it does. The fact that market timing must be unpredictable, but that investors nonetheless clamor to know when things will happen, is probably the single main reason why so much nonsense is written about the stock market. It is an old English adage that if you ask a silly question, you will get a silly answer.[34]

In other words, don't trust anybody who thinks they know more than the markets. Trust the markets themselves. Invest whenever you have investable funds and adhere to your investment plan (asset allocation).

The Royalty of Portfolio Management

In his book *How to Pick Stocks,* Fred Frailey, the deputy editor of *Kiplinger's Personal Finance* magazine, offers a series of "insightful interviews with leading mutual-fund managers"—the so-called legendary market gurus. Kiplinger himself, in an introduction to the book, calls them the "royalty of portfolio management." What I find most interesting are his commentaries, which followed each interview. Examples follow.

On Mario Gabelli: "The flagship Asset and Value funds did okay (in 1995), but not spectacularly, producing returns of almost 30 percent." Unfortunately, the S&P 500 Index was up over 37 percent, and the large-value index was up over 38 percent. In fact the performance of Gabelli Asset Management has been so poor, underperforming the S&P 500 Index in six of the last eight years, that the April 28, 1997, edition of *Fortune* carried this headline: "Super Mario's Super Slump."

On John Neff: "Neff confessed to some disappointment. . . . The Vanguard Windsor Fund matched the S&P 500 Index in 1994 and trailed the index by 7 percent in 1995."

On Kent Simmons and Larry Marx: "Whatever else you can say of 1996, it was not a Marx-and-Simmons kind of year. By November Guardian's year-to-date return had crept up to 13 percent—not bad in itself, but still far short of the S&P 500 Index, which was up almost 20 percent."

On Larry Auriana and Hans Utsch: "Kaufman Fund returned 37 percent in 1995." Of course this trailed the S&P 500 Index. "Alas, 1996 was another story altogether. Kaufman shot out of the starting gate like a bullet. But it was caught by the mid-year crash of high tech stocks and trailed the S&P 500 thereafter."

On Robert Bacarella: "Monetta perked up in 1995, ultimately

returning 28 percent to the S&P 500's 38 percent." This marked "four straight years of underperforming the S&P 500 Index." Interesting that the fund's performance can be termed "perked up" when it underperformed by 10 percent.

On Elizabeth Bramwell: "It's a pity that 1996 ultimately disappointed Bramwell's investors (Bramwell Growth Fund). The fund trailed the S&P 500 substantially."

James Craig (Janus Fund) said: "I need a big year. I'm paid on performance and I haven't had a bonus since 1991."

On James Stowers III (Twentieth Century): "The fund laid a goose egg. Both funds ended November with returns in single digits—this when the overall market was up by 25 percent."

On Ralph Wagner (Acorn Fund): "Its 1994 total return was −7.5 percent, when most small-company growth funds had about broken even. Then in 1995 it returned 21 percent, or 17 percent lower than the S&P 500 Index."

On Jerome Dodson: "For all of 1995—the best year for stocks in more than three decades—Parnassus merely broke even, returning less than 1 percent. The substandard performance continued throughout 1996. It was as if Dodson had steered his fund into a tree."

On Brad Lewis: "Disciplined Equity's new brain seemed to suffer memory lapse. For the year 1995, the fund trailed by more than 8 percent. In 1996, the shortfall was another 2 percent."

There were many other similar tales. Keep in mind that these quotes are from the very author who not only chose these experts as the royalty of fund managers but also is the deputy editor of a magazine that recommends to investors which funds should receive their investment dollars.

While James Craig, manager of the Janus Fund, was highlighted in the above tale, if Wall Street had a "royal family," the Janus family of funds would certainly have worn the crown during the bull market of the late 1990s. Let's examine the returns of the flagship Janus Fund, as well as those of three of its royal siblings, during the ensuing bear market. The following table speaks volumes about placing your trust in royalty.

	2002 Return (%)	2001 Return (%)	2000 Return (%)
S&P 500 Index	−22.1	−11.9	−9.1
Janus Fund	−27.6	−26.1	−14.9
Janus Enterprise	−28.3	−39.9	−30.5
Janus Twenty	−24.0	−29.2	−32.4
Janus Venture	−27.3	−11.9	−45.8

The relative performance of the four Janus funds did improve somewhat in the bull market of 2003, with three of the four funds outperforming the S&P 500 Index. One can only wonder how many investors were left to benefit from that performance?

When Even the Best Aren't Likely to Win the Game

Your golf club hosts a charitable event. Each member donates one thousand dollars to a charity. A slip of paper with each participant's name on it is dropped into a hat, with the winner getting a chance to play eighteen holes with Tiger Woods. It is your "lucky day" and you win! On one of the holes you both hit a poor shot, with the balls landing right next to each other under a large tree. There is a small opening between branches that a great shot just might make it through and you would head right for the hole. Alternatively, you can decide to take the safe route and chip out into the clear. Tiger, being the greatest player in the world, decides to go for the great shot. He proceeds to miss, landing pretty much back where he began. Confident of his skills he tries again, and again, and again. Finally, on his tenth attempt he puts the ball through the branches and it lands right near the cup. It's now your turn. Do you try to make the great shot, knowing the best player in the world failed in 90 percent of his attempts or do you play it safe? The prudent approach, and thus the winning strategy of course, would be to play it safe, as the odds of your success are surely very low. Let's now look at the analogy to investing.

It would seem logical to believe that if anyone could beat the market, it would be the pension funds of the largest U.S. companies. These pension plans control very large sums of money. They have access to the best and brightest portfolio managers, each clamoring to manage the billions of dollars in these plans (and earn those big fees). The pension plans certainly have access to managers most individuals don't have access to because they don't have sufficient assets to meet the minimums of these superstar managers. I think it safe to say that these pension plans never hired a manager who did not have a track record of outperforming their benchmarks. Certainly they would never hire a manager with a record of underperformance. I think it is also safe to say that they never hired a manager who did not make a great presentation, explaining why they had succeeded and why they would continue to succeed. In addition, pension plans often hire professional consultants, such as Frank Russell, SEI, and Goldman Sachs, to help them perform due diligence in interviewing, screening, and ultimately selecting the very best of the best. As individuals it is rare that we would have the luxury of being able to personally interview money managers and perform as thorough a due diligence. And we generally don't have professionals helping us to avoid mistakes in the process. As individuals we are generally stuck relying on Morningstar's ratings—and we have seen that their track record on identifying future outperformers is abysmal. I hope you agree that just as it would be imprudent to try to make a shot that Tiger Woods failed to make 90 percent of the time, it would be imprudent to try to succeed if institutional investors, with far greater resources, had also failed about 90 percent of the time.

The consulting firm FutureMetrics studied the performance of 203 major U.S. corporate pension plans for the sixteen-year period 1987–2002.[35] Since it is estimated that the average pension plan has an allocation of 60 percent equities and 40 percent fixed income, we can compare the realized returns of these plans to a benchmark portfolio with an asset allocation of 60 percent S&P 500 Index and 40 percent Lehman Brothers Intermediate Government/Credit Bond Index. This passive portfolio could have been implemented by each of the plans as an alternative to active strategies. Out of 203 pension plans playing the game of attempting to outperform the market, 22 (10.8 percent) succeeded. While each pension plan obviously believed they were likely to outperform (otherwise, why would they have played?), in a colossal triumph of hope over experience (and perhaps the all-too-human trait of overconfidence), nearly 90 percent failed in the attempt.

Philip Halpern, the chief investment officer of the Washington State Investment Board (a very large institutional investor), and two of his coworkers wrote an article on their investment experiences. They wrote the article because their experience with active management was less than satisfactory and they knew, through their attendance at professional associations, that many of their colleagues shared, and therefore corroborated, their own experience. The article included a quote from a Goldman Sachs publication: "Few managers consistently outperform the S&P 500 Index. Thus, in the eyes of the plan sponsor, its plan is paying an excessive amount of the upside to the manager while still bearing substantial risk that its investments will achieve sub-par returns." The article concluded: "Slowly, over time, many large pension funds have shared our experience and have moved toward indexing more domestic equity assets."[36]

Outfoxing the Box

The following hypothetical situation should also lead you to the winning strategy. Called "outfoxing the box," it was created by my good friend Bill Schultheis, author of *The Coffeehouse Investor.* Like our golfing example, it is a game that you can choose to either play or not. In this game you are an investor with the following choice to make. You are shown nine boxes, each representing a rate of return you are guaranteed to earn for the rest of your life on your assets. The returns each box represents are presented in this table.

%	%	%
0	5	23
6	**10**	14
−3	15	20

You are told that you have the following choice: You can choose to accept the 10 percent rate of return in the center box or you will be asked to leave the room, the boxes will be shuffled around, and you will then get to choose a box, not knowing, of course, what return the box holds. You quickly calculate that the average return of the other eight boxes is 10 percent. Thus if thousands of people played the game and each one chose a box, the expected average return would be the same as if they all chose not to play. Of course, some would earn a return of negative 3 percent, while others would earn 23 percent. This is like the world of investing, where if you chose an actively managed fund and the market earns 10 percent, you might be lucky and earn as much as 23 percent per annum or you might be unlucky and lose 3 percent per annum. A rational, risk-neutral, or risk-averse investor should logically decide to "outfox the box" and accept the average (market) return of 10 percent.

In my years as an investment advisor, whenever I present this game to an investor, I have never once had an investor believe that it would be better to play. While they might be willing to spend a dollar on a lottery ticket, when it comes to their life's savings, they become more prudent in their choice.

Now consider the following. In the "outfox the box" game, the average return of all choices was the same as the choice of not playing, and 50 percent of those choosing to play would be expected to earn an above-average return. The real world study on the returns of pension plans demonstrated that among supposedly sophisticated institutional investors, with access to all the great money managers in the world, about 90 percent of the players received a below-market return and thus would have been better off not playing. If individuals would choose to not play a game when they have a 50 percent chance of success, what logic is there in choosing to play a game where the most sophisticated investors have a 90 percent rate of failure? Yet that is exactly the choice those playing the game of active management are making. You, of course, don't have to play; you can outfox the box and accept market returns by investing passively. Charles Ellis, author of *Investment Policy: How to Win the Loser's Game,* put it this way: "In investment management, the real opportunity to achieve superior results is not in scrambling to outperform the market, but in establishing and adhering to appropriate investment policies over the long term—policies that position the portfolio to benefit from riding with the main long-term forces of the market."[37]

Ignorance Is Bliss

In the face of this tremendous and ever-mounting body of evidence, why do investors continue to pour their hard-earned investment dollars into actively managed funds? One explanation is that it is the triumph of hope over wisdom and experience. Another explanation is that investors are simply overconfident. While they recognize that 90 percent or more of the players are likely to fail, they believe that they will succeed. A third explanation is that perhaps they are simply unaware of the facts—an explanation that *you* can no longer use. And, certainly, it isn't in the interest of active managers (or the financial press) to inform investors that there is a better way when they are deriving huge fees for producing negative results compared to their benchmarks. Patrick Regnier, associate editor of *Morningstar Investor* magazine, said: "Mutual fund fees are unconscionably high. They get higher every year, while funds get bigger every year—and that should make the fees smaller"—by virtue of the economies of scale.[38] And, as Rex Sinquefield of DFA says: "We all know that active management fees are high. Poor performance does not come cheap. You have to pay dearly for it." In the investment business, while investors don't always get what they pay for, they always pay for what they get.

Whose Interest Do They Have at Heart?

The mutual fund and brokerage industries belittle indexing because it is deadly competition for their higher margin products. The financial media ignore it because it makes such lousy copy.
—Gregory Baer and Gary Gensler, *The Great Mutual Fund Trap*

The brokerage industry services investors like Bonnie and Clyde serviced banks.   —William Bernstein

A stockbroker is someone who invests other people's money until it's all gone.   —Woody Allen

Why do brokers exist? Why is there a whole industry devoted to helping individual investors pick out stocks when every jot of financial wisdom in the past 50 years, including Nobel prize-winning work, suggests that this is a mug's game?
—Holman Jenkins Jr., member of the
editorial board of the *Wall Street Journal*

Jean Baptiste Colbert, finance minister to Louis XIV, summed up his views on taxation with the following: "The art of taxation consists in so plucking the goose as to obtain the largest possible amount of feathers with the least possible amount of hissing." The same can be said of active managers—they want to keep plucking those large management fees from the pockets of individual investors with the least possible amount of hissing. In order to continue doing so, they must keep alive the myth that active management is likely to produce outperformance. Frank Knight, a professor of economics at the University of Chicago from 1928 to 1958, said it best when he claimed that economic theory was not at all obscure or complicated, but that most people had a vested interest in refusing to recognize what was "insultingly obvious."[39]

If you believe that Wall Street places your interests at the top of its priorities, the following excerpt from an internal memo of a large brokerage firm disseminated to its sales force should convince you otherwise. I have omitted the name of the firm, not to protect the guilty, but because the memo could just as easily have come from any other firm. The memo was in response to requests from its sales force for the firm to offer index funds. The sales force was simply responding to similar requests from clients who had heard about the superior performance of these passively managed funds.

Index funds are passively managed mutual funds. They simply buy and hold all the stocks of a popular index such as the Standard and Poor's 500 . . . Because their turnover is low and they don't require large research staffs, most have low operating expenses . . . The performance of an index fund is a function of two factors: the performance of the index itself, and the fees to operate and DISTRIBUTE the fund. *For a fund to be successful in the brokerage community it must adequately compensate brokers through either an up-front commission or an ongoing service fee. As a result, a broker sold index fund would underperform no-load index funds. This is why most index funds are offered by no-load fund groups.* (Emphasis mine).

Index funds are not sold by brokers, but not because they do not perform well. They are not sold because investors can buy them cheaper elsewhere. In addition, there is just not enough revenue available to compensate the broker, whose first priority might be generating fees, not obtaining the best possible results for his clients. In other words, mutual-fund sponsors avoid indexing because, while the record makes clear it is the winning strategy for *investors,* it is not very profitable for fund sponsors. They see indexing as the losing *business* strategy.

For these reasons Wall Street does not educate consumers about the virtues of passive management and continues to extol the dubious virtues of active management. It is clearly in the interest of Wall Street to charge you 1.5 percent for an underperforming actively managed fund rather than about 0.15 percent to 0.5 percent for a domestic passively managed fund (and generally a bit higher for international funds as they are more expensive to operate) with superior performance.

Nor is it in the interests of the trade magazines and publications to inform investors of what is in their best interests. If they simply offered you the information provided in this book, who would buy their publications? And what would happen to all those market gurus who appear on CNBC and MSNBC if everyone regarded them as investment panderers?

That Giant Sucking Sound

Individual investors have not been totally blind to the underperformance of active managers. That giant sucking sound you've been hearing isn't the sound of jobs disappearing as Ross Perot predicted would happen with the passage of the North American

Free Trade Agreement (NAFTA); it is the sound of money being siphoned out of actively managed funds and into passively managed funds. The reason for the stampede couldn't be clearer—index funds have outperformed actively managed funds in virtually every asset class over both the short and the long term. For example, for the five-year period 1998–2002, encompassing both a huge bull and a terrible bear market, the S&P 500 (large-cap index), 400 (mid-cap index), and 600 (small-cap index) outperformed 62 percent, 91 percent, and 66 percent of actively managed funds, respectively.[40]

The Bear Market Myth

One of the more persistent myths perpetuated by the Wall Street establishment is that active managers will protect you from bear markets. The following is a perfect example. In 1997 Susan Byrne, of the Westwood Equity Fund, when asked by *Fortune* magazine about index funds responded: "An index fund doesn't have a conscience. It doesn't think. That's how you get overvalued stocks. The reason index funds are beating everybody is that the market has been going straight up. When we are not in a straight-up market everyone will beat them."[41] Let's look at the historical record to see if Susan Byrne was right and whether active managers actually protect investors in bear markets. Once again, you will see that accountability ruins the game.

- Just prior to the second worst (at the time it was the worst) bear market in the postwar era (1973–74), mutual-fund cash reserves stood at only 4 percent. Cash positions reached about 12 percent at the ensuing low.[42]

- In the market correction of mid-1990, when the S&P 500 Index fell 14.7 percent, actively managed funds fell an average of 17.9 percent.[43]

- In mid-1998, when the Asian Contagion bear market arrived, cash reserves were just 5 percent. Compare this to the 13 percent level reached at the market low in 1990, just prior to beginning the longest bull market in history.[44] In the bear market of July 16–August 31, 1998, the average equity fund lost 22.2 percent. This compares to losses of just 20.7 percent and 19.0 percent for a Wilshire 5000 Index Fund and an S&P 500 Index Fund respectively.[45]

- The S&P 500, S&P Midcap 400, and S&P SmallCap 600 Indices outperformed 54 percent of large-cap funds, 77 percent of mid-cap funds, and 72 percent of small-cap funds, respectively, during 2000–02, the worst three-year bear market in the post–Depression era.[46]

- In 2002 alone, the S&P 500, S&P MidCap 400 and S&P SmallCap 600 Indices outperformed 61 percent of large-cap funds, 70 percent of mid-cap funds, and 74 percent of small-cap funds, respectively.[47]

- Lipper Analytical Services studied the six market corrections (defined as a drop of at least 10 percent) from August 31, 1978 to October 11, 1990 and found that while the average loss for the S&P was 15.12 percent, the average loss for large-cap growth funds was 17.04 percent.[48]

It seems that not only was Susan Byrne proven wrong, but that fund managers are very good at executing a buy *high* and sell *low* strategy. Susan Dziubinski, editor of Morningstar's *FundInvestor* newsletter, put it this way: "The average fund can't keep up with its index when it's sunny or rainy."[49]

The Competition Is Too Tough

Academics would say that "experts" are highly unlikely to beat the market because it is "efficient" (a term we will explore later). A less technical way of saying the same thing (and also explaining why hard work is not its own reward) is that there are so many bright, hard-working individuals trying to beat the market that the competition is awfully tough. Remember that because all stocks must be owned by someone, outperforming the market must be a zero-sum game—if one investor outperforms, another must underperform. Benjamin Graham, undoubtedly our most famous author on security analysis (legendary investor Warren Buffett is an almost religious devotee of Graham), felt that the results of security analysts depended more on the level of their competition than on the level of their skill. The tougher the competition, the tougher it is to beat the market. Today, institutional investors account for as much as 80 to 90 percent of all trading. Charles Ellis noted: "Half of all trading on the NYSE is done by the fifty most active institutional investors, all of which are fully staffed by the very best people available. Every investor in the market is competing with these giants all the time."[50] In order to win this game you have to believe that others are making mistakes in how they price securities. In other words, the market (which represents the collective wisdom of all investors) is wrong, and you are right. Burton Malkiel provides the following insight:

> Stock trading among institutional investors [because they are the market] is like isometric exercise: lots of energy is expended, but between one investment manager and another it all balances out, and the commissions the managers pay [as well as the other expenses they incur] detract from

performance. Like greyhounds at the racetrack, professional money managers seem destined to lose their race with the mechanical rabbit.[51]

I took the liberty of adding my thoughts to Malkiel's excellent analogy.

Being Smart Is Not Good Enough

When I was a child we played with a very popular device known as Chinese handcuffs. It was a cylindrical device, about six inches long, into which you inserted the forefinger of each hand. Once your fingers were inside the bamboo cylinder, you were instructed to try to remove them. As the effort expended in pulling your fingers apart increased, the bamboo cylinder tightened and your fingers were even more entrapped. Active management is a lot like Chinese handcuffs. The greater the effort expended, the more entrapped you become in a losing struggle.

Active managers not only must be smarter than the market but much smarter, since active management—with all the research, trading, and other expenses that are incurred—puts them at a large cost disadvantage relative to passive managers. And the more effort they expend, the greater the expense burden becomes. Active managers must overcome not only the burden of the operating-expense ratio of their fund but also the burdens of trading costs, what is called the "cost of cash," and for taxable accounts the taxes caused by the realization of gains. We will discuss in the next chapter just how great a hurdle these expenses create.

Given the poor performance of actively managed funds, you might ask how do they get away with such high fees? It's simple: Investors let them. Amy Arnott of Morningstar suggested that one explanation for this seemingly irrational behavior is that investors don't focus on fees because they never receive a bill from the fund labeled "management fee." The money is simply deducted from the fund's total assets and thus never shows up on an account statement—except, of course, in the form of lower net returns.[52] Given the total indifference shown by shareholders, it's hardly surprising that fees have remained stubbornly high; what is amazing is the twisted logic that funds use to justify a raise even after years of poor performance. Take Seligman Income, which produced only two-thirds of the average returns of similar funds for the years 1994–95. Despite the poor performance, the board proposed raising fees by 22 percent. Its explanation: "To remain competitive and invest in people and resources necessary to continue to provide a high level of service." In 1996 the fund provided a return of only 8.2 percent versus the 13.3 percent produced by its peers. One can only imagine how badly the fund would have done without the extra help.[53]

Summary

Peter Bernstein, the founder of the *Journal of Portfolio Management,* said: "The essence of investment theory is that being smart is not a sufficient condition for being rich."[54] Rex Sinquefeld, the cochairman of DFA, put it this way: "Just because there are some investors smarter than others, that advantage will not show up. The market is too vast and too informationally efficient."[55] As we have seen, being smart is not enough to beat the market. The research and trading expenses and the tax consequences of active managers giving it the "old college try" create hurdles that prove to be just too great to overcome in the vast majority of cases. I hope that all this evidence has convinced you that active management is a loser's game. It certainly convinced the American Law Institute that the odds are against active management, as described below.

The Prudent Investor Rule

There are well-dressed foolish ideas just as there are well-dressed fools. —Nicholas Chamfort

Embedded within the American legal code is a doctrine known as the Prudent Investor Rule. Basically, this rule states that if you are responsible for the management of someone else's assets, you must manage those assets in a manner appropriate to the financial circumstance and tolerance for risk of the beneficiaries—as would a prudent investor. For example, if you are the trustee of the assets of an elderly widow, you should be investing her money in safe assets, not in a commodity trading account. At one time stocks were considered to be so risky that trustees believed bonds to be the only appropriate investments; even corporate pension funds reflected that view. That attitude has obviously changed, and equities are considered appropriate investments (as long as the investment horizon is not very short). As a result, the average U.S. pension fund now has an equity allocation of about 60 percent.

During the 1970s pension fund administrators began to discern that the collective performance of the active managers they hired to manage their pension fund assets was poor. This realization created the initial demand for the creation of index funds. Even though a few index funds became available, it wasn't until 1990, and the awarding of the Nobel Prize to Merton Miller, William Sharpe, and Harry Markowitz, that the benefits of modern portfolio theory (MPT) became more widely known.

In May 1992, in response to both the overwhelming body of academic evidence about the overall unsatisfactory performance of active managers and the benefits of passive asset-class investing, the American Law Institute rewrote the Prudent Investor Rule. Here is some of what the institute had to say in doing so:

- The restatement's objective is to liberate expert trustees to pursue challenging, rewarding, non-traditional strategies and to provide other trustees with clear guidance to safe harbors that are practical and expectedly rewarding.

- Investing in index funds is a passive but practical investment alternative.

- Risk may be reduced by mixing risky assets with essentially riskless assets, rather than creating an entirely low-risk portfolio.

- *Active strategies entail investigation and expenses that increase transaction costs, including capital gains taxation.* Proceeding with such a program involves judgments by the trustee that gains from the course of action in question can reasonably be expected to *compensate for additional cost and risks,* and the course of action to be undertaken *is reasonable in terms of its economic rationale.*

By rewriting the Prudent Investor Rule, the American Law Institute recognized both the significance and efficacy of MPT and that active management delivers inconsistent and poor results. The institute had the following to say about market efficiency, in summary:

- Economic evidence shows that the major capital markets of this country are *highly efficient,* in the sense that available information is rapidly digested and reflected in market prices.

- Fiduciaries and other investors are confronted with potent evidence that the application of expertise, investigation, and diligence in efforts to "beat the market" ordinarily promises little or no payoff, or even a negative payoff after taking account of research and transaction costs.

- Empirical research supporting the theory of efficient markets reveals that in such markets skilled professionals have rarely been able to identify under-priced securities with any regularity.

- Evidence shows that there is little correlation between fund managers' earlier successes and their ability to produce above-market returns in subsequent periods.

The Uniform Prudent Investor Act, currently the law in the vast majority of states, sets forth standards that govern the investment activities of trustees. It adopts MPT as the standard by which fiduciaries invest funds. The act does note that trustees do have the authority to delegate their responsibilities as a prudent investor would.[56] Thus trustees/investors who do not have the knowledge, skill, time, or interest to prudently manage a portfolio should delegate that responsibility to an advisor who does. However, prudence in delegating the responsibilities must be observed. Section 9 (a) of the act states:

The trustee shall exercise reasonable care, skill, and caution in (1) selecting an agent, (2) establishing the scope and terms of the delegation, consistent with the purposes and terms of the trust, and (3) periodically reviewing the agent's actions in order to monitor the agent's performance and compliance with the terms of the delegation.

For those with fiduciary responsibility, adopting MPT makes sense because:

- It can provide the maximum expected return for a given level of risk.
- It provides relief from liability for fiduciaries who are not in the investment business by appointing competent managers or advisors who invest according to its tenets.

Faced with this restatement, and recent legislative changes, trustees began a major switch from active to passive portfolio strategies. As recently as twenty years ago, around $1 billion was invested in passive funds. Today the amount invested is over $3 trillion and may represent as much as 40 percent of institutional funds (i.e., pension plans and endowment funds).[57] One reason for this rapid shift is that pension fund managers must now ask themselves: "Do I want to invest in a way that has been recognized as prudent by the American Law Institute? Or would I rather try, with historical evidence against me, to beat the market through an active management strategy, knowing that if I fail I may be forced to justify why I engaged in such a strategy in the face of an overwhelming body of academic evidence?" Consider this baseball analogy. The score is tied in the bottom of the ninth. The lead-off runner singles. Not wanting to be second-guessed in the light of all the historical evidence, the manager will likely play it by the book and attempt to bunt the runner into scoring position. Like the baseball manager, institutional fund managers and other trustees are faced with a wealth of historical evidence that is leading them to "play it by the book." Given the risk/reward trade-off, the growing trend toward the use of passive asset-class investing by institutional investors is not only inevitable but will likely continue to accelerate. Frederick Grauer, cochairman of Barclays Global Investors, the world's largest institutional fund manager, put it this way: "There are trends that have been major market drivers for the decade. Indexing people are looking to reduce costs, control exposures to the marketplace and to get exact implementation of pension policies. They are fed up with out-of-control outcomes."[58]

The trend to passive investing is not only apparent in the institutional market but is also rapidly gaining momentum in the retail market. It took Vanguard, by far the largest provider of retail-oriented passively managed funds, eleven years (1976–87) to cross $1 billion with its S&P 500 Index Fund. In early 1997 it crossed $30 billion. As of July 9, 2004, the fund had $97 billion under management.[59] It had also long surpassed Fidelity Magellan to become the largest retail fund in the world. While active managers will probably never go the way of buggy whip manufacturers, their market share will inevitably decline.

Filling in the Void

The balance of this book will provide you with a theoretical understanding of both the interaction between risk and return and how markets work. Having seen how markets work, you will have the skills to make them work for you. You will see that active management does not make sense theoretically and is not justified empirically. When you complete this book, you will be able to emulate the Nobel Prize–winning strategy used by the most knowledgeable institutions. It will no longer be necessary for you to watch CNBC, read *Money* magazine, or spend time analyzing investment advice from your broker, who only makes money when you trade—whether or not the trade was in your best interest. You will begin to let the markets work for you. Instead of listening to the latest hot tip from your friend, broker, or barber, you will be investing in a way recommended by the brightest academic minds in the field of economics. It should also comfort you to know that your investment strategy is based on research that was awarded a Nobel Prize. Your newly acquired knowledge will allow you to play the winner's game of managing risks. You will no longer play the loser's game of trying to pick stocks and time the market. Finally, since the ultimate objective of investing is consumption, you will probably eat a lot better, too. Wouldn't that make a pretty good story to tell at the next cocktail party? In fact instead of having that one great cocktail party story to tell, you will probably be the one throwing the party.

PART TWO

◆

Efficient Markets and Modern Portfolio Theory

I am no longer an advocate of elaborate techniques of security analysis in order to find superior value opportunities. This was a rewarding activity, say forty years ago, when Graham and Dodd was first published; but the situation has changed . . . [Today] I doubt whether such extensive efforts will generate sufficiently superior selections to justify their cost. . . . I'm on the side of the "efficient" market school of thought.
— Benjamin Graham, the father of fundamental security analysis (the art of trying to identify securities that the rest of the market has mispriced—under or overvalued) in an interview in the *Financial Analysts Journal* shortly before his death in 1976. Quoted in *A Random Walk Down Wall Street* by Burton G. Malkiel

It isn't what people think that is important, but the reason they think what they think. — Eugene Ionesco

There is only one good, knowledge, and one evil, ignorance. — Socrates

Blinding ignorance does mislead us. O! Wretched mortals open your eyes! — Leonardo da Vinci

CHAPTER 3

◆

Efficient Markets I—
Information and Costs

There is one thing stronger than all the armies in the world; and that is an idea whose time has come. —Victor Hugo

Only liars manage to always be out during bad times and in during good times. —Bernard Baruch

I have personally tried to invest money, my client's and my own money, in every single anomaly and predictive result that academics have dreamed up. And I have yet to make a nickel on any these supposed market inefficiencies. An inefficiency ought to be an exploitable opportunity. If there's nothing investors can exploit in a systematic way, time in and time out, then it's very hard to say that information is not being properly incorporated into stock prices.
—Richard Roll, financial economist and principal of the portfolio management firm, Roll and Ross Asset Management

The evidence clearly indicates that active managers as a group produce results that are consistently below that of their benchmarks, such as the S&P 500 Index. In addition, just as in Las Vegas—where the longer gamblers stay at the tables, the smaller the number of winners—the longer the investment horizon, the lower the percentage of active managers who manage to beat their benchmarks. The efficient market hypothesis (EMH) explains this phenomenon: current market prices reflect the total knowledge and expectations of all investors, and it is highly unlikely that one investor can know more than the market does collectively. For this

57

hypothesis to hold true, one condition must be met: any new information must be disseminated to the public rapidly and completely so that prices instantly adjust to new data. If this is the case, an investor can consistently beat the market only with the best of luck.

While the information condition is at the core of the EMH, there are two other factors related to market efficiency that affect the development of a winning investment strategy: cost and risk.

If the investor's cost to enter into a market transaction is relatively low, the market can be considered efficient from a cost perspective, and the trading costs incurred by active management are relatively low. The more cost inefficient the market (the greater the spread between the bid and offer), however, the greater are both the costs of trading and the barriers active managers must overcome in order to beat their benchmarks.

Market efficiency must also be considered from a *risk* perspective. In brief: Do investments that entail greater risk provide investors with greater *expected* returns as compensation for the greater risk assumed?

Once you have a grasp of these three elements of market efficiency—information, cost, and risk—you will realize not only why active management is a loser's game but, more important, why MPT and the EMH provide the winning investment strategy.

This chapter addresses the information and the cost components of efficient markets; the next chapter addresses the risk component.

Efficient Markets and Information

One of my favorite films is *The House of Rothschild,* with George Arliss playing the role of the patriarch of the family. In the film's climactic scene, he has placed his entire family fortune on the line in an attempt to save the British financial system. There is a tidal wave of selling, with shares being dumped at any price, as British traders are anticipating a Napoleonic victory. Just as the great resources of the House of Rothschild are about to be exhausted, Arliss demands the attention of all the traders, announcing that Wellington is victorious. The traders mock him, saying that he is just trying to save his own fortune with this false rumor. At this point he must disclose the great family secret. (One reason the Rothschilds were able to amass their fortune was that they were always a step ahead of the public in terms of information.) While the fastest ships in the British Fleet are just beginning to sail with the news of Napoleon's defeat, carrier pigeons had already delivered the news into the Rothschilds' hands. With this disclosure prices soar, and the Rothschilds emerge richer than ever.

Today the Rothschilds' advantage is not possible, as information is carried all over the globe in seconds. And you will see that markets adjust to news almost instantaneously.

An efficient market exists when trading systems fail to produce returns in excess of the market's overall rate of return because stocks are already trading at what they are worth based on all *available* information. When a market is efficient, information moves rapidly, prices immediately reflect new information, and no investor can consistently know more about an individual security than does the market as a whole. If this is true, then there are only two ways individual stock selection can be productive. The first is that an individual possesses insider information, that is, facts and figures about a company that should only be known by its board of directors, officers, and, perhaps, key upper-level managers. To trade on such privileged information is a violation of the securities laws of the United States. The second is to somehow interpret that same information more correctly than does the market. As we have seen, the investment results of both individual and institutional investors demonstrate that it is highly unlikely that anyone can persistently identify securities that have been mispriced by the market.

There is one more important issue about information that we need to discuss—investors confuse information with knowledge that they can exploit.

The Information Paradox

Something that everyone knows isn't worth knowing.
—Bernard Baruch

People overconfidently confuse familiarity with knowledge. For every example of a person who made money on an investment because she used a company's product or understood its strategy, we can give you five instances where such knowledge was insufficient to justify the investment.
—Gary Belsky and Thomas Gilovich, *Why Smart People Make Big Money Mistakes and How to Correct Them.*

When it comes to investing, information is a fact, data, or an opinion held by someone. Knowledge, on the other hand, is information that is of value because it can be exploited to generate above-market returns. Confusing the two is perhaps the most common misperception investors have about investing. Let's take a look at what I call the "information paradox."

If information is valuable, it is highly likely that it has no value from an investment perspective because either the market already knows it and has incorporated it into prices or it is illegal on which to trade. Keep in mind that the only other way you can exploit information is to interpret that information differently (and more correctly) from the way in which the market collectively interprets it—the market has mispriced the security.

The following example illustrates the logic of the information paradox. It is also one that any investor who has ever purchased a stock based on a recommendation from a broker (or from a financial publication, a CNBC guest, and so on) will be able to relate to. The example is a hypothetical phone conversation between a broker and an investor. While the conversation is hypothetical, it will probably sound familiar (though perhaps exaggerated) to those who have dealt with brokers.

Broker: We just have to buy IBM. (Note: the broker will never say, "I just have to *sell* you IBM")

Investor: Why should I buy IBM?

Broker: Our analyst who covers IBM is a genius. She graduated first in her M.B.A. class at Harvard. She then graduated first in her class at Stanford, receiving a Ph.D. in electrical engineering. She then worked for ten years at IBM in product development and then ten more in marketing and sales. She then joined our firm and has been our technology analyst. She has personally visited all IBM plants and research facilities. She has also visited with all competitors. She even visited with all of IBM's major customers to check on how they perceive IBM products and service and to check on the status of new orders. She even met with IBM's suppliers to check on the quality of their work. The stock is currently selling at 100. Given the great new pipeline of fifty great new products and the growth in sales that will result, the stock is worth 200 if it's worth a penny.

Investor: That sounds great. Let's buy one thousand shares.

Let's assume that everything the broker said was absolutely true. Even in that event, there is a very logical reason for you to ignore all such prognostications. Simply put, there is something very wrong with the picture. An alternative version of our hypothetical phone call will illustrate why. This version, however, will not only be totally unfamiliar to all investors it is also one they will never hear. The reason is that while the broker will also be telling the truth, in this case the truth is not in the broker's interests to disclose.

> *Broker:* While we have a very smart analyst covering IBM, there are seventy other very smart analysts covering IBM. They each have an M.B.A. from a top school and lots of experience. They are all highly paid and motivated. They all work diligently to gather the facts. They all have the same information our analyst does. If the other analysts thought IBM was worth 200, obviously the stock would already be trading there. Do you think all those smart people would let a stock that is obviously worth 200 sit there at 100 without rushing to buy it at this obviously undervalued level? The reason IBM is trading at 100 is that the market as a whole thinks that it is only worth 100, not 200. However, our analyst thinks the rest of the world has got it *wrong*. Our analyst is *right* and the rest of the world is *wrong*. Only our analyst really knows this stuff, and the rest of the smart analysts are simply misinterpreting the information. We really need to buy IBM.
> *Investor:* Dial tone.

I think it is safe to say that if you had heard the second conversation instead of the first, instead of buying IBM you would have laughed at the broker's *ill*logic and simply hung up. Despite knowing that the second conversation is far more likely to be the truth, because brokers know how any intelligent person would respond, the alternative conversation never occurs. The reason is that it is simply not in the broker's interest for you to know the truth. He wouldn't make any money.

It is also important to keep the following in mind. Beating the market is a zero-sum game—for one fund manager to outperform, another must underperform. Is it really logical to believe that an analyst at, for example, Merrill Lynch is superior and knows more than the analyst at Goldman Sachs or Janus?

The next time you watch CNBC (or read any financial publication) and listen to an analyst or fund manager explain all the good reasons why to buy a specific stock, sector, or equities in general, keep the information paradox in mind. Even though you might be impressed with the intellectual capacity of the person and the information presented, as well as the logic of the recommendation, remember these points before you leap into action:

- Capturing *incremental* insight is very difficult, if not impossible, to achieve. The reason is that security analysts are competing with so many other smart and highly motivated people researching the same stocks. It is this tough competition that makes it so difficult to gain a competitive advantage. Imagine an art auction where you are the only expert among a group of amateurs. In that circumstance, it might be possible to find a bargain. On the other hand, if you are one of a group of mostly experts, it is far less likely that you will find bargain prices. The same is true of stocks. Competition among all the professional active managers ensures that the market price is highly likely to be the correct price. Binkley Shorts, a portfolio manager at Wellington Management, put it this way: "When you're looking at companies like Microsoft,

IBM, Merck, and Coca-Cola, the ability to capture *incremental* insight is so damn challenging because so many people are looking at those stocks and it takes so long to get through the body of knowledge."[1]

- Think about where you just heard the new insightful information—*on national television.* In the unlikely scenario that this information *was* a secret, it no longer *is.* The same analogy could be made for recommendations from any of the high-profile publications such as *Barron's, BusinessWeek, Fortune, Forbes, Money,* or *SmartMoney.*

Author Harry Dent makes the same mistake—failing to understand the important difference between information and knowledge you can exploit—in his book *The Roaring 2000s.* Dent is a demographer whose investment advice is based on the following thought process:

- The population of the United States is rapidly aging.
- An aging population will boost the demand for certain products and services, benefiting these sectors (i.e., health care).
- Individuals can benefit from these obvious trends by investing in stocks of companies in these sectors of the economy.

Dent, being an excellent demographer, makes a very compelling case. When you understand the information paradox, however, it is easy to see that Dent is presenting information and not providing investors with knowledge they can exploit. For example, it is hard to imagine that there was even a single institutional investor who was unaware of the fact that the population was aging, that the demand for health care and related services would rise, and that certain companies would likely benefit from those trends. Therefore, unless you believe that the entire market was "asleep at the switch," it is obvious that this information must already have been built into prices and thus could not be exploited.

It is important to make one last point on trying to benefit from "obvious" trends. Even if you "know" the demand for a certain product or service will rapidly rise, that information tells you very little about future profits in the industry. For example, certainly the demand for cell phones continued to rise at a very rapid pace from 2000 through 2003. Despite the rapid rise in demand, investors who were able to correctly forecast this trend would have experienced severe losses had they invested in stocks of providers of this product. The reason is that the supply greatly exceeded demand and prices for the service collapsed, taking stock prices with them.

Institutions Are Now the Market

It is estimated that over 80 percent of all trading is now done by institutional investors such as mutual funds and pension funds. The managers of these funds are highly paid, intelligent, hard-working individuals who spend a considerable amount of time doing research, mainly to discover securities that they assume have somehow been mispriced by all their equally intelligent and just as hard-working competitors. Not only does it seem illogical and futile in this light, but study after study has confirmed the failure of efforts to beat the market. (In fact not a single credible academic study, of which I am aware, has shown that active management is *likely* to produce above benchmark results.) Efforts to beat the market are thus highly likely to prove counterproductive—not because of poor research, but because the research is done so well by so many people that no one individual is likely to gain an advantage over another. Therefore, the costs of research are unlikely to be recouped through improved returns.

Do Markets Value Stocks Correctly?

Some people have a problem with the efficient market concept when they see the price of a particular stock go from 30 one day to 20 the next. If the markets are so efficient, how can a company's worth vary by billions of dollars from one day to the next? The problem stems from the question itself; it confuses the concept of market efficiency with the concept of current valuation. Defining a market as efficient once again means that the market incorporates everything that is *currently* known about a stock (including forecasts of future earnings, and so on) into its valuation, or price.

Louis Bachelier, a French economist, long ago remarked: "Clearly the price considered most likely by the market is the true correct price: if the market judged otherwise it would not quote this price, but another price higher or lower."[2] Prices will not change if the *expected* happens. It is the *unexpected* that causes prices to move. In an efficient market, any new information the market receives will be random, not in the sense of being good or bad, but in the sense of whether or not it surpasses or falls short of the expectations that are built into the current price. The market quickly incorporates the new information and revalues the security. The volatility of both the stock and bond markets is evidence of the frequency with which the expected fails to occur. Let's examine the evidence on how quickly markets, both fixed income and equities, incorporate new information.

A study on U.S. fixed-income markets found that a considerable portion of the changes in interest rates can be attributed to scheduled macroeconomic announcements, such as employment reports and inflation data. The major adjustment to the information release (and the window for trading profits) lasts about forty *seconds*.[3] The speed of the stock market's response to new information is almost as startling. A study on the after-trading-hours quarterly earnings announcements of one hundred New York Stock Exchange (NYSE) and one hundred National Association of Securities Dealers (Automated) Quotations (NASDAQ) firms found that the majority of the price response is realized during the *opening* trade. Earnings announcements that occurred during trading hours caused adjustments to occur very quickly. For NYSE stocks the price adjustment occurred during the first several postannouncement trades; for NASDAQ stocks the price adjustment was concentrated in the first postannouncement trade.[4] One can only conclude that the U.S. markets are very efficient at processing information and incorporating that information into valuations.

Let's look at the evidence from an international market. Perhaps they are less efficient, providing fertile ground for active managers. A study examined the impact of nine major economic announcements (such as inflation data, retail sales, etc.) on stocks of the Financial Times Stock Exchange 100 (FTSE 100), a U.K. equivalent of the S&P 500 Index. The study also examined the impact on fixed-income instruments. The authors concluded that the U.K. equities markets took seventy-five to ninety seconds, or about seven trades, to adjust to the new data. The fixed-income markets took about the same amount of time.[5] One can conclude that both the U.K. and U.S. markets are very efficient at processing information and incorporating that information into valuations.

Let's look at an example. On the evening of January 23, 1997,

Cascade Communications reported that its fourth-quarter earnings had risen more than 100 percent from the previous quarter. The stock had closed the previous day at just over 64. "In a private off-the-record conversation, Cascade's president indicated to a select group of Wall Street analysts that the next quarter would be flat—a devastating setback for a company whose share price was predicated on a vision of almost unending growth." Before the market could even open the next day, in after-hours trading on Instinet, Cascade dropped over 30 percent to $44.[6] Market efficiency is not about valuation; it is about how quickly market prices incorporate available information. It is about the effectiveness of active versus passive management.

Good News, Bad Results

On February 4, 1997, after the market had closed, Cisco Systems reported that its second-quarter earnings had risen from 31 cents per share in the prior year period to 51 cents, an increase of 65 percent. Certainly no one would suggest that a rise in earnings of that magnitude is bad news. Yet the price of Cisco's stock fell the following day from its prior close of just over 67 to 63, a drop of 6 percent. The market's reaction can be explained by the EMH. Simply put, the market was anticipating a greater increase in earnings than the company reported. Prior to a company's release of information, outsiders do not know whether it will report earnings higher or lower than market expectations. In other words, whether subsequent information will affect the price of a stock in a positive or negative manner is random. The market incorporates new information and appropriately adjusts a stock's valuation.

Bad News, Good Results

A similar phenomenon occurs when a company's stock price rises after a "bad" earnings report. For example, the day IBM released its earnings for the second quarter of 1996, the price of its stock rose 13 percent. Based on the price movement, one would have thought that IBM had announced spectacular results. Their earnings were, in fact, down about 20 percent from the same period of the prior year. The stock rose because the market was expecting IBM to announce far worse results. The market's valuation was correct before the news release (based on everything that could then be known about the company) and was also correct after adjusting to the new information.

Active Management and Efficient Markets

While whether or not the market is efficient is an important question because it has practical implications in determining the winning investment strategy, the only real question about which investors should be concerned is: Can anyone persistently outsmart the market through active portfolio management? In commenting on active management, Paul Samuelson, one of our most well-known and respected economists (you probably used his textbook in Economics 101), wrote: "A respect for evidence compels me to the hypothesis that most portfolio managers should go out of business. Even if this advice to drop dead is good advice, it obviously will be not be eagerly followed. Few people will commit suicide without a push."[7] Simply eloquent.

Timing the Market

I'm the lousiest market timer in the history of the world.
> —Charles Clough, Chief Market Strategist,
> Merrill Lynch, *Wall Street Journal*, October 29, 1997

My favorite time frame is forever.　　　—Warren Buffett

Our stay-put behavior reflects our view that the stock market serves as a relocation center at which money is moved from the active to the passive.　　　—Warren Buffett

It has been a problem since the dawn of the retail brokerage business: Brokers have a strong incentive to get customers to trade when it might be in clients' interests to do nothing.
> —*BusinessWeek*, July 14, 1997

Seventy percent of success in life is just showing up.
> —Woody Allen

We have seen that it is highly unlikely that portfolio managers can add value by finding mispriced securities. But perhaps they are able to add value by trying to time their investment decisions? In order to believe in this approach, a manager must believe that he/she knows more—has better information—than the rest of the market; the market is either under- or overvalued (i.e., the rest of the market is wrong). There is one simple piece of historical data I believe will convince even the most ardent of skeptics that trying to time investment decisions is an exercise in futility.

During the 3,541 trading days of 1980–93, an investor who built and held a portfolio consisting of the S&P 500 Index would have realized annualized returns of 15.5 percent per annum. If, in an attempt to time the market, an investor missed out on just the best ten days, the annualized return dropped to 11.9 percent. This investor, by being absent from less than 0.3 percent of the trading days, would have lost over 23 percent of the returns available for the entire period. If the same investor had the misfortune of missing out on the best forty days (or about 1 percent of the total trading days), his or her annualized returns would have dropped to 5.5 percent, a loss of almost two-thirds of the passive investor's returns. Another way of looking at this is that the returns of the investor who missed out on just the best forty days could have been matched by owning risk-free certificates of deposit at a local bank.

Why Market Timing Doesn't Work

Annualized Returns for the S&P 500

1980–93	Returns*
3,541 Trading Days	15.5%
Minus 10 Best Days	11.9
Minus 20 Best Days	9.5
Minus 30 Best Days	7.4
Minus 40 Best Days	5.5

*S&P 500 Index (price appreciation only: returns don't include dividends).

Source: Smith Barney Research Department

Trying to time investment decisions just doesn't work because most of the action occurs over such brief, and unexpected, periods of time. Despite that, there are "professional" Wall Street market timers who claim they can pick the best 1 percent of all trading days and who will spend much of their time, and your money, on this futile endeavor. "These professionals would do well to learn from deer hunters and fishermen who know the importance of 'being there' and using patient persistence—so they are there when opportunity knocks."[8] Let's examine some further evidence on the failure of market-timing efforts.

A study of one hundred large pension funds and their experience with market timing found that while they all had engaged in at least some market timing, *not one* had improved its rate of return as a result. In fact, eighty-nine of the one hundred lost as a result of their efforts, and their losses averaged an incredible 4.5 percent over the five-year period.[9]

MoniResearch studied the performance of eighty-five market-timing managers with a total of $10 billion under management.[10] They found that the timers' annual average return ranged from 4.4 percent to 16.9 percent, that the average return was 11.0 percent, and that *none of the market timers beat the market.*

The following may be my favorite story on market timing. A Morningstar study evaluated 199 no-load growth mutual funds for which they had performance data for the period 1989–94. The average total return for the 199 funds over this six-year period was 12 percent. The individual owners of those same funds (keeping in mind that the average no-load mutual-fund investor holds his/her funds for only twenty-one months) for their various periods of ownership received a return, however, of just 2 percent. Either market timing or chasing the hot manager turned their 12 percent returns into 2 percent.[11]

Here is some further evidence that the most likely winning strategy is passive investing. Using the Center for Research in Security Prices (CRSP) database, out of the 936 months in the period 1926–2003, the returns for the best sixty-six months (just 7 percent of the time) averaged over 11 percent. The returns for the remaining 870 months (93 percent of the time) averaged less than two one-hundredths of 1 percent per month. Richard Thaler put it this way: "If you are prepared to do something stupid (attempt to time the market) repeatedly, there are many professionals happy to take your money."[12]

How Legends Are Made

Another of my favorite films is *The Man Who Shot Liberty Valance,* a story about a greenhorn, pacifist lawyer (Jimmy Stewart) who stands up to and then shoots and kills the villain, Liberty Valance (Lee Marvin). When Stewart, now a U.S. senator, returns to his hometown to attend the funeral of his best friend (John Wayne), he relates the tale of the legendary gunfight in an interview with a young newspaper reporter. The reporter eventually learns that it was not Stewart but John Wayne who actually killed Liberty Valance; excited about his great discovery, he races off to his editor. When the editor finishes reading this incredible tale, he rips the reporter's notes to shreds and tells him: "When the legend becomes fact, print the legend."

In an attempt to generate business, investment firms also build legends; they go out of their way to create auras of greatness around their prognosticators who, having made one or two accurate predictions, are promoted as experts capable of forecasting market movements. My college professor and mentor gave me this advice as I was about to embark on my career: "If you are going to forecast, forecast often; eventually you will get it right. And if you forecast a number, never give a date." And Winston Churchill said: "The greatest lesson in life is to know that even fools are right sometimes." Investors, of course, generally only hear about an "expert's" accurate forecasts. Investors almost never hear anything when the experts inevitably fall from grace. As investment advisor

John Merrill says: "Strict and thorough accountability would ruin the game—so it is ignored."[13] The self-interested Wall Street establishment does, indeed, print the legend.

There is no better example of this than the rise and inevitable fall of market guru Elaine Garzarelli. While working at Shearson Lehman, Ms. Garzarelli was deemed a market guru when she correctly forecasted the 1987 crash based on a model that used a proprietary group of indicators that were thought to be able to predict market movements. Shearson Lehman began to widely tout her ability to call market moves; she also received considerable attention from the print and electronic media. Remember, the media creates gurus so that their audiences feel privileged to receive their insights. Ms. Garzarelli's forecasts even began to receive credit for moving the market itself. Eventually, Shearson Lehman rewarded her for her successful prognostications with a mutual fund of her own to manage. Let's look at her record.

By June 30,1994, the fund she was managing, the Smith Barney Shearson Sector Analysis Fund, had risen in value by 38 percent over the five years she was in charge. During this same period the Dow Jones Industrial Average (DJIA) had risen in value by 74 percent. In other words, she managed to underperform that benchmark by about 50 percent. As Casey Stengel said, "You could look it up."

In May 1996, with the Dow surpassing 5,700, this well-known market guru, who had "left" Shearson Lehman to form her own firm, advised her clients to invest aggressively since she foresaw the market heading for a new high of 6,300 by year-end. Almost immediately the market underwent a sharp correction, falling over 400 points. Perhaps Ms. Garzarelli's crystal ball began to cloud over because at this point she reversed direction. Now she advised her clients to sell because her indicators called for a further large negative correction. Once again the market reversed course. By November the DJIA had crossed 6,500.

In November 1996, despite her misreadings of the market, Ms. Garzarelli touted her "successful track record" in a major direct-mail promotional campaign. The mailing claimed that she had predicted every bear market in the past twenty years. The *Wall Street Journal* called it "one of the most alarming pieces of junk mail in Street history," and noted that "there has been only one crash in that time, but let's not get picky. If the market crashes any time in the next twenty years, the guru, or at least her public relations people, can say she had it right again."[14]

Continuing the saga, in January 1997, with the market approaching 7,000, Ms. Garzarelli reversed position once again and advised her clients to buy. By April the market had dropped to under 6,400.

Not yet convinced? For ten years the *Wall Street Journal,* with assistance from two research firms, Wilshire Associates and Carpenter Analytical Services, studied the asset allocation advice of strategists at the nation's largest brokerage houses, including Lehman Brothers, Goldman Sachs, Paine Webber, Prudential, Smith Barney, Merrill Lynch, and others. The *Journal* concluded that "a decade of results throws cold water on the notion that strategists exhibit any special ability to time the markets. The average annual gain from their allocation decisions was a mere 0.18 percent." This figure ignored the transaction costs and taxes incurred as a result of the trading decisions. Once these were taken into account, the value these strategists added would clearly have been negative.[15]

There are temptations everywhere, especially tempting when offered by notable market gurus. But remember that market timers simply run too great a risk of being absent when the market makes one of its very infrequent but very large moves that are the big determinants of performance. Peter Lynch provided this very useful insight: "If it were truly possible to predict corrections, you'd think somebody would have made billions by doing it." He also noted that he had never once seen the name of a market timer on *Forbes*'s annual list of the richest people in the world.[16] Lynch got it almost right. While no individual has made billions from efforts to time the market, Wall Street firms that peddle this type of economic pandering certainly have made billions from the commissions on the trades of the individuals who listened to, and acted on, this type of fortune-telling.

Market Timing Strategists and Weathermen

One of the most respected people on Wall Street is Barton Biggs, Morgan Stanley's director of global strategy. Mr. Biggs appeared on the cover of the July 19, 1993, issue of *Forbes* wearing a bear costume, warning investors: "Except for that nasty jolt in October 1987, most investors under forty have never experienced a bear market. We have all been spoiled by twelve fat years." Convinced that the U.S. market had gotten way ahead of itself (meaning that investors were wrong to have bid the market up to such lofty levels), Biggs advised his clients to reduce their exposure to the U.S. market to 18 percent of their portfolio and to move their money overseas. He argued that the U.S. market was near its top and was due for a fall that could range from 20 to 50 percent. "If the DJIA registers one of its average cyclical declines . . . it could have a precipitous drop . . . to somewhere between 2800 and 2275. We are due for a secular bear market . . . the decline could be 50 percent." He added: "While the U.S. has had a tremendous bull market, the European markets have been sluggish or worse. It doesn't take a genius to see that this relationship is due for a change."

It took almost seven years before the bear market Biggs called for finally arrived. During this period the United States experienced its greatest bull market ever (one that Mr. Biggs's clients presumably missed out on). In addition, despite his claim that "it doesn't take a genius to see that this relationship is due for a change," the U.S. market far outperformed the European and emerging-country markets—markets in which Mr. Biggs was advising his clients to invest—by margins of about two to one. If you can't trust Mr. Biggs or the venerable Morgan Stanley, whom can you trust? In fact, Mr. Biggs himself stated: "God made global strategists so that weathermen would look good."[17] It seems he has a similar view to Warren Buffett, who said, "The only value of stock forecasters is to make fortune-tellers look good."[18]

Investors would do well to consider timing the market to be a lot like playing slot machines. While it may be entertaining, the risk/reward trade-off is very poor. While we know that over the short term some slot machine players win, we neither attribute any skill to them nor expect them to win over the long term. The same is true of market timers. In the short term there will always be some who will make correct forecasts. Evidence has shown, however, that we should neither attribute any skill to the short-term winners nor expect them to beat the market in the future. The problem for investors is that market gurus who have made the most recent correct forecasts end up being interviewed by the financial press and the media. This attention somehow gives them an aura of credibility. It also, unfortunately, fuels the hopes of investors that there is a way to beat the market.

The body of evidence on the failure of efforts to time the market is so overwhelming that *Fortune* magazine reached this conclusion: "Let's say it clearly: No one knows where the market is going—experts or novices, soothsayers or astrologers. That's the simple truth."[19] Despite reaching this conclusion *Fortune* advises you on when to increase your allocation to stocks and when to "Sell Stocks Now!" Listen carefully to Steve Forbes, publisher of the magazine that bears his name, quoting his grandfather, who founded the publication eighty years ago: "You make more money selling the advice than following it."[20]

Whenever I am asked if it is a good time to invest, my advice is simple: the best time to invest is always whenever you have funds available to do so. Any other advice would simply be advising someone to play the loser's game. Remember that "the direction of the next 20 percent market move is both unknowable and immaterial to the success of a lifetime investment program. It's the direction of the next 100 percent move that matters, and we know perfectly well which way that'll be, now don't we?"[21] Benjamin Disraeli said it best: "Patience is a necessary ingredient of genius."

The Emperor Has No Clothes

The fairy tale of the emperor's new clothes provides an appropriate analogy to the belief in active management. In the children's fairy tale, a tailor convinces the emperor of the beauty of his nonexistent clothes. In the end the emperor is embarrassed when he goes before the people believing in what is obviously not there. Just as the emperor was tricked by the tailor, investors are tricked by the investment community into believing in active management. The tailor relied on the emperor's ego. The emperor didn't want to admit that he couldn't see the tailor's miraculous cloth. Investors don't want to admit that neither they nor the investment managers they choose are likely to outperform the market. They don't want to admit that they have been needlessly paying transaction costs and management fees. Charles Mackay, author of *Extraordinary*

Popular Delusions & the Madness of Crowds, said: "Every age has its peculiar folly: some scheme, project, or fantasy into which it plunges, spurred on by the love of gain, the necessity of excitement, or the force of imitation." He said this in 1841. It is just as true now as it was then.

Various academic studies provide evidence on the inability of professional investment managers to outperform the market. Mark Carhart studied mutual-fund performance, analyzing 1,892 funds for the period 1961–93. The following is a summary of his findings.

- The average actively managed fund has underperformed its appropriate passive benchmark on a pretax basis by about 1.8 percent per annum. On an after-tax basis, the performance is even worse.

- There is no persistence in performance beyond that which would be randomly expected—the past performance of an individual active manager is a very poor predictor of his/her future performance.

- Expenses reduce returns on a one-for-one basis and thus they explain much of the persistent long-term underperformance of mutual funds.

- Turnover reduces pretax returns by almost 1 percent of the value of the trade.

Carhart's conclusion: "While the popular press will no doubt continue to glamorize the best-performing mutual fund managers, the mundane explanations of strategy (asset class allocation, not individual stock selection) and investment costs account for almost all of the important predictability in mutual fund returns."[22]

Russ Wermers's study on mutual-fund performance confirmed the results of Carhart's study, while also providing some valuable insights. Wermers's study covered the twenty-year period 1975–94 and included a universe of 241 funds at the start of the period and 1,279 by the end.[23] In order not to inject survivorship bias (funds that perform poorly close because of redemptions by investors or they are merged out of existence by their sponsors) into the data, Wermers's total database included 1,788 funds that existed at any time during the period. Here is a summary of his findings:

- The stocks active managers selected actually outperformed by 0.7 percent per annum.
- Unfortunately for investors, in their efforts the funds ran up total expenses of about 2.3 percent per annum.
- The net result was an underperformance of 1.6 percent per annum.
- Even worse, because the stocks they bought were, on average, riskier than the average stock, on a risk-adjusted basis the underperformance increased to 2.2 percent per annum.

It seems that the emperor really has no clothes.

Does Active Management Work in "Inefficient Markets"?

Because of the overwhelming body of evidence, heretofore skeptical practitioners have started to concede that the market is highly efficient, at least with respect to the stocks of the companies with a large market capitalization; there are so many analysts following these companies that information about them is available to everyone and the competition is too tough. On the other hand, the same practitioners hold that the efficient market thesis is not true for the stocks of smaller companies, which are less widely followed and on which less information is available. In fact the case in favor of market efficiency is just as compelling for the smaller capitalization stocks as it is for the larger capitalization stocks. Statistics show that active managers in the asset class of small-cap companies perform no better than do active managers in the asset class of large-cap companies. For example, as was stated earlier, for the five-year period 1998–2002, encompassing both a huge bull and a terrible bear market, the S&P 600, a small-cap index, outperformed 66 percent of actively managed funds.[24]

As further evidence consider the following. For the ten-year period ending March 2004, the passively managed DFA Micro Cap and Small Cap Funds provided annualized returns of 15.4 percent and 13.1 percent, respectively. Actively managed small-cap funds earned annualized returns of just 11.9 percent. The passively managed DFA Small Value Fund provided an annualized return of 16.2 percent, while actively managed small-value funds, on average, provided annualized returns of just 13.6 percent. Also note that this data is biased in favor of actively managed funds because the Morningstar database from which it is drawn is not free of survivorship bias.

Emerging Markets

The same practitioners also cling to the belief that stock selection can add value in the underresearched and "inefficient" capital markets of the emerging industrial countries such as Mexico, Brazil,

Singapore, or Turkey. If active management can produce superior results to a passive strategy, it should certainly be able to do so in these "inefficient" markets, where research can theoretically uncover undervalued securities.

First let's deal with the myth that the financial markets of the emerging countries are underresearched. The Turkish Stock Exchange, for example, as of May 2003, had 288 listed stocks and 114 brokerage firms. It also had a modern, totally computerized trading system. It doesn't sound like the Turkish market lacks coverage for its securities or that its market is backward. However, if the financial markets of the emerging markets are truly inefficient, then we should find that active managers are beating the market averages. Once again, the evidence is to the contrary.

The Morningstar database provides us with a list of only eleven actively managed emerging-market funds with a full ten-year track record covering the period 1994–2003. Even with the obvious survivorship bias in the data, during this period the DFA Emerging Markets Fund outperformed the average actively managed fund by over 1 percent per annum, providing an annualized return of 2.27 percent. Only four of the eleven that managed to survive the full period outperformed the passively managed DFA fund, and one did so by just 0.02 percent per annum. It is important to note that in addition to its Emerging Markets Fund (which is a large-cap fund), DFA also runs two other passively managed Emerging Markets funds, a Small Cap Fund and a Value Fund. Its Emerging Markets Small Cap Fund returned 5.88 percent per annum, outperforming all but one actively managed emerging-markets fund. The one outperformer was the GMO Emerging Markets Fund, and it outperformed by just 0.04 percent per annum. The GMO fund is, however, a value fund, and thus a better benchmark would be the DFA Emerging Markets Value Fund. It provided an annualized return of 7.16 percent, and was the top performer of all funds with a full ten-year track record. It is important to note that on the other end of the spectrum stood the Fidelity Emerging Markets Fund. It "rewarded" believers in active management in supposedly highly inefficient markets with an annualized return of negative 5.19 percent, and underperformed the DFA Emerging Markets, Emerging Markets Small, and Emerging Markets Value Funds by 7.46, 11.07, 12.35 percent per annum, respectively, for ten full years! That is a high price to pay for belief in active management. The other underachievers were funds of Wells Fargo, Merrill Lynch, JPMorgan, Morgan Stanley, Frank Russell, and the legendary Templeton.

The Efficiency of International Markets

Thanks to David Booth of DFA, we have further empirical evidence against the often heard argument that because international markets are not as well researched and therefore not as efficient as the U.S. markets, active managers can add value when investing globally.

Booth compared the performance of single country funds to an appropriate benchmark, a country index. His study covered nine countries and twenty-six funds in developed markets, and eighteen countries and thirty funds in emerging markets. If active managers are able to add value, we would see them consistently outperforming market indices. All results are for periods ending December 1996. Booth found that the average developed-market country fund underperformed its benchmark by 7.9 and 1.4 percent per annum over three- and five-year periods, respectively. The average emerging-market country fund also underperformed its benchmark country index by 5.8 and 1.6 per annum over three- and five-year periods, respectively. The average underperformance for all fifty-six funds covering twenty-seven countries was 6.6 and 1.5 percent per annum for three- and five-year periods, respectively. The value added by active managers is clearly negative. In addition, the negative value added was greatest in the emerging markets, the very markets where active managers claim to add the most value (because they believe these markets to be the most inefficient).

The main reason for this result is that the costs of trading in the less efficient overseas markets are greater than in the more efficient U.S. markets—and the more inefficient the market, the greater the trading costs. Again we see that despite the claims of active managers, there is no evidence that active management works in either efficient or inefficient markets. Booth concluded: "Even these dismal results overstate the value of active managers since the benchmark indices are price-only indices, rather than total return indices, which would include dividends." Even Booth's insight on total returns is not the whole story. For taxable accounts, the value added by active managers is likely to be even more negative due to the greater turnover, and probably greater distributed income, of an active versus a passive management strategy.[25]

Another study covering the U.K. market for the ten-year period ending in 1995 found that only two of seventy-nine growth and income mutual funds outperformed the market.[26] As W. Scott Simon pointed out in his book *Index Mutual Funds,* this means that less than 3 percent of these funds that employ money managers who take themselves seriously and pay themselves accordingly were able to achieve what they were paid to do. Since these figures did not even take into account the negative impact of taxes, it could very well be that none of the managers were able to beat what they claim to be a "no-brainer"—match the market on a tax-adjusted basis."

The Bottom Line

Since over 80 percent of all equity trading is carried out by institutions through their skilled, knowledgeable traders, it is very difficult to secure an advantage over the competition. I do not claim that it is impossible to beat the market. In fact, as we have seen, about 30 percent of active managers do so every year. However, as was so aptly put by active manager Robert Stovall: "Of course, each year it's a different group." Moreover, academic studies have demonstrated that the longer the time frame, the lower the number of active managers who succeed at this loser's game.

One of the most impressive pieces of data on the inability of active management to beat the market (thereby strengthening the argument that the markets are efficient) is contained in the chart that follows. It shows an incredibly high similarity between the ability of active managers to beat the market and the outcome of a coin-flipping contest.

If you put enough people together, some will flip ten heads in a row. Similarly, if you have thousands of active managers, some will beat the market, possibly even ten years in a row. Attributing a particular level of skill to the managers who beat the market, however, is the equivalent of attributing a particular skill to the winner of the coin-flipping contest. Put another way, believing that the winner of the coin-flipping contest will repeat his or her performance is comparable to believing that an active manager who beats his or her benchmark in one period will do so in the next period. If the markets were truly inefficient, one would observe far more successful money managers than just the handful of Peter Lynchs and Warren Buffetts.

Active vs. Passive Management

Security Selection: Do active managers perform better than a random flipping of coins?

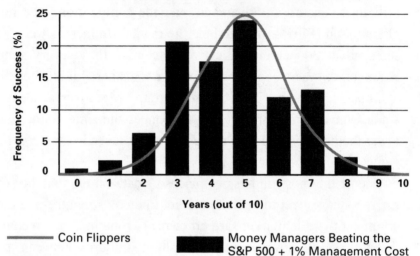

Number of Years (out of ten) Active Money Managers
beat the S&P 500 + 1% Management Cost and
Number of Times (out of ten) Coin Tosses Produce "Heads"

———— Coin Flippers ■ Money Managers Beating the S&P 500 + 1% Management Cost

Source: SEI Investments (1984–1993)
Manager returns are calculated without subtracting fees.

Technical Analysis

If fifty million people say a foolish thing, it is still a foolish thing. —Anatole France

Technical analysis is anathema to the academic world. We love to pick on it. Our bullying tactics are prompted by two considerations: the method is patently false; and it's easy to pick on. And while it may seem a bit unfair to pick on such a sorry target, just remember: it's your money we are trying to save. —Burton Malkiel, *A Random Walk Down Wall Street*

As we have seen, active managers have had little success adding value through superior research. Before turning to the discussion in the next chapter on risk, let's take a look at one other strategy individual investors and active managers believe they can use to beat the market: technical analysis.

Millions of people believe in astrology. They believe that astrologists, by interpreting the alignment, or charts, of the planets and stars, can predict the future. Astrologists make forecasts such as the following:

> Bill Meridian, writing in the *Mountain Astrologer,* believes that the bear will likely visit the stock market as Jupiter soon completes the most bullish part of its 12-year passage from Virgo through Sagittarius. Don't be downhearted, though. Jupiter moving into conjunction with Uranus in mid-February will touch off one of those bursts of technological creativity that accompany this planetary alignment in 14-year cycles.[27]

Millions of people also believe in technical analysis. They believe that technical analysts can predict future stock-price movements by interpreting charts of past prices. Unfortunately for investors, technical analysis has no more basis in reality than astrology.

Technical analysts are a unique group. Like proponents of the EMH, they believe that fundamental security analysis, which focuses on predicting the performance of stocks based on predicted future earnings, is a futile endeavor. On the other hand, the EMH states that no trading system can generate returns in excess of the market's return. Technical analysts believe, however, that they can identify mispriced assets based on historical price movements.

Technical analysts look at charts of historical prices to find patterns they believe will enable them to identify which direction, and by how much, prices will move in the immediate future. People engaged in this "art" used to be called "chartists." In order to give them an air of authority and respectability, they are now called "technicians." If this style of analysis worked, one would be able to see managers who use this style of analysis beating the market. As already shown, no such evidence exists. While this lack of evidence should be sufficient to convince you, there is one dramatic story I believe will convince anyone, except those trying to sell you their technical analysis services.

In 1959 Harry Roberts, of the University of Chicago, had a computer generate a series of random numbers that would have a distribution matching the average weekly price change of the average stock (about 2 percent). Since the numbers were randomly generated, there was no pattern and therefore no knowledge that could be obtained by studying a chart of this nature. In order to create the illusion that his charts were those of particular stocks, Roberts placed a starting price of $40 on each chart. He then took a group of these charts to the leading technical analysts of his day. He asked for their advice on whether to buy or sell these unnamed hypothetical stocks. He told them that he did not want them to know the name of the stock since this knowledge might bias them. Each technical analyst had very strong advice on what Roberts should do but since the numbers were randomly generated the patterns were only in the minds of the observers. I am sure that you will never hear about this story from a technical analyst.

Despite the fact that the results of this study were published in the *Journal of Finance* in 1959, certainly embarrassing the technical analysis "profession," you can still observe technical analysts dispensing advice on CNBC. And, unfortunately, investors are presumably acting on that advice.[28] In actuality, the only thing their advice is good for is entertainment. Taken any other way, it is dangerous to the financial health of the listeners because it causes them to veer from the prudent passive strategy. As a test, see if you can pick out the randomly generated chart from the actual chart of weekly stock prices for 1956. The charts are replicas of ones that appeared in the aforementioned *Journal of Finance* article. Be sure to cover up the legend at the bottom.

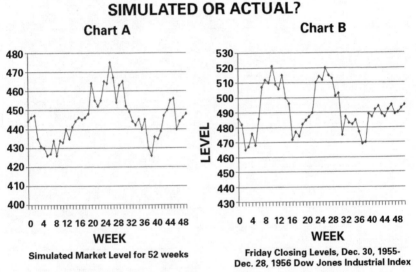

SIMULATED OR ACTUAL?

Chart A

Chart B

WEEK

WEEK

Simulated Market Level for 52 weeks

**Friday Closing Levels, Dec. 30, 1955-
Dec. 28, 1956 Dow Jones Industrial Index**

Source: *The Journal of Finance* XIV, No.1, March 1959, "Stock Market "Patterns" and Financial Analysis: Methodological Suggestions," Harry V. Roberts. University of Chicago

It is worth noting that Roberts's experiment has been repeated using the results of a computer-generated coin-toss game. As you can see in the following chart, the computer output will produce a randomly generated chart that moves around the expected 50 percent heads and 50 percent tails. It does look suspiciously like the chart of a stock's price movement. This is, by the way, further support for the EMH. As was just explained, stock prices do move in a random fashion as they respond to new information, which is random in whether it will be better or worse than the

Effects of Random Wandering on Coin-Tossing Game

$1 Gain or Loss per Toss
Expected Return: $0.00

95% Confidence Limits(+/−)

Number of Tosses	Average Return per Toss		Total Gain or Loss
	Low	High	
100	−20 to	20	+/− $20
10,000	−2 to	2	+/− $200
1 million	−.2 to	.2	+/− $2,000
100 million	−.02 to	.02	+/− $20,000
10 billion	−.002 to	.002	+/− $200,000

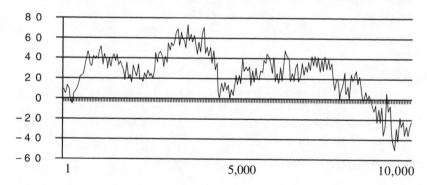

markets have anticipated. Technical analysts, if shown this chart, will give you a strong opinion on the future direction of the "stock" the chart is supposedly representing. And George Bush thought that Ronald Reagan was practicing "voodoo economics."

What I hope you have learned from this story is that while a picture (or chart) may be worth a thousand words, it is not worth even one of your investment dollars.

The following story is one of my favorite examples of the gibberish of technical analysis. The November 16, 1992, edition of *USA TODAY* carried the following forecast in Dan Dorfman's column. Being in Mr. Dorfman's column, of course, gave it immediate credibility. "Technical analyst Jerry Favors sees the DJIA plunging 400 points in the next few weeks, and dropping from 3,233 to 1,700 or less between May and June of 1993. The forecast is based on a 'three-peaks-and-a-dome-house' technical indicator he claims has never been wrong in the twenty-five or so times it has been activated in the last two hundred years." Mr. Dorfman presumably carried this story because he thought that Mr. Favors was providing real value added for his clients. Mr. Dorfman also presumably thought his readers might want to consider acting on this advice (otherwise why print the story). Five years and over 4,000 points later, investors who sold their investments based on Mr. Favors's forecast were still waiting for the correction that was predicted. If you are not yet convinced that three-peaks-and-a-dome house and a technical indicator that never failed in over two hundred years is gibberish and investment pandering, I certainly am not accomplishing my mission. I hope that you have learned that even if such a thing ever existed, it was just another example of a random pattern with no predictive value.

As Burton Malkiel points out: "If you examine past stock prices in any given period, you will always find some kind of system that would have worked in a given period. If enough different criteria for selecting stocks are tried, one will eventually be found that selects the best ones for that period." Malkiel cites a study in which a computer was programmed to draw charts for 548 stocks traded on the NYSE over a five-year period. It was instructed to scan all the charts and identify any one of thirty-two of the most popularly followed patterns. Whenever the computer identified a bearish or bullish chart pattern, it recorded the appropriate sell or buy signal. The conclusion of the study was that there was no relationship between technical signals and subsequent performance. After trading expenses, the performance of the technical indicators was no better than a buy-and-hold strategy. In fact the strategy that came closest to producing above-average results was to buy after one of the bear signals.[29]

If technical analysis has no basis in reality, why do many Wall Street firms hire people to perform this particular brand of fortune-telling? Wall Street firms hope to persuade investors to generate greater trading activity and therefore more commission income. Unfortunately, the media contribute to the appearance that technical analysts add value by giving them space in print and time on the air.

Efficient Markets and Bond Funds

Basically, we were guessing on interest rates. . . . What we've come to believe is that no one can guess interest rates.
—Fred Henning, head of fixed-income investing at Fidelity
Investments, *Los Angeles Times,* July 7, 1997

The exact same logic on market efficiency relative to equity investing applies to fixed-income investing. In fact it is much harder for active managers to add value in fixed-income investing than it is with equity investing. Let's see why this is true.

First, with U.S. government debt, all bonds of the same maturity will provide the same return. There will be no differentiation in performance. When we look at corporate or municipal bonds of the highest credit rating (AAA or AA), bonds that have the same rating and the same maturity are highly likely (but not 100 percent certain) to provide very similar returns. The reason is that securities in these rating categories experience almost no defaults. Thus there is a very limited ability to add value by security selection (which is at least theoretically possible with equities). And because the main purpose of the fixed-income portion of a portfolio is to provide stability and/or certainty of cash flow, allowing you to sleep well while taking the risks of equity ownership, investors should limit their purchases to securities within the top two investment grades.

The total (with U.S. government securities) or very minimal (with AAA- and AA-rated securities) lack of differentiation between securities leaves the ability to correctly forecast interest rates as the only way for active fixed-income managers to add value. William Sherden reviewed the leading research on forecasting accuracy from 1979 to 1995. The research covered forecasts made from 1970 to 1995. He concluded that:

- *Economists cannot predict the turning points in the economy.* He found that of the forty-eight predictions made by economists, forty-six missed the turning points.

- *Economists' forecasting skill is about as good as guessing.* Even the economists who directly or indirectly run the economy (the Federal Reserve, the CEA [Council of Economic Advisors], and the CBO [Congressional Budget Office]) had forecasting records that were worse than pure chance.

- *There are no economic forecasters who consistently lead the pack in forecasting accuracy.*[30]

Obviously, if you cannot forecast the economy correctly, you cannot forecast interest rates with any degree of accuracy. As you will see, the evidence supports Sherden's findings.

A study covering the ten-year period ending 1998 found that the average actively managed bond fund underperformed the Lehman Brothers Aggregate Bond Index by 0.7 percent per annum.[31] A similar 1994 study found that only 128 (16 percent) out of 800 fixed-income funds beat their relevant benchmark over the ten-year period covered.[32]

Just as we saw with equities, the evidence is overwhelming that active management is a loser's game. Of course, just as is true with equities, being a loser's game does not mean there are not some winners. That leaves the question: Can we identify the few winners ahead of time? In other words, is there persistence of outperformance? Again, let's look at the evidence.

John Bogle of Vanguard studied the performance of bond funds and concluded that "although past absolute returns of bond funds are a flawed predictor of future returns, there is a fairly easy way to predict future relative returns." After he separated the bond funds into their major categories of quality and maturity, he analyzed returns in terms of their expense ratios. Bogle placed funds into four categories: those with expenses of less than 0.5 percent, those with expenses between 0.5 and 1 percent, those with expenses between 1 percent and 1.5 percent, and those with expenses of over 1.5 percent. Bogle found that "in every case, and in every category, the superior funds could have been systemically identified based solely on their lower expense ratios. At the extremes, the lower expense funds outpaced the higher expense funds by between 1 and 2.2 percent annually. The ability to predict interest rates played no part in the performance of the bond funds."[33]

William Reichenstein's study, "Bond Fund Returns and Expenses: A Study of Bond Market Efficiency," covered the five-year period 1994–98 and found similar results.[34] He sorted bond funds by investment quality (low, medium, high) and by maturity structure (short term, intermediate, and long term). His conclusion:

There is virtually a perfect inverse relationship between expenses and returns—increases in expenses lead to a direct proportional 1:1 reduction in returns.

And finally, a study by Dale L. Domian and William Reichenstein sought to determine if the municipal bond market is as efficient as the taxable fixed-income market. They studied the performance of municipal bond funds for the period 1991–2000.[35] The authors came to the following conclusions, all of which are consistent with the EMH.

- Across similar-style funds (by maturity and credit quality) there is a consistent negative relationship between expense ratios and net returns.

- Expense ratios consistently predict relative fund returns over one- to five-year horizons—lower expense ratios produce a persistent advantage year after year.

The authors concluded: "Net returns are driven almost exclusively by fund expenses." They also concluded that the longer the horizon, the better the expense ratio predicts returns.

In the face of this body of evidence, we can draw some conclusions as to the winning investment strategy. First, because bonds, within each investment grade, are relatively homogenous investments (have relatively similar risk characteristics), there is little opportunity for fund managers to distinguish themselves. Since different bonds of the same investment grade are good substitutes for one another, costs only reduce returns. This is particularly true of short-term fixed-income investments, where little or no value can be added by guessing right on the future direction of interest rates. The implication for investors is that the winning strategy in fixed-income markets, whether taxable or tax exempt, is either to choose the lowest cost fund (and passive funds are likely to be the lowest cost) that meets your credit and maturity criteria or if your portfolio is large enough to build your own individually tailored portfolio (thus avoiding the fund's fees).

Efficient Markets and Costs

Beware of false prophets, which come to you in sheep's clothing, but inwardly they are ravening wolves.
—Matthew 7:15, King James Version

While the question of whether or not the market is efficient from an information perspective has important implications, it is not the only criterion one needs to consider in order to develop the appropriate investment strategy. As we have seen, the efficiency of the market in processing information makes active management a loser's game. Another factor that makes it a loser's game is that any advantage gained by exploiting alleged market inefficiencies may not be great enough to overcome the trading, research, and other costs incurred. As you will see, the costs incurred by active managers play a very important role in determining the winning investment strategy.

The Bid-Offer Spread

A market can be said to be efficient when the cost to enter into a transaction is relatively low. Since managers incur the cost of the difference between the bid (the price received when they sell) and offer (the price paid when they buy) when they trade, the bid-offer spread is a reasonably good *initial* estimate of the trading costs of a mutual fund. Using data provided by Bridge from November 8, 2001, the average spread between the bid and the offer for the stocks of the first decile (the top 10 percent) of companies, ranked by market capitalization (size), is 0.12 percent. In addition, these large-cap stocks traded almost $300 million worth of shares each day. However, while the trading costs are relatively low, we have seen that the high degree of information efficiency surrounding these stocks (e.g., GE, Microsoft, etc.) makes it extremely difficult to gain a competitive advantage that can be exploited. On the other hand, in the very smallest of the small-cap stocks (the bottom 10 percent), the average trading volume was under $200,000, and the bid-offer spread was 4.03 percent.[36] Thus while it may be possible to gain a competitive advantage in terms of information (because fewer analysts and traders follow these stocks), the cost of exploiting any such advantage is much greater—almost 4 percent, or over thirty times greater. Thus, from a trading cost perspective, we can conclude that the market for the largest cap stocks is over thirty times as efficient as that for the smallest cap stocks.

Markets characterized by large numbers of buyers and sellers, and the resulting small spreads, are called liquid or efficient markets. Markets with fewer buyers and sellers are less liquid and therefore less efficient from a cost perspective. It is logical that the greater the number of buyers and sellers, the tighter will be the spreads and the lower the trading costs. The lower level of liquidity available in the smallest cap stocks makes trading in this asset class riskier and more expensive than trading in the more liquid asset class of large-cap stocks. In the next chapter I will show that the markets are efficient in pricing for risk. In other words, if an asset class is riskier, investors must be compensated with higher returns for accepting that higher level of risk.

Turnover

Let's now examine just how great an impact the bid-offer spread can have on the performance of active managers in their search for securities that the rest of the market has somehow mispriced. The average mutual fund has a turnover rate of about 100 percent. While turnover is best defined in dollar terms, it can also be thought of in the following way. If a fund held the stocks of eighty companies at the beginning of the year, the fund must bear the expenses of selling eighty stocks and buying eighty new ones. One can approximate the cost of turnover by multiplying the turnover rate by the bid-offer spread. For the first decile of stocks, the cost is 0.12 (100 percent times the bid-offer spread of 0.12 percent). For the tenth-decile stocks, the cost is 4.03 percent.

Passively managed funds generally have very low turnover rates in comparison to actively managed funds. A passively managed small-company fund might have turnover of perhaps 30 percent per annum. Using this assumption, we can compare the trading cost hurdle (for the asset class of the smallest cap stocks) that active management imposes on itself, as compared to a passive strategy.

	Active Management (%)	Passive Management (%)
Turnover Rate (a)	100	30
Bid-offer Spread (b)	4	4
Trading Costs (a × b)	4	1.2

The trading costs of active management create a significant hurdle of 2.8 percent per annum (4 −1.2) that must be overcome in order to match the performance of passive managers. And this figure excludes trading commissions (and the fund's operating-expense ratio). In reality, the impact of the turnover of active managers is greater than just illustrated because the example ignores the market impact of the trading activity of active managers. If an active manager attempts to buy (or sell) in excess of the daily trading volume, the result will probably be that his/her actions will drive up (or down) the price. Barra, a research organization, did an extensive study on market-impact costs and found that while market-impact costs will vary, depending on many factors (fund size, asset class, turnover, etc.), they can be quite substantial. Barra noted that a fairly typical case of a small- or mid-cap stock fund with $500 million in assets and an annual turnover rate of between 80 and 100 percent could lose 3 to 5 percent per annum to market-impact costs—far more than the annual operating expenses of most funds. Even large-cap funds can have large market-impact costs.[37] Given that they have such great hurdles to overcome, one might say that it is to the credit of the managers of actively managed small-company funds that their performance is not worse than it actually is. The only problem is that since they are still delivering results below those delivered by passively managed funds, they would be better off not trying in the first place. So would their investors. That is why it is a loser's game.

As you can see, the more illiquid the market (the larger the bid-offer spread), the greater the hurdle an active manager has to overcome in order to add value. One can only imagine how much wider the spreads must be, and higher the transactions costs, when trading in the emerging markets of Brazil, Mexico, and so on. These wide spreads and high-transaction costs go a long way toward explaining the poor performance of actively managed emerging-market funds as compared to their passively managed counterparts.

Costs Create Hurdles

The burden of overcoming the costs of active management is a major reason why active management doesn't work, even if the markets, as many claim, are relatively inefficient from a classical economic (i.e., information) perspective. While market efficiency from an informational perspective is a very important ingredient in both understanding how markets work and in determining whether active or passive management will be the winning strategy, what we learn from this is that the whole debate about whether or not the markets are "efficient" is really somewhat irrelevant to the investment policy process. What really matters to investors is whether or not active management can overcome its expenses and add value over a passive strategy. Let's look at the evidence from a Morningstar study. Over the ten-year period studied, Morningstar found that low-turnover funds (those with an average holding period greater than five years—or less than a 20 percent turnover rate) rose an average of 12.9 percent per annum, while high-turnover funds (those with an average holding period of less than one year—or a turnover rate of greater than 100 percent) gained only 11.3 percent per annum on average. Trading costs and the impact on prices of trading activity reduced returns of the high-turnover funds by 1.6 percent per annum.[38] As we have seen, the more illiquid the market, the more difficult it will be for active managers to succeed in their objective. To summarize, active management doesn't work well in efficient (liquid) markets, and it doesn't work well in inefficient (illiquid) markets. It doesn't work well, period. It is a loser's game.

The Large Hurdle Created by Taxes

We have seen how great a hurdle the costs imposed by active management can create. Unfortunately, at least for investors holding equities in taxable accounts, we have not yet discussed what is often the greatest hurdle created by active management—the negative impact of the burden of taxes as a result of IRS form 1099 fund distributions. Whenever a fund realizes gains, it must distribute them to investors. Because dividend and realized capital-gain distributions are subject to state, local, and federal taxation, for taxable accounts after-tax returns are the only returns that matter. It is the greater turnover of actively managed funds that makes them tax inefficient relative to passively managed funds.

The study titled "How Well Have Taxable Investors Been Served in the 1980s and 1990s?" in the *Journal of Portfolio Management* investigated:

- The pre- and after-tax efficiency of actively managed funds,
- The likelihood of pre- and after-tax outperformance,
- The relative size of outperformance versus the relative size of underperformance.

The study, covering the twenty-year period 1979–98, included all funds with over $100 million in assets. Here is a summary of its findings:[39]

- Just 22 percent of the funds beat their benchmark on a *pretax* basis. The average outperformance was 1.4 percent, with the average underperformance being 2.6 percent. On an after-tax basis, however, just 14 percent of the funds outperformed.

The average after-tax outperformance was just 1.3 percent, while the average after-tax underperformance was 3.2 percent. The risk-adjusted odds against outperformance are about *seventeen to one.*

- The average fund underperformed its benchmark by 1.8 percent per annum before taxes but by 2.6 percent on an after-tax basis.

The story is actually worse than it appears because the data above contains survivorship bias. For example, for the full twenty-year period, the average fund underperformed its benchmark by 2.6 percent on an after-tax basis. However, thirty-three funds disappeared during the time frame covered by the study. When we adjust for survivorship bias, the underperformance increases to 2.8 percent. Thus the risk-adjusted odds of outperformance were even lower than the dismal figures presented above. One more point on survivorship bias: since the study only covered funds with more than $100 million in assets, it is likely that the survivorship bias is understated. Funds that have successful track records tend to attract assets. Funds with poor records tend to lose assets or are "put to death," never reaching the $100 million threshold of the study. So it seems logical to conclude that if the study covered all funds, instead of just those with assets over $100 million, the survivorship bias would have been even greater. We do know that far more than thirty-three funds disappeared during the period covered.

The Really Dirty Secret

Before concluding this chapter, I would like to relate the following story. It is a highly unusual one, as you will see. Aronson + Partners is an actively managed institutional fund that, as the plus sign in its name suggests, uses a quantitative (mathematically based rules as opposed to subjective judgment) approach to stock selection. In an interview with *Barron's,* Theodore Aronson made some very interesting statements:[40]

- I never forget that the devil sitting on my shoulder [is the] low-cost passive funds. They win because they lose less.

- None of my clients are taxable. Because, once you introduce taxes *active management probably has an insurmountable hurdle.* We have been asked to run taxable money—and declined. The costs of our active strategies are high enough without paying Uncle Sam.

- Capital gain taxes, when combined with transaction costs and fees, *make indexing profoundly advantaged,* I am sorry to say.

- All of the partners are in the same situation—our retirement dough (tax deferred accounts) is here. But not our taxable investments.

- If you crunch the numbers turnover has to come down, not low, but to super-low, like 15–20 percent, or taxes kill you. That's *the real dirty secret in our* business: *Mutual funds are bought with and sold with virtually no attention to tax efficiency.*

- My wife, three children and I have taxable money in eight of the Vanguard index funds.

In an interview with Jason Zweig, a columnist for *Money,* Aronson was asked: "You're an active fund manager, and most of your money is in index funds?" He responded: "Personally, I think indexing wins hands-down. After tax, active management just can't win."[41]

Listen carefully to the advice of Jonathan Clements, columnist for the *Wall Street Journal:* "If index funds look great before taxes, their performance is almost unbeatable after taxes, thanks to their low turnover and thus slow realization of capital gains."[42] In light of the evidence, a logical conclusion for investors is that for taxable accounts the already low probability of actively managed funds outperforming a passive alternative are dramatically reduced. (Appendix G addresses the investment implications of the tax act of 2003.)

Explaining the Performance of the Superstars

One of the two most asked questions I am posed is: "If the markets are so efficient, how do you account for the performance of such superstars as Peter Lynch and Warren Buffett?" The answer lies in the chart of coin flippers we explored earlier. We only know that Mr. Lynch and Mr. Buffett are the superstars of the investment world after the fact. With many thousands of investment managers trying to beat the market, we know that it is almost inevitable that some will succeed. We also have seen that because of the many hurdles that these managers face in their efforts to beat the market, far fewer succeed than would randomly be expected to do so. The surprise, therefore, is not that a few managers did beat the market but rather that so few succeeded in doing so. While we fully expect some to succeed, the problem is that it is impossible to know ahead of time which will be the lucky few. In other words, twenty years from now we will be talking about a few superstar investment managers who are the successors to Lynch and Buffett, but there is no way to predict who they will be.

Fortunately, you do not need the next Michael Jordan of investment managers to have a positive investment experience. The gains are, literally, there for the taking. As you will see, the key to success is gaining exposure to the right asset classes, diversifying your risk, and having the discipline to stick with the strategy.

CHAPTER 4

◆

Efficient Markets II—Risk

Though this be madness, yet there is method in 't.
—Shakespeare, *Hamlet* II: ii

The third concept related to market efficiency, in addition to informational efficiency and trading-cost efficiency—and probably the most important factor to be used in developing the winning investment strategy—is risk. Fortunately, most find this concept is the easiest to grasp. It can really all be summed up in the cliché, "Nothing ventured, nothing gained." It is important to understand that markets are efficient—riskier assets must provide higher *expected* returns as compensation for their greater risk. If less risky assets produced higher *expected* returns, then you would have what economists call a "free lunch." The important word is "expected." If the higher returns were instead guaranteed, then there would not be any risk. In other words, sometimes the risk shows up—the ex-post (after-the-fact) results don't match the ex-ante (before-the-fact) expectations.

Imagine a world in which a U.S. government security carried a higher yield than a corporate bond with a similar maturity; this world would not make any sense. The government security carries no credit risk. The corporate bond carries with it some degree of default risk. Being riskier, the corporate bond must provide a higher yield to attract investors. However, if such an anomaly existed, investors would immediately sell corporate bonds, driving their price down (and yield up), and buy government bonds, driving their price up (and yield down), until the anomaly no longer existed. Their actions would drive the price differential between the two securities to the level at which investors were exactly compensated for the perceived difference in risk. We will now examine how an investor can utilize this knowledge about the relationship between risk and return to develop his/her own winning strategy.

Returns and Cost of Capital

We know that corporations must pay a higher rate of interest (they have a higher cost of capital) than the U.S. government. We also know that corporations with low credit ratings must pay more (have a higher cost of capital) than corporations with high credit ratings. We know, too, that the flip side of a high cost of capital is a high *expected* return to those who provide that capital (a very important piece of knowledge). Why, then, shouldn't an investor in search of high returns buy the bond of just one company with a low credit (junk bond) rating? The answer is that the investor might be unlucky enough to buy the bond of a company that will eventually go bankrupt. In order to eliminate what economists call *uncompensated risk,* an investor needs to, in effect, buy the bonds of all the companies within that risk category (asset class). The risk of owning a single security (or small number of securities) within an asset class is called uncompensated risk because the expected return of any one security is the same as that of all securities with similar risk characteristics. By owning just one security (or a small group of securities), an investor is taking risk that can be diversified away. Risk that cannot be diversified away, like the risk of owning stocks, is called compensated risk. Effective diversification results in the elimination (or at least reduction) of uncompensated risk.

Returns and Risk

For the period 1926–2003, totally riskless one-month Treasury bills produced less than a 1 percent annualized real (after inflation) rate of return. U.S. government bonds (average maturity of twenty years), which entail no credit risk, but do carry interest-rate risk (if rates rise, they will fall in value), provided an annualized real rate of return of a little more than 2 percent per annum. The S&P 500 Index (a proxy for an investment in the stock market) provided a much greater return; it increased at an annualized after-inflation rate of over 7 percent per annum.

The above data is a very clear example of the riskier the asset, the greater the return to investors. Markets price efficiently for risk. Of course, investors did not receive those greater returns each and every year. There were many periods of very poor performance, periods that tested investor discipline. And, importantly, there was no guarantee that those high returns would be achieved. However, the higher expected returns are why savers (those who save in the form of cash or substantially equivalent investments like money market accounts, Treasury bills, or CDs) may sleep well, but investors (those who invest, or risk, their savings in equity investments) are highly likely to eat well (if their horizon is long and they have the discipline to stay the course).

Savings versus Investments

The differentiation between savings and investments is a very important concept to understand. Savings, because of low risk, and therefore low return, should be accumulated to meet emergency needs, cash flow needs, and shorter term spending requirements (e.g., college tuition, purchase of a home or car). Once you have created this safety net, the balance of your capital should be invested. This combination of savings and investments (your portfolio's asset allocation) will help you to ride out the often dramatic fluctuations in the market if you have confidence in the long-range success of your investment strategy.

There is no one right portfolio for everyone. Each individual's needs for savings are different. Everyone's investment time horizons are also different. In addition, not everyone can have peace of mind and accept the virtually inevitable bad years. One purpose of this book is to give you the information necessary to empower you to make your own asset-allocation decisions.

Equities Provide the Highest Expected Returns

As just shown, over the long term equities historically have provided much higher returns than either short- or long-term fixed-income investments. In order to be confident that they will continue to provide superior returns, we need to question whether this superior performance was logical. We need to ask the question: Why do equities produce greater returns? The answer is simple: they must, at least in an ex-ante sense—if they didn't, then investors wouldn't accept the greater risk that equities entail compared to fixed-income instruments. Taking it one step further, companies that the markets perceive as riskier have a higher cost of capital. The bonds of Wal-Mart, for example, carry a lower rate of interest than do the bonds of JCPenney. Said another way, riskier companies have to give away more of their expected future earnings in order to raise capital than do their safer counterparts. Investors demand these greater returns as the compensation for taking greater risk.

Identifying High Expected Returning Asset Classes

The more original a discovery, the more obvious it seems afterwards.
                                                    —Arthur Koestler

Identifying high expected returning asset classes is a simple exercise. Since it is known that risk is associated with expected return, all one has to do is identify the riskiest asset classes. One starts by comparing the asset classes of stocks and bonds. We know that because equities are riskier than bonds, they must provide greater expected returns. We can, therefore, move on to trying to identify the highest cost of capital equity asset classes. The answer is intuitive. Companies that have the highest cost of capital are risky small companies and risky "lousy" (or "value") companies.

"Lousy" or distressed companies are those trading closest to their liquidation value. One can identify these companies by their BtM (book value-to-market value) ratio. "Book value" is a term for a firm's net worth (assets minus liabilities) from an accounting perspective. The higher the BtM ratio, the closer a company is to being worth more dead than alive. Investors, through their market-trading activities, have driven down the prices of value companies because these companies have produced poor track records. Therefore they are perceived to be risky. Supporting this conclusion is that academic studies have found that value companies are typically characterized by simple intuitive risk interpretations, including a high degree of leverage (debt) and a high standard deviation of earnings.[1]

Small companies are also generally perceived as risky. One reason is that they have a smaller capital base and fewer alternatives for raising capital, reducing their ability to deal with economic adversity. (General Motors, a large company, may or may not be perceived as a great company, but it has a large cash reserve that it could use to carry it through a prolonged recession.) Small companies, like value companies, also typically have greater leverage and, as we will see, lower levels of profitability. In addition, they generally do not have long proven track records of success. Lousy or value companies, in contrast, have proven track records, only they are currently poor ones.

Robert Merton, a prominent financial economist at Harvard, provided this further explanation on why small companies are riskier, have higher costs of capital, and therefore provide higher returns. He postulated that the neglect of analysts and institutions results in a lack of information—increasing the risks to investors and therefore the cost of capital to the firm. This hypothesis has been confirmed by studies focusing on investor relations. He also stated that a key determinant of the size of the spread quoted by market makers (a proxy for the cost of trading) is information asymmetry facing the market maker. In other words, when market makers believe that some investors have superior knowledge, the bid-offer spread widens (increasing the cost of active management) as a form of protection.[2]

Think of risk and the market in these terms: Microsoft is now a much larger company and a lot less risky investment than it was twenty years ago. It also has many more analysts following the company. If it were to raise capital today, it would pay a lot less for that capital than it did when its stock first went public. Since it is a safer investment today, investors should expect to receive a lower future return.

Citigroup is a safer investment today than it was not too long ago when some thought its credit losses might even bring it down. Today, because it has returned to profitability and restored its capital base, its cost of equity capital is lower than it paid to investors just a few short years ago (when it was a value company). Therefore, investors who purchase Citigroup stock today can expect to earn a lower return than did investors in the recent past. Returns are compensation for risk.

The fact that investments in the stocks of both Microsoft and Citigroup are likely to produce lower expected returns than they did when they were small and value companies, respectively, does not make them bad investments. It does mean, however, that investors seeking a lower risk profile should expect lower returns. Investors must decide for themselves whether they want higher expected returns, and will accept the risk that goes along with those higher expected returns, or whether they want a lower level of risk, and are willing to accept the lower expected returns associated with that reduced level of risk.

We have just seen that lousy (distressed) companies must provide higher expected returns. However, if you are not yet convinced that great companies don't make great investments, here is one story that should convince you that one of the most fervently held beliefs about investing is not correct.

Great Companies Do Not Make Great (High-Returning) Investments

Let's go back in time to December 1963. John Doe is the best security analyst in the world. He is able to identify, with uncanny accuracy, the companies that will produce the highest rate of return on assets over the next thirty-eight years. While he cannot see into the future as it pertains to the stock price of those companies, following the conventional wisdom of Wall Street he builds a portfolio of the stocks of these great companies because he has confidence that these great-performing companies will, obviously, make great investments.

Jane Smith, on the other hand, believes that markets are efficient. She, therefore, bases her strategy on the theory that if the market believes that a group of companies will produce superior results, then the market must believe that they are relatively safe investments and will already have bid up the price of those stocks to reflect those great expectations and the low level of perceived risk. While the *companies* are likely to produce great financial results, the *stocks* of these great companies are highly likely to produce relatively low returns. Jane, expecting (though not being certain) that the market will reward her for taking risk, instead buys a passively managed portfolio of the stocks of value or lousy companies. She even anticipates the likelihood that, on average, these companies will continue to be poor performers; but she expects the stocks to provide superior returns, thereby rewarding her for taking risk. Jane believes that markets work. John does not.

Faced with the choice of buying the stocks of "great" companies or buying the stocks of "lousy" companies, most investors would instinctively choose the former.

Let us now jump forward to 2003. How did John's and Jane's

113

investment strategies work out? Who was right? In a sense, they were both right. For the thirty-eight-year period ending in 2001, the ROA (return on assets) for John's great growth stocks was 9.1 percent per year. This was over twice as great as the 4.2 percent ROA for Jane's lousy value stocks. Over the thirty-nine-year period ending in 2002, however, the average annual return to investors in Jane's value stocks was 15.5 percent per annum—53 percent greater than the 10.1 percent average annual return to investors in John's great growth stocks.

If the major purpose of investment research is to determine which companies will be the great performing companies, and if you are 100 percent correct in your analysis yet still produce inferior results, why bother? Why not save the time and the expense and just let the markets reward you for taking risk?

If the theory that markets provide returns commensurate with the amount of risk taken holds true, one should expect to see similar results if Jane invested in a passively managed portfolio consisting of those risky small companies. When one compares the performance of the asset class of small companies with the performance of the large company asset class, one gets the same results produced by the great company versus value company comparison. While small companies produced returns on assets about 40 percent below those of large companies (5.9 percent versus 3.4 percent), the annual average investment return on the stocks of small companies exceeded the return on stocks of large companies by about 25 percent (15.2 percent versus 11.5 percent). This seeming anomaly actually makes our point that markets work. The riskier investment in small companies produced higher returns.

The simple explanation for this anomaly is that investors discount the future expected earnings of value stocks at a much higher rate than they discount the future earnings of growth stocks. This more than offsets the faster earnings growth rates of growth companies. The high discount rate results in low current valuations for value stocks and higher expected future returns relative to growth stocks. Why do investors use a higher discount rate for value stocks when calculating the current value? The following example should provide a clear answer.

Let's consider the case of two pieces of investment property that are for sale in your town. Property A is in the heart of the most desirable commercial area, while Property B borders the worst slum in the region. Clearly it is easy to identify the more desirable property. If you could buy either property at $10 million, the obvious choice would be Property A. This world could not exist as investors would bid up the price of Property A relative to Property B.

Now let's imagine a slightly more realistic scenario, one in which Property A is selling at $20 million and Property B at $5 million. Based on the projected cash flows from rents, you project that (by coincidence) both properties will provide an expected rate of return of 10 percent—the higher rental income tenants pay for the better location is exactly offset by the higher price you have to pay to buy the property. Faced with the choice of which property to buy, the rational choice is still A as it provides the same expected return with less risk. Thus this world could not exist either.

In the real world A's price would continue to be bid up relative to B's. Perhaps A's price might rise to $30 million and B's might fall to $4 million. Now A's expected rate of return is lower than B's. Investors demand a higher expected return for taking more risk. It is important to understand that the fact that A provides a lower expected rate of return does not make it a worse investment choice—just a safer one. The market views it as less risky and thus discounts its future earnings at a lower rate, driving up the price and lowering the expected return. The price differential between the two will reflect the perceived differences in risk. Risk and ex-ante reward must be related. It is somewhat surprising to me that everyone understands this simple example of risk and expected reward being related, but it is almost universally forgotten when thinking about stocks and how they must be priced.

To provide the appropriate analogy to stocks, we can think of Property A as Wal-Mart and Property B as JCPenney. By any financial measure, Wal-Mart is clearly the superior (safer) company. The market valuation differential between the two companies will reflect the market's perception of differences in risk. The market's high relative valuation of Wal-Mart simply reflects investor perception of low risk. Wal-Mart's future earnings are being discounted at a very low rate, reflecting that low perceived risk. This low discount rate translates into low future expected returns. Risk and reward are directly related, at least in terms of *expected* future returns. It is important to include the word *expected* since we cannot know the future with certainty. Because JCPenney is viewed as a much riskier company, its future earnings are discounted at a very high rate. It therefore has a low relative valuation, reflecting the greater perceived risk. However, it also has high expected future returns.

International Markets Produce the Same Results

If the international markets are efficient in pricing for risk, one should see the same results there that the U.S. markets produced. The riskiest asset classes, not the "great companies," should produce the highest returns. There are now several academic studies on this subject, all coming to the same conclusion: Investors around the globe demand a premium for investing in the stocks of riskier small and value companies. For example, the study in the *Journal of Investing,* "The Dimensions of International Equity

Style," confirmed the existence of both the size and value effects in international markets. The study divided the market into four categories: value (top 50 percent as ranked by BtM); growth (bottom 50 percent as ranked by BtM); small (bottom 30 percent as ranked by market cap); and large (top 30 percent as ranked by market cap). The study covered the period 1975–96, twenty countries, and six geographic regions.

The following table presents annualized returns of each asset class.

Asset Class	World (%)	World ex-U.S. (%)
Value	17.0	16.9
Growth	12.4	12.1
Small	16.4	15.4
Large	13.9	14.0

It is also worth noting that for all six geographic regions, value stocks outperformed growth stocks. Markets work. It's that simple.[3]

At this point you may be wondering whether I am advocating investing in *only* the high-risk asset classes of small and value. This is certainly not the case. However, I am suggesting that you consider including an allocation to them in your portfolio—the size of that allocation is dependent on your own unique ability, willingness, and need to take risk. In addition, it is important to understand that the risk of an asset class should not be viewed in isolation. Instead, it should be based on how it impacts the overall risk of the portfolio. In later chapters we will explore how to reduce the risk of investing in risky asset classes through the building of a broadly diversified global portfolio using the tenets of MPT.

Fixed Income Assets—Risk and Return

So far we have focused our attention on the equity side of a portfolio; to complete the picture, we need to develop an understanding of, and then a strategy for, fixed-income assets.

As was shown earlier, active management of fixed-income portfolios is the same loser's game as for equity portfolios, a fact that was demonstrated in a study that found that actively managed bond funds underperformed their benchmarks by an average of 0.85 percent per annum.[4] That is certainly an expensive price to pay for the privilege of trying to beat the market. It is also evidence that the markets are highly efficient. Trying to guess the direction of interest rates is a loser's game. Once again, the winner's game is passive management. Buy and hold bonds of the maturity and risk characteristics that meet your risk profile.

Academic research has found that over long periods of time, while investors have been compensated for accepting the risk of owning longer maturity fixed-income assets, this relationship has broken down beyond five years or so.[5] Research on the relationship between risk and return has shown that for the period 1964–2002:

- The annualized return on one-month Treasury bills was 6.2 percent with a standard deviation of just 1.3 percent per annum.

- Extending the maturity to one year increased the annualized rate of return by about 1 percent, while increasing the standard deviation to about 2.3 percent.

- Extending the maturity to five years increased the annualized return by only another 0.6 percent (total premium above the annualized return on one-month Treasury bills of about 1.6 percent), yet the standard deviation increased by more than two-thirds to 6.4 percent.

- Extending the maturity to twenty years caused annualized returns to actually *fall* 0.1 percent (total premium above the annualized return on one-month Treasury bills of about 1.5 percent), yet the standard deviation almost *doubled* again to 11.1 percent.

The above data is based upon what is called a constant maturity (see glossary).

The Sharpe Ratio is a measure of return relative to risk taken. It is derived by first subtracting the risk-free rate from the annual rate of return earned on the asset, then dividing the result by the standard deviation of the asset. The higher the Sharpe Ratio the more efficient is the investment in delivering returns *relative* to the risk taken. The Sharpe Ratio has been about 0.5 at the one-year maturity but falls to less than 0.3 if we extend the maturity to about five years, and it continues to fall as we extend the maturity. Thus, in general, holding assets with a maturity of about one to two years is the prudent strategy.

It is important to discuss the issue of why investors in long-term bonds have not been compensated for the greater risk they have taken (using standard deviation as a measure of risk). I believe that there is a good explanation for this seeming risk/return anomaly. There are many investors, such as pension plans, that have fixed long-term obligations. In order to create a match between the term of their defined liabilities (the pension obligations due to past and current employees) and the term of their assets (thereby *eliminating* risk), they are willing to accept the price risk of the assets themselves. The investor demand for these longer maturity bonds exceeds the demand by issuers for liabilities of that length. Prices rise (and yields fall) when demand exceeds supply. In this case, the price of long-term bonds has risen sufficiently to make them relatively poor investments for those investors not needing them to match a liability of similar length.

There is another reason to consider not owning longer term fixed-income instruments. As stated earlier, the main reason for holding fixed-income assets is to provide a safety net to anchor your portfolio during bear markets, allowing you to stay disciplined. In order for the safety net to be effective, the assets it holds must have low correlation to the risky equity portion of the portfolio.

Unfortunately, the longer the maturity, the higher the correlation of fixed-income assets to equities. Also, unfortunately, that high correlation with the equity portion of your portfolio can appear at just the wrong time. There may be times when interest rates rise, bond prices fall, and the stock market falls at the same time. Just when you need low correlation, you may get high correlation. The following are the correlations between government instruments of various maturities and the S&P 500 and EAFE Indices.[6] Remember that the lower the correlation, the more effective the diversification and the lower the overall risk of the portfolio. Note also that there is basically no correlation between short-term maturities (up to one year) and both U.S. and international equities.

Quarterly Correlation Data

Maturity	Correlation with S&P 500 Index 1964–2003	Correlation with EAFE Index 1970–2003
One month	−0.05	−0.12
Six months	0.02	−0.05
One year	0.05	−0.02
Five years	0.17	0.12
Twenty years	0.25	0.17

As the above figures demonstrate, the risk of having relatively higher correlation between equities and fixed-income instruments can be avoided by buying short-term fixed-income instruments— they have essentially no correlation with equities.

Before concluding our discussion on fixed-income investing, we need to cover two relatively new types of fixed-income securities. In 1997 the U.S. Treasury introduced two new types of debt instruments that every investor should consider. Investors should become familiar with them as they are excellent investment vehicles that can reduce the risk of investing. They are called Treasury Inflation-Protected Securities (TIPS) and I bonds.

Inflation-Protected Securities

A TIPS is a bond, sold at auction, that receives a fixed *real* rate of return but also increases its principal by the changes in the nonseasonally adjusted U.S. city average all items Consumer Price Index for All Urban Consumers (CPI-U), published by the Bureau of Labor Statistics. Its fixed-interest payment is calculated on the inflated principal, which is eventually repaid at maturity. This gives an investor protection against inflation by providing a guaranteed *real* return over a predetermined investment horizon. Interest is paid (the real rate) and accrued (the inflation adjustment) semiannually. At maturity the bondholder will receive the greater of the inflation-adjusted value or par. A further benefit of TIPS is that, like all Treasury debt, they are exempt from state and local taxes. There is another important benefit of TIPS that should not be overlooked. Because equities actually have a slightly negative correlation to inflation (inflation has a negative impact on equity returns as it increases business risk), TIPS should logically have a negative correlation to equities (because they should be highly correlated to inflation). This negative correlation helps reduce the overall risk of the portfolio. This is a distinct advantage over intermediate to longer term bonds.

Investors should note that TIPS, like most fixed-income instruments with a long maturity, are subject to price risk. Another potential negative is that an investor must pay the tax on both the real and the "unrealized" income (the amount of each year's inflated principal). Thus the best place to hold TIPS is in a tax-deferred account.

The other inflation-protected security is called an I bond. An I bond works like a TIPS in that it provides a fixed real rate of return and an inflation-protection component. There are, however, significant differences. The fixed rate on an I bond is announced by the Treasury in May and November and applies to all I bonds issued during the following six months. Like zero coupon bonds, they accrue in value their total return (fixed rate plus inflation adjustment). I bonds increase in value on the first of each month and compound semiannually. They pay interest for up to thirty years. They can be bought and redeemed at most financial institutions. The redemption value can never go below par. All income is deferred for tax purposes until funds are withdrawn from the account holding the bond. The tax-deferral feature makes an I bond a more attractive candidate than TIPS for a taxable investor. A further benefit of I bonds is that they are exempt from state and local taxes.

Although I bonds can be redeemed at any time after one year of issuance, they are meant to serve as long-term investments. Therefore there is a prepayment penalty of three months' interest if not held for a minimum of five years. Also note that there is an annual $30,000 per social security number limitation on the amount of I bonds that can be purchased.

For investors with either short investment horizons or a concern for stability of value prior to maturity, the preferred alternative to inflation-protected securities is a short-term fixed-income investment vehicle. Keep in mind that while traditional short-term fixed-income vehicles do not contain a specific inflation-protection component, their short-term nature offers similar protection from inflation. If inflation picks up, interest rates will rise, and the short maturity structure will allow these vehicles to quickly capture the new higher rates. This is not true of long-term bonds. The other important characteristic of short-term investment vehicles is their highly stable value.

Investors considering inflation-protected securities should evaluate the decision on which is the preferred vehicle based on current yields, their current tax situation, their ability to hold to maturity, their ability to accept principal risk, and whether the investment is for their taxable or tax-deferred account. These investments should also be compared to the yields on alternative short-term fixed-income securities.

With the preceding information, we can now determine the winning strategy for the fixed-income portion of our portfolio. For the vast majority of investors using fixed-income assets to reduce the risk of an equity portfolio, the winning strategy seems obvious: own very short-term fixed-income assets (of the highest investment quality). Here's why.

Since the main purpose of fixed-income assets for most investors is to reduce the volatility of the overall portfolio, investors should include fixed-income assets that have low volatility. Short-term fixed-income assets have the benefit of both low volatility and low correlation with the equity portion of the portfolio. By limiting the maturity of the fixed-income portion of the portfolio to one to two years, we get most of the yield benefit and accept only moderate risk (very low standard deviation). The benefit of the low volatility of the short-term fixed-income asset class, combined with the benefit of the reduced volatility of the overall portfolio, seems a small price to pay for giving up the relatively small increase in returns that could be gained by extending the maturity of the fixed-income assets to five years or longer. From the perspective of risk reduction, short-term investing is far more effective than long-term investing. For those investors willing to accept their greater price volatility, TIPS should also be considered—as should I bonds as well.

Summary

At this point you have been exposed to most of the theory and facts behind the winning investment strategy. We know that if we want and/or need high returns, and are willing to accept greater risk, we should invest in high-risk asset classes. Conversely, if we are unwilling and/or unable to accept a high degree of risk, we must accept lower expected returns and should invest in low-risk securities, such as Treasury bills or short-term bonds. Or, as we will discuss in later chapters, we can combine asset classes in a way that will achieve a level of risk anywhere in between the two extremes.

If we seek high returns, we start with a preference for equities over bonds. Within the equity asset class, we know to buy the stocks of small companies and lousy, or value, companies. We know to buy and hold passively managed mutual funds that basically buy and hold all of those stocks that fall within our chosen asset class. Within the fixed-income asset class, we purchase short-term instruments or inflation-protected securities, not long-term, instruments.

I promised early in the book that you would not need an extensive knowledge of financial markets to understand the body of work that is called modern portfolio theory (MPT). We have now covered two of the four major tenets of MPT. Summarizing, we have learned:

- Markets process information so rapidly when determining security prices that it is extremely difficult to gain a competitive edge by exploiting market anomalies. This causes active management to be a loser's game and passive management to be the winning strategy.

- Riskier assets provide higher expected returns as compensation to investors for accepting greater risk.

With this knowledge, financial economists have built a model that has been utilized to demonstrate that the vast majority of the returns that one can expect a portfolio to generate is determined by the percentage of assets allocated to each of five factors. This paradigm is known as the five-factor model. In the next chapters we will see how this model works and how you can put it to work for you.

CHAPTER 5

◆

The Five-Factor Model

Knowledge is power.
—Sir Francis Bacon, *Meditationes Sacrae. De Haeresibus*

Baseball scouts, when sent to look at the latest hot prospect, are trained to evaluate a player's skills in five areas; speed, throwing arm, fielding, batting for average, and hitting with power. How a prospect rates in these five skills has proven to be an excellent predictor of whether or not he will make it to the major leagues.

Similarly, financial economists have determined that there are five factors that determine the vast majority of expected returns from a diversified portfolio. Three factors are related to the portion of the portfolio that is allocated to equities, and two factors are related to fixed-income assets. When one combines these into the five-factor model, one can determine the expected return of a balanced-equity and fixed-income portfolio. We will first examine the three-factor equity model. In succeeding chapters we will explore how this model is used to build portfolios.

The Three-Factor Equity Model

The fundamental concept of risk and return in equity investing is embodied in what economists call the three-factor model, which states that the returns one can expect from an equity portfolio are virtually unrelated to either the ability to pick stocks or to time the market. Instead, the degree of exposure to three *risk factors* determines the vast majority of returns. (As used here, "returns" refer to annual premiums above the benchmark risk-free rate of return on short-term U.S. Treasury bills, i.e., one-month government obligations that have neither credit nor interest rate risk, hence the term "risk free.")

The first risk factor in the three-factor equity model is the amount of exposure of a portfolio to the risk factor of the overall stock market. All equities have some exposure to this risk factor (the more volatile the stock, or portfolio of stocks, the greater the exposure, and vice versa). Since equities are riskier than fixed-income investments, they should provide greater returns. And, in fact, they have. Note that when discussing risk premiums financial economists use annual, not annualized (meaning compound) returns. From 1927 through 2003, the average annual equity risk premium, the return above riskless one-month Treasury bills, has been just over 8 percent. It is important to note that because of the high volatility of equities the 8 percent annual premium was reduced to about 6 percent on an annualized basis (the next chapter focuses on the effects of volatility).

The second risk factor is the size of a company as determined by market capitalization. Intuitively we know that small companies are riskier than large companies. And they have provided an annual risk premium of just over 3 percent (volatility reduced this to 2.5 percent per annum) over the rate of return on large companies.

The third risk factor takes value into consideration. High book-to-market (BtM) (value) stocks are intuitively riskier than low BtM (growth) stocks. And they have provided an annual risk premium of just over 4 percent (volatility reduced this to 3.5 percent per annum) over that provided by growth stocks.

It is important to note that studies have not only verified the existence of these risk premiums in international markets and even emerging markets as well as domestic markets, but they also found that the premiums are similar in size.

Every equity portfolio (be it an index, asset class, or mutual fund) has some degree of exposure to each of the three risk factors. It is important to understand that the exposure to each factor may be larger or smaller than one. In addition, it may be negative as well. For example, for the period 1927–2003, the S&P 500 Index, while it had an exposure to the equity risk factor of 1.04, because it is basically a large-cap portfolio it had an exposure to the risk factor of size of a negative 0.14. As another example, from January 1979 (its inception) through 2003, the Russell 2000 Index (a small-cap index), which also had exposure to the equity (or market) factor of one (actually 0.99), had an exposure to the risk factor of size of 0.85. The percent exposure to each risk factor is called a "loading factor." The loading factor is then multiplied by the risk premium to determine either any excess (if the loading factor is positive) or underperformance (if the loading factor is negative) relative to the market that can be explained by the asset allocation.[1] In this manner the risk premiums are additive. Exactly how much of each premium a portfolio (or mutual fund) earns is calculated through three-factor linear regression, a statistical tool used in many branches of science and technology. For those interested, regression can be performed relatively easily, for example, in an Excel spreadsheet. The only inputs required are the monthly premiums (market, size, and value), the monthly return of one-month Treasury bills (the risk-free return), and the monthly returns of the portfolio.

The above data on risk premiums presents the historical returns to both equities and the risk factors. However, it is important not to make the very common mistake of simply extrapolating historical equity returns into the future. The reason is that the price you pay matters. The higher the current price, the lower the expected future returns; and the lower the current price, the higher the expected future returns. But before learning how to estimate future returns based on current valuations we need to cover the two-factor fixed-income model, which when combined with our three-factor equity model provides us with the five-factor portfolio model.

The Two-Factor Fixed-Income Model

Financial economists have determined that there are just two factors that determine the returns that can be expected from a fixed-income portfolio. As noted earlier, neither of these two factors have anything to do with the ability to predict the direction of interest rates nor the ability to identify mispriced securities. The underperformance of bond mutual funds provides clear evidence that trying to time fixed-income investments based on predictions of the future direction of interest rates is just as much a loser's game as trying to select individual stocks or time equity investments. Passive management is the winning strategy. The real question that faces fixed-income investors is the same one that faces equity investors: How much risk are you willing to accept in search of higher returns?

The two fixed-income risk factors are maturity and default (or credit risk). The fixed-income model works in the same manner as does the equity model. We begin with the risk-free rate of return, the rate of return on one-month Treasury bills. These instruments, once again, carry neither credit nor interest rate risk. As we saw earlier, historically the risk premium for investing in longer term securities has been about 1.6 percent.

It is important to note that, at least for bond mutual funds, the premium for taking the risk of investing in investment-grade corporate debt instruments (versus U.S. government, U.S. government agency, or what are called GSEs—government-sponsored entities such as Fannie Mae or Freddie Mac) has historically been very close to zero. This calculation is based on comparing the results of long-term government bond funds and long-term corporate bond funds. While corporate bonds carry higher note rates than do government issues, the incremental yield has historically been offset by credit losses, probably higher expense ratios (resulting from the need to analyze the credit risk of corporate issuers), and other features incorporated into corporate bonds, such as a call option. A call option gives the right to the issuer to call in (prepay) the bonds. The issuer will do so if interest rates drop sufficiently to warrant the expense of the recall and reissuance of new bonds at the then-prevailing lower rate. The investor in such a security, having the high-yielding bond paid off, will then have to purchase a new bond at the new lower rates. There are very few Treasury issues with call features.

It is important to remember that, as with equities, using historical returns to estimate future returns is a very common mistake. Academic research has determined that the best estimate of future yield curves is today's yield curve. Thus we can estimate fixed-income returns simply by observing today's rates.

Estimating Future Returns

While estimating expected equity returns is not a science, the approach most often used by financial economists is known as the

Gordon constant growth dividend discount model. While it is a mouthful, it is actually fairly easy to understand. The Gordon model assumes that expected *real* (after inflation) equity returns are equal to the current dividend yield plus estimated real growth. A logical assumption for the estimate for growth might be to assume that it would equal the long-term growth of the gross national product (GNP). The long-term real growth of GNP has been about 3 percent per annum. However, some of that future growth will go to companies that are not yet public or do not yet even exist. Thus part of the growth in future GNP will provide returns to venture capitalists, not public equity owners. Because of this "leakage," I recommend using 2 percent as a conservative estimate for growth. Thus if the current dividend yield is 2 percent, the expected real return to U.S. equities (the total market) is 4 percent (not the 7 percent experienced from 1927 through 2003). This methodology assumes the market's valuation of equities (one example of a valuation metric is the price-to-earnings P/E ratio) will remain unchanged (the best assumption we can make). If valuation metrics actually improve (the P/E ratio increases), then future returns will likely be greater than estimated, and vice versa. Estimates of risk premiums for each respective asset class must also be made and appropriately weighted based on the specific asset allocation of the investment policy statement. While each fund/index has a different exposure to the size and value risk factors, making a general rule an imperfect approach, for simplicity purposes I suggest you consider using the following estimated risk premiums (above the market return). They are based on the annualized long-term historic premiums in the U.S. market. Unfortunately, there is no better methodology.

Small Cap:	1 percent
Micro Cap:	2 percent
Large Value:	2 percent
Small Value:	4 percent
Real Estate:	1 percent

For international asset classes I would use the same estimates. For emerging markets I would use 4 percent. Thus for international large-cap stocks use the same estimated real return as you use for U.S. large-cap stocks (4 percent). And for international small-cap stocks use the same estimated return as you use for U.S. small-cap stocks (4 percent + 1 percent). Keep in mind that the above are returns for the asset class, and asset classes have no expenses—but the investment vehicles used to invest in an asset class do have expenses. And, as we have seen, the greater the expenses, the lower the expected return. All fund expenses should be considered when estimating returns.

For fixed-income investments, the best estimates for future returns are current yields. However, this is true only if the investment has no credit risk—which is true only for obligations that carry the full faith and credit of the U.S. government. For securities that do not carry such a guarantee, an estimate of credit losses must be subtracted. Of course, the lower the credit rating, the greater should be the estimate of credit losses. If you use mutual funds to invest in fixed-income assets, you should reduce the expected return by the expense ratio of the fund.

In order to estimate nominal returns we have to estimate inflation. We can observe the market's estimate of future inflation by subtracting the current yield on Treasury Inflation-Protected Securities (TIPS) from the yield on a similar term U.S. government coupon bond. For example, if the rate of return on a ten-year

Treasury note is 4 percent and the rate of return on a ten-year TIPS (which is a real rate) is 2 percent, then expected inflation is 2 percent (4 −2).

Having estimated returns for each asset class, you must then determine the impact that the return of each asset class has on the portfolio in order to estimate the expected return of the overall portfolio. You can then determine how the expected return of the portfolio relates to the return needed to achieve your objective. Using the following assumptions, we can create a simple example.

- Estimated real return to U.S. equities: 4 percent
- Current ten-year Treasury bond yield: 4 percent
- Current ten-year TIPS yield: 2 percent
- Expected inflation: 2 percent (4 percent minus 2 percent)

We can now estimate that an investment in a total stock market fund will provide a real rate of return of 4 percent and a nominal rate of return of 6 percent. If we created an all-equity portfolio that was 50 percent large-cap stocks and 50 percent small value then the expected nominal returns would be 6 percent on the large-cap stock allocation and 10 percent (4 percent real return on equity plus 4 percent risk premium for small value and 2 percent inflation) on the small-value allocation for a weighted average return of 8 percent for the portfolio.

Keep in mind that the resulting weighted-average expected return of the portfolio is the median return expected and not a single-point estimate. Half the time we would expect the outcome to exceed the median and half the time to fall short. (Actually, the probability of achieving the returns is even a bit worse—but the math is too complicated to go into.) And I don't know many investors who would be satisfied with a plan that had just a 50 percent chance of success.

It is extremely important that investors not make the mistake of treating the expected return as a single-point estimate. In fact, it is highly unlikely that the estimated return will turn out to be the same as the ex-post return. To get a more accurate picture of the possible outcomes, we need to use a Monte Carlo Simulator (see appendix B).

An Important Lesson

Now that you understand the risk factors that determine expected returns, you should understand that beating the market, at least when the market is defined as the S&P 500, is not difficult. Since the S&P 500 represents the stocks of the largest U.S. companies, an investor in this asset class can expect to receive the risk-free rate of return plus the equity premium. This investor is missing out, however, on the risk premiums of small companies and value companies. Keep this in mind as I relate this next tale.

Fortune reporter Terence Pare claimed: "The truth is that you can beat the market. A claim like that goes straight to the infamous efficient market theory like a stake to a vampire's heart."[2] Mr. Pare uses "infamous" in a way that implies that passive management, resulting from the EMH, is almost un-American. Investors reading this statement would be led to believe that active management actually works. Unfortunately for Mr. Pare and his readers, he just doesn't get it; he was comparing apples to oranges. Beating the market (the S&P 500 Index) is simple, as you just learned. All you have to do is load up a portfolio with stocks from the high-risk asset classes of small companies and value companies; you can then expect to be compensated for accepting higher risk with higher expected returns, just as the EMH states. Thus active managers should be judged, not against the S&P 500 Index, but against a passively managed asset-class benchmark. In other words, a small-cap active manager should be judged against a small-cap index or a small-cap passively managed fund; an active manager investing in value stocks should be judged against a value benchmark, and so on. When put to this test, statistics show that active managers fail badly because the markets are efficient. Remember: Beware of all claims that active managers can beat the market. What Mr. Pare really should consider as infamous is that despite his claims about being able to beat the market, 70 percent or more of active managers regularly underperform the S&P 500 Index every year.

Summary

We can project the expected long-term rate of return of a portfolio by examining its exposure to the five dimensions, or factors, of risk. This ability is one of the major benefits of passive asset-class investing. Investing with active managers means you cannot make projections about future returns since you do not know in which asset classes they will choose to invest.

Our next step is to learn how to construct a portfolio that fits an individual's unique tolerance for risk—the third and fourth tenets of MPT.

- Adding high-risk, low-correlating asset classes to a portfolio can actually reduce volatility and increase expected rates of return.

- Passive asset-class fund portfolios can be designed with the expectation of delivering, over time, the highest returns for a chosen level of risk.

We will cover all you need to know about building just such a portfolio in the following chapters.

CHAPTER 6

◆

Volatility, Return, and Risk

Everything's got a moral, if only you can find it.
—Lewis Carroll, *Alice's Adventure in Wonderland*

We have already discussed how the risk factors of equities, size, value, maturity, and credit quality impact returns. There is another important issue we need to understand before we can implement the winning strategy—volatility and how it impacts returns. One needs to understand how to control that impact because it is powerful.

Volatility and Returns

Statistics are like a bikini. What they reveal is suggestive, but what they conceal is vital.   —Aaron Levenstein

To illustrate the impact of volatility on a portfolio, let's look at a hypothetical example. Suppose you were offered the choice between two portfolios, one with an average *annual* return of 15 percent and one with an average *annual* return of 12 percent. I am sure that the vast majority of people would not even think twice before choosing the portfolio with the 15 percent *annual* average return. Surprisingly the better approach is to first determine the volatility of the two portfolios. Before I explain why, you must first understand how standard deviation is used as a measure of risk.

Standard deviation, a statistical term, is used to measure volatility. It is not a difficult concept to understand. St. Louis and Honolulu might have the same average temperature. However, the standard deviation, or variability, of the temperature in St. Louis is far greater than it is in Honolulu. In terms of investing, standard deviation measures the amount by which annual returns vary, or deviate, from average returns. The greater the variability, the higher the standard deviation. For example, a portfolio with a 15 percent annual average return and an annual standard deviation of 35 percent can be expected to generate annual returns between a negative 20 percent (15 −35) and a positive 50 percent (15 +35) in thirteen out of every twenty years (about two-thirds of the time). A portfolio with a 12 percent annual average return and an annual standard deviation of 15 percent can be expected to generate annual returns between a negative 3 percent (12 −15) and a positive 27 percent (12 +15) in thirteen out of every twenty years. Clearly the portfolio with the 15 percent annual return and a standard deviation of 35 percent is much more volatile or risky than the portfolio with a 12 percent annual return and a standard deviation of 15 percent. You can see why standard deviation is used as a measure of risk. (It is important to understand that standard deviation is just one measure of risk and that there may be risks about which investors care other than volatility.)

Surprisingly, despite the fact that the average annual rate of return on the first portfolio (15 percent) exceeded the average annual return of the second portfolio (12 percent), it only produced a compounded growth rate of each dollar invested of 9 percent, as compared to 11 percent for the second portfolio. As shown in the following table, over a twenty-year period, each dollar invested in the first portfolio grew to $5.49, while each dollar invested in the second portfolio grew to $8.06. The explanation for this anomaly is the higher volatility of the portfolio with the higher annual return. Put simply, volatility reduces returns. And the greater the volatility, the greater the negative impact.

Effect of Volatility

Average annual return	15%	12%
Standard deviation	35%	15%
Compound growth rate	9%	11%
Growth of each dollar invested	$5.49	$8.06

Using a simpler example, let's compare two portfolios with exactly the same average annual return but with different levels of volatility.

John Doe's portfolio increases 50 percent one year, decreases 50 percent the next, and then repeats the pattern. Jane Smith's portfolio neither increases nor decreases in value (she might be holding cash). Both portfolios provide average annual returns of zero. Since both portfolios show the same average return, you might expect that at the end of a four-year period, John and Jane would have portfolios of equal value at the end of the period. You may be surprised to see that the result is quite a bit different. Assuming they both began with $100, John's original investment would grow in the first year to $150, decline in the second to $75, increase in the third to about $112, and decline in the fourth to about $56. Since Jane's portfolio never varied, her $100 investment has held its original value. The 50 percent standard deviation of John's portfolio negatively impacted the outcome.

In yet another example, two portfolios have much closer standard deviations. John Doe's portfolio increases 20 percent one year and then has no growth in the second year. This portfolio has an average annual return of 10 percent and a standard deviation of 10 percent. Jane Smith's portfolio also averages an annual return of 10 percent, but because it increases 10 percent every year its standard deviation is zero. After the first year, John's original investment will grow to $120; it will remain there the second year. Jane's investment will grow to $110 after the first year and to $121 after the second. Once again, the portfolio with the lower standard deviation produced higher growth. Note that the smaller standard deviation in this example produced a much smaller difference in return than in the prior example. This demonstrates that the greater the volatility, the greater the impact on compound returns of a portfolio.

These two examples point out the powerful impact that volatility can have on a portfolio and the relative irrelevance of "average annual rates of return." Investors can't spend average rates of return. What should be of concern to investors is the compound growth rate of an invested dollar.

If an investor can find a way to reduce the volatility of a portfolio, the return of that portfolio can be increased. The solution to this problem was provided by Harry Markowitz, and was a major reason why he was awarded the Nobel Prize in economics in 1990 (along with William Sharpe and Robert Merton). It is also the third major tenet of MPT.

We will now see how investors can reduce the volatility of a portfolio, thereby improving the risk/return trade-off—one of the few cases where you can have your cake and eat it too. By applying the principles of MPT, investors can increase returns without increasing risk, or conversely, they can reduce risk without having to accept lower returns. In fact you will learn that despite what you have always heard, there is a free lunch—diversification.

Diversification of Risk

*There are two times in a man's life when he should not spec-
ulate: when he can't afford it, and when he can.*
— Mark Twain, *Following the Equator*

Every investor is familiar with the saying, "Don't put all your eggs
in one basket." No matter how good an investment seems, few individuals would construct a portfolio that consists of just one asset.
Even if one believes that the risk of being wrong is very small, the
cost of being wrong is too great to make that big a bet. Conversely,
even when the odds are stacked against them, as at the racetrack or
in a lottery, individuals will make an "investment" if the cost of being wrong is small. This type of behavior demonstrates that investors are not risk neutral; in fact they are risk averse, and prudent
investors spread their investment dollars across various investment
alternatives. This process is called diversification of risk. We will
now explore, using three easy steps, how one can most effectively
use the principle of diversification to reduce risk.

Let's begin with a portfolio that consists of only the stock of
one company, General Motors. Despite the size and strength of the
company, that would be a very risky, and potentially very volatile,
portfolio. In order to reduce the risk of the portfolio, we need to
diversify. We can do so by adding Ford, but this type of diversification is not very effective because both companies are susceptible to the same types of business risk. Since both are likely to
respond to changes in the economic environment in a very similar
manner, their stock prices are likely to move in a highly correlated
manner. (If they moved in exact tandem, they would have a correlation of +1.) Not only are they likely to move up and down at the
same time, but the size of their price movements are also likely to

be similar (but not identical). While we slightly reduced the risk of our portfolio by adding a second security, we did not really accomplish our objective.

We can more effectively reduce the risk and the volatility of our portfolio by adding the stocks of companies from different industries, preferably ones that do not respond in exactly the same way to business cycles. If assets tend to do well or poorly at the same time, they have high correlation. If the opposite is true, then their correlation is lower, and it may even be negative. Ideally, we would like to find assets with negative correlation. The addition of assets that have perfect negative correlation could completely eliminate the volatility of the portfolio. Although assets that have negative correlation are very hard to find, risk can be reduced by including in a portfolio assets whose correlation is less than perfect—and the lower the better.

Even without any understanding of the math, I think you can accept that an investor would have reduced the risk of our sample portfolio by adding Merck (a drug company), Citigroup (a financial institution), or AT&T (a communication company) to the portfolio. This type of diversification works because these companies are not susceptible to *exactly* the same business risks as an automobile manufacturer (such as changes in the price of gasoline). The more companies from different industries one adds to the portfolio, the more one reduces its volatility and therefore its risk.

It is difficult for individual investors using individual stocks to construct an equity portfolio that achieves a broad enough diversification to reduce overall risk to an acceptable level. Fortunately, mutual funds solve this problem. The use of mutual funds can be a very efficient method of achieving the required degree of risk diversification. Some mutual funds hold thousands of different securities. The following steps can help you achieve broad diversification.

Step 1: Buy low-cost, no-load, passively managed mutual funds instead of individual securities.

Further steps are, however, in order. If we bought two or more mutual funds that all invested in the same type of companies (such as technology companies or health care companies), we would make the same type of mistake as if we bought two automobile manufacturers. And if we bought two or more funds that invested in the same asset class (such as small, large, value, or growth companies), we would make a similar, though not as grievous, mistake. Two funds comprised of securities from the same asset class— groups of companies with similar risk characteristics—tend to move with high degrees of correlation. While we have diversified away business risk, unfortunately we have not diversified away asset-class risk—and Professors Eugene Fama and Kenneth French demonstrated that asset-class diversification is more important than sector (industry) diversification.

Asset classes move in and out of favor in the securities market. In some years, small companies are the best performers. In other years, value or large companies may rise to the top. The top-performing asset class in one year is just as likely to repeat as fall to the bottom. Most important, no one knows which asset class will top the list next year. In order to reduce risk, we need to diversify across a broad group of asset classes.

Step 2: Create a portfolio of mutual funds that is diversified across several asset classes.

Even taking this step would not complete the process of effective diversification. We also need to diversify country risk. Investing in only the U.S. market, because foreign markets are perceived as risky, is similar to the mistake of investing in only the automobile industry. Since the main determinant of the performance of foreign markets is local conditions, foreign markets do not move in perfect correlation to the U.S. market. The following table shows the correlation, on a monthly basis, of various asset classes for the period 1975–2003.

Asset Class	Correlation with S&P 500 Index
U.S. Large Value	.87
U.S. Small Value	.74
U.S. Small Cap	.79
U.S. Micro Cap	.71
U.S. Real Estate	.54
EAFE (International Large Cap)	.55
International Large Value	.53
International Small	.40

Emerging markets, for which the data is only available for the period 1987–2003, had a correlation with the S&P 500 Index of just .60.[1]

Investors who avoid the risk of foreign markets make the mistake of looking at these asset classes in isolation. If these asset classes have less than perfect correlation with the rest of the portfolio, the addition of risky asset classes can actually reduce a portfolio's volatility. In particular, emerging-markets stocks make excellent diversifiers because they not only have low correlation to U.S. stocks but they also have low correlation to other international stocks.

To achieve the most effective diversification, a portfolio should include mutual funds that invest not only in the United States but also in Europe, the Far East, and emerging markets. This type of portfolio not only diversifies business risk but also country risk. Diversifying both business risk and country risk can dramatically reduce the volatility, and therefore risk, of a portfolio.

Step 3: Include international mutual funds in your portfolio.

In following steps 1–3, remember to buy only mutual funds that are passively managed. As we will see, it is the only way to ensure that a portfolio maintains its desired asset allocation.

The next chapter shows you how to build a portfolio that can provide above-market returns. In other words, you will see that passive management does not mean you have to accept "average" returns (and we have seen that the vast majority of active managers provide below-average returns). You will also discover that you can achieve these superior returns without necessarily taking greater risk and how this can be accomplished in six easy steps.

PART THREE

◆

Play the Winner's Game: Make Modern Portfolio Theory Work for You

Anybody can win, unless there happens to be a second entry.
—George Ade

CHAPTER 7

◆

Six Steps to a Diversified Portfolio— Using Modern Portfolio Theory

Not only is there but one way of doing things rightly, there is but one way of seeing them, and that is seeing the whole of them. —John Ruskin, *The Two Paths*

In baseball the general manager's job is to put together a team that is well balanced between hitting, fielding, pitching, and running speed. If he builds a team with great power but little speed or pitching, it is likely to suffer from too many strikeouts, double plays, and batting slumps to win a championship. If he focuses on pitching and defense, the team probably will be unable to score enough runs to compensate for the days its pitching or defense is poor. While teams that are built around one area of strength may go on brief winning streaks when everything is going right, they are unlikely to win often enough over a long season to be champions. A general manager succeeds by building a team with diversified strengths. Similarly, individual investors succeed by building and properly managing diversified portfolios.

Jonathan Clements, a columnist for the *Wall Street Journal,* noted: "Indexing is a wonderful strategy. It's a shame most folks get it wrong."[1] He was referring to his belief that most investors who use index funds limit themselves to funds that mimic the S&P 500 Index. In this chapter you will see how to expand on a simple S&P 500 indexing strategy and embark on the winning investment strategy by applying the principles of MPT. We will see how an investor can build a well-diversified investment portfolio by:

- utilizing only passively managed mutual funds;
- utilizing the high expected return asset classes of small and value companies;
- eliminating the use of long maturities from the fixed-income portion of the portfolio; and
- utilizing global diversification to improve the efficiency of the portfolio (reduce volatility without reducing returns).

The power of MPT will be demonstrated by following the performance of a "control" portfolio, with a traditional asset allocation of 60 percent equities and 40 percent fixed income over the period 1975–2003. This 60/40 allocation is typical of the asset allocation of U.S. pension plans, so-called balanced mutual funds, and many individual investors. We will assume that our investor, knowing that passive management is the winner's game, will use only passively managed asset-class funds.

Unaware of the benefits of MPT, that is, passive asset-class investing combined with broad diversification, the portfolio has just two investments: the S&P 500 Index for the equity allocation and the Lehman Government/Credit Bond Index (range one through thirty-plus years) for the fixed-income allocation. The Lehman Index is a popular fixed-income index that is often used as a benchmark against which active managers are measured.

First, we will see how the portfolio performed if the investor had the patience to stay with this allocation from 1975 through 2003. Then we will determine how the portfolio's performance could have been improved (made more efficient) by using broadly diversified, passive asset-class funds. We will do so in six easy steps, using six variations on the control portfolio, so that you can clearly see MPT at work.

The Control Portfolio

Let us now check the performance of our control portfolio over the period 1975–2003 to see how our basic 60 percent equity and 40 percent fixed-income allocation performed. It is important to note that the figures showing the growth of dollar invested assumes no taxes on distributions or income.

Control Portfolio: Portfolio 1

S&P 500 Index   60%

Lehman Index   40%

1975–2003

Annualized Return	Annualized Standard Deviation	Growth of a Dollar	Sharpe Ratio
12.3%	11.0%	$28.75	0.58

Source: See sources and descriptions of data

This simple portfolio provided an annualized return of 12.3 percent. Its standard deviation, a measure of volatility, was 11.0 percent. And the Sharpe Ratio was 0.58. A dollar invested in 1975 grew to $28.75 by the end of 2003, a return that would have satisfied most investors.

By changing the composition of the control portfolio through a step-by-step process, we will see how the application of MPT allows investors to improve returns without increasing risk (volatility) relative to the basic 60/40 strategy.

Step 1: Apply the principle of diversification.

While maintaining the equity allocation at 60 percent, we reduce the allocation to the S&P 500 Index to 40 percent and allocate 20 percent to an EAFE (Europe, Australasia, and the Far East) Index fund (an index of large companies, similar to the S&P 500). We maintain our equity allocation of 60 percent but shift the equity portion from 100 percent U.S. to two-thirds U.S. and one-third international. This revised allocation produced the following results:

Portfolio 2: The International Effect

S&P 500 Index	40%
EAFE Index	20%
Lehman Index	40%

1975–2003

	Annualized Return	Annualized Standard Deviation	Growth of a Dollar	Sharpe Ratio
Portfolio 1	12.3%	11.0%	$28.75	0.58
Portfolio 2	12.2%	10.6%	$28.29	0.60

Source: See sources and descriptions of data

As you can see, while the portfolio produced slightly more than 99 percent of the returns, it also produced only 96 percent of the volatility, resulting in a slightly higher Sharpe Ratio (a more efficient portfolio). The growth of each dollar invested did fall slightly from $28.75 to $28.29 (a fall of about 2 percent).

Step 2: Add a small-company asset-class fund to our portfolio.

With our next step we reduce our S&P 500 Index (large

domestic company) allocation from 40 percent to 20 percent and replace this portion with a 20 percent allocation to a U.S. small-company fund. In doing so, we maintain both our 60 percent equity allocation and our two-thirds U.S. allocation.

Portfolio 3: The U.S. Small-Company Effect

S&P 500 Index	20%
U.S. Small	20%
EAFE Index	20%
Lehman Index	40%

1975–2003

	Annualized Return	Annualized Standard Deviation	Growth of a Dollar	Sharpe Ratio
Portfolio 1	12.3%	11.0%	$28.75	0.58
Portfolio 2	12.2%	10.6%	$28.29	0.60
Portfolio 3	13.4%	10.6%	$38.33	0.71

Source: See sources and descriptions of data

The addition of the high expected return asset class of small companies increased returns from 12.2 percent to 13.4 percent (a 10 percent increase in returns) without increasing the volatility of the portfolio at all. The growth of each dollar invested improved from $28.29 to $38.33 (a 35 percent increase) while the volatility actually fell. Note also that the Sharpe Ratio rose from 0.60 to 0.71 (an increase in the efficiency of the portfolio of 18 percent). It is also worth noting that while the volatility of Portfolio 3 is the same as the volatility of Portfolio 2, its volatility is less than that of the control portfolio.

Step 3: Add the asset classes of small-cap value and large-cap value.

We now split our 20 percent allocation to U.S. small into 10 percent U.S. small and 10 percent U.S. small value, and we split our 20 percent S&P 500 Index (large-cap) allocation into 10 percent S&P 500 Index and 10 percent U.S. large value.

Portfolio 4: The U.S. Value Effect

S&P 500 Index	10%
U.S. Large Value	10%
U.S. Small	10%
U.S. Small Value	10%
EAFE Index	20%
Lehman Index	40%

1975–2003

	Annualized Return	Annualized Standard Deviation	Growth of a Dollar	Sharpe Ratio
Portfolio 1	12.3%	11.0%	$28.75	0.58
Portfolio 2	12.2%	10.6%	$28.29	0.60
Portfolio 3	13.4%	10.6%	$38.33	0.71
Portfolio 4	13.8%	10.6%	$42.26	0.75

Source: See sources and descriptions of data

Adding the asset classes of U.S. small value and U.S. large value increased the rate of return from 13.4 percent to 13.8 percent (an increase of about 3 percent) while volatility remained unchanged. The growth of each dollar invested increased from $38.33 to $42.26 (an increase of over 10 percent). Note that the

Sharpe Ratio again rose from 0.71 to 0.75, an increase in the efficiency of the portfolio of almost 6 percent.

Step 4: Replace the 20 percent allocation to the EAFE Index, which provides a large company exposure to the international markets, with the high expected return (and lower correlating) asset classes of international large value (10 percent) and international small (10 percent). The international exposure, therefore, remains unchanged at one-third of equities.

Portfolio 5: The International Small and Value Effect

S&P 500 Index	10%
U.S. Large Value	10%
U.S. Small	10%
U.S. Small Value	10%
International Large Value	10%
International Small	10%
Lehman Index	40%

1975–2003

	Annualized Return	Annualized Standard Deviation	Growth of a Dollar	Sharpe Ratio
Portfolio 1	12.3%	11.0	$28.75	0.58
Portfolio 2	12.2%	10.6%	$28.29	0.60
Portfolio 3	13.4%	10.6%	$38.33	0.71
Portfolio 4	13.8%	10.6%	$42.26	0.75
Portfolio 5	14.8%	10.5%	$55.21	0.85

Source: See sources and descriptions of data

This portfolio increased the annualized return from 13.8 percent to 14.8 percent (an increase of over 7 percent). At the same time, the power of diversification reduced the volatility of the portfolio from 10.6 percent to 10.5 percent (a decrease of about 1 percent). The growth of each dollar invested increased from $42.26 to $55.21 (an increase of over 30 percent). With greater returns and lower risk, we certainly improved the efficiency of our portfolio as the Sharpe Ratio rose from 0.75 to 0.85, an increase of over 13 percent.

Step 5: Replace the 40 percent allocation to the Lehman Index with a 20 percent allocation to a two-year fixed-income fund.

We do so because long-term fixed-income securities have not appropriately compensated investors for risk and the longer term securities have higher correlation to the equity portion of the portfolio.

Portfolio 6: The Short-Term Fixed-Income Effect

S&P 500 Index	10%
U.S. Large Value	10%
U.S. Small	10%
U.S. Small Value	10%
International Large Value	10%
International Small	10%
Two-Year Fixed Income	40%

Six Steps to a Diversified Portfolio

1975–2003

	Annualized Return	Annualized Standard Deviation	Growth of a Dollar	Sharpe Ratio
Portfolio 1	12.3%	11.0%	$28.75	0.58
Portfolio 2	12.2%	10.6%	$28.29	0.60
Portfolio 3	13.4%	10.6%	$38.83	0.71
Portfolio 4	13.8%	10.6%	$42.26	0.75
Portfolio 5	14.8%	10.5%	$55.21	0.85
Portfolio 6	14.5%	9.9%	$50.26	0.87

Source: See sources and descriptions of data

The shift from long-term fixed-income investments to shorter term fixed-income investments has a very positive effect on the volatility of the portfolio, with a much smaller negative impact on returns. Volatility of the portfolio decreased from 10.5 percent to 9.9 percent (a decrease of almost 6 percent), while returns decreased slightly from 14.8 percent to 14.5 (a decrease of .3 percent). The growth of each dollar invested only declined from $55.21 to $50.26 (a decrease of about 9 percent). Note that the Sharpe Ratio rose again from 0.85 to 0.87, an increase of over 2 percent. It is also worth noting that while replacing the allocation to long-term bonds with an allocation to a much shorter term fixed-income asset did lower returns, one should be careful in relying on this particular bit of data. The reason is that the yield on the twenty-year government bond fell from almost 8 percent at the start of the period to just about 5 percent at the end. This produced capital gains for investors. The incremental return, however, was accompanied by much higher volatility, resulting in the reduced efficiency of the portfolio (a lower Sharpe Ratio). It does not seem likely that similar capital gains can be repeated going forward, while the volatility of the longer term bond is likely to continue to be much greater.

Step 6: Add an allocation to the asset class of real estate.

Real estate, via an investment in Real Estate Investment Trusts (REITs), has been found to be an excellent diversifier as it has relatively low correlation to both equities and fixed-income instruments.

Portfolio 7: The Real Estate Effect

S&P 500 Index	8%
U.S. Large Value	8%
U.S. Small	8%
U.S. Small Value	8%
U.S. REITs	8%
International Large Value	10%
International Small	10%
Two-Year Fixed Income	40%

1975–2003

	Annualized Return	Annualized Standard Deviation	Growth of a Dollar	Sharpe Ratio
Portfolio 1	12.3%	11.0%	$28.75	0.58
Portfolio 2	12.2%	10.6%	$28.29	0.60
Portfolio 3	13.4%	10.6%	$38.83	0.71
Portfolio 4	13.8%	10.6%	$42.26	0.75
Portfolio 5	14.8%	10.5%	$55.21	0.85
Portfolio 6	14.5%	9.9%	$50.26	0.87
Portfolio 7	14.3%	9.4%	$48.67	0.89

Source: See sources and descriptions of data

While the rate of return fell slightly (about 1 percent), the volatility of the portfolio fell by over 5 percent, resulting in an increase in the Sharpe Ratio from 0.87 to 0.89 (an increase of over 2 percent). The slightly lower annualized return did produce a slightly lower growth of a dollar.

At this point it is worth comparing the control portfolio to Portfolio 7. Despite maintaining our equity/fixed allocation at 60/40, we managed to increase our rate of return from 12.3 percent to 14.3 percent (an increase of over 16 percent). We accomplished this increase in returns while actually decreasing the volatility, or risk, of our portfolio from 11.0 percent to 9.4 percent (a decrease of almost 15 percent). The growth of each dollar invested grew from $28.75 to $48.67 (an increase of over 69 percent). The Sharpe Ratio rose from 0.58 to 0.89, an increase of 53 percent. Thus Portfolio 7 was 53 percent more efficient at producing a unit of return for each unit of risk (as measured by volatility). We accomplished these once seemingly incompatible objectives by applying the principles of MPT—that is, adding the high expected returning asset classes of small and value together with broad global diversification.

Does Passive Investing Produce Average Returns?

Through the step-by-step process described above, it becomes clear that one of the major criticisms of passive portfolio management—that it produces *average* returns—is just not true. There was nothing "average" about the returns of any of the seven portfolios we explored. Certainly they produced far greater returns than did the average investor, be it individual or institutional. It is important to understand that passive investing produces *market,* not average returns—and it does so in a relatively low-cost and tax-efficient manner. Remember that the average actively managed fund produces well below market results and does so with great persistency. Thus by simply playing the winner's game of accepting market returns, investors will almost certainly outperform the vast majority of both individual and institutional investors who choose to play the active game.

Summary

Let's quickly review. First, markets are efficient. With this understanding, we concluded that attempts to either select individual securities that were under/overvalued or to time the market would be highly likely to be nonproductive. Therefore, we chose a passive management approach. We then identified the asset classes that would produce the highest expected returns and saw that because the markets are efficient at pricing for risk, the highest expected returning asset classes are those that have the highest risk. These asset classes were small capitalization companies and value companies. We showed how to spread risk by owning a large number of these companies (all companies within the given asset class) through the purchasing of passive asset-class funds. Finally, we saw how to lower risk and improve the risk/reward trade-off by diversifying across a broad spectrum of asset classes, including international and real estate. In the next chapter we will explore several different model portfolios. We will start with a conservative portfolio and gradually add risk and expected return. We will then provide an investment approach that will help you choose the portfolio that best meets your objectives and your tolerance for risk. It is important to keep in mind that the model portfolios are not recommendations. At the risk of being redundant, there are no right portfolios, just one portfolio that is right for each individual—based on his/her own unique ability, willingness, and need to take risk. The models are, therefore, offered *only as starting points*. How much you allocated to each asset class is a personal decision the implications of which should be thoroughly considered prior to implementation.

CHAPTER 8

◆

How to Build a Model Portfolio

Fortune favors the bold. —Virgil, *Aeneid* X

It's Super Bowl Sunday, you are the head coach of one of the combatants, and your team is trailing 17–14. The good news is that your team has the ball on the opponent's one-yard line. But it's fourth down, and only one second is left on the clock. Do you play it safe and kick the tying field goal to send the game into overtime, or do you go for broke and try for the winning touchdown? Many questions rush through your mind. How much confidence do I have in my offense? If we kick the field goal, can my defense hold the opponent if they win the coin toss? Even a field goal isn't a sure thing. Which is the correct decision?

Different coaches will come to different conclusions based on their assessments of such questions. Perhaps the deciding factor will be the personality of the coach. The extent to which the coach is a risk taker may ultimately be the deciding factor on whether to kick the field goal or go for the glory.

Choosing an appropriate asset allocation when creating an investment portfolio is, in many ways, like the decision facing the Super Bowl coach. First, there is no right answer. As we have discussed, there are many factors that should be considered in the decision-making process. One example is that a major determinant should be the ability to accept and deal with the possibility of a negative outcome. In football the price of going for the glory is the possibility of living with the agony of defeat. In the field of investments, the price of seeking high returns is the possibility, if not probability, of accepting long periods of poor or even negative returns.

How does an investor choose a portfolio that will meet his/her unique tolerance for risk and unique time horizon? To show how to do so, we will explore several different model portfolios, starting with a conservative approach, gradually adding risk and then return to the portfolio.

We will examine four model portfolios and discuss how they performed over the thirty-one-year period 1973–2003. The portfolios will range in their equity allocation from 40 percent to 100 percent and be characterized as: conservative (40 percent equity/ 60 percent debt); moderate (60 percent equity/40 percent debt); moderately aggressive (80 percent equity/20 percent debt); and highly aggressive (100 percent equity). These categories should cover the risk spectrum of most investors. Then we will examine the annual compound returns and standard deviations of these portfolios. We will also look at the worst single year as well as the *cumulative* returns for the worst two– and three–calendar year periods. These measurements should be used as the benchmarks against which an investor can measure his/her willingness and ability to absorb the "stomach acid" these periods produce. Finally, we will examine the growth of each dollar invested if the investor stayed the course and rebalanced the portfolio at the end of each year in order to maintain the chosen percentage allocation to each asset class.

Note that the data for our model portfolio intentionally extends back to include 1973–74, two of the worst investment years since the Depression. Including these years allows us to see the performance of our portfolios in the worst of times as well as the best of times. This information is particularly relevant to investors who find it easy to stick with an investment plan when everything is going well but have more difficulty doing so in bear markets.

Before proceeding with our look at model portfolios, we need to address the important issue of how much to allocate to international assets.

How Much to Allocate to International Equities?

Today, the U.S. markets account for approximately 50 percent of the global equity markets total capitalization. Since one interpretation of the EMH is that the asset allocation should be determined by a particular country's share of the global equity markets, this would result in a U.S. investor's international allocation being as high as 50 percent of the portfolio. Although there is certainly logic to this argument, such a large allocation completely ignores an important psychological (and very real) problem—most investors are far more willing to tolerate poor performance from the equity markets of their home country than they are from international assets (which they incorrectly view as more risky). This leads to the loss of discipline and panic selling almost always at the wrong time. Thus the model portfolios contain an allocation to international assets of 30 percent. Investors less susceptible to this psychological risk should consider an even higher allocation (and vice versa). Before you decide on the appropriate allocation, however, you should consider the academic evidence demonstrating that adding international assets is a very effective way of improving the efficiency of a portfolio. The following is a summary of one study, covering the period 1970–96:[1]

- Increasing the international allocation to as much as 40 percent *increased* returns and *reduced* risk as measured by standard deviation (volatility).
- An allocation of 40 percent international produced the highest Sharpe Ratio.
- Increasing the international allocation from 0 to just 20 percent reduced the likelihood of negative returns by one-third.
- Investors with a 10 percent international allocation could be 98 percent confident that they would reduce risk by raising the international allocation.
- Investors with an allocation as high as 22 percent could be 90 percent confident that they would reduce risk by raising their international allocation.

Other studies have come to very similar conclusions.

We can now turn to examining the model portfolios. It is important to remember that these portfolios are just illustrations and not necessarily optimal portfolios. In addition, your portfolio should be tailored to your own unique situation. Your portfolio, therefore, may look very different from the ones shown below.

Model Portfolios Allocations

	Conservative	Moderate	Moderately Aggressive	Highly Aggressive
Equity (%)	40	60	80	100
U.S. stocks (%)	28	42	56	70
Large (%)	6	9	12	15
Large Value (%)	6	9	12	15
Small (%)	6	9	12	15
Small Value (%)	6	9	12	15
Real Estate (%)	4	6	8	10
Int'l Stocks (%)	12	18	24	30
Large (%)	2	3	4	5
Large Value (%)	4	6	8	10
Small (%)	4	6	8	10
Emerging Markets (%)	2	3	4	5
Fixed Income (%)	60	40	20	0
U.S. Two-Year (%)	60	40	20	0

How to Build a Model Portfolio

Model Portfolios 1973–2003

	Conservative	Moderate	Moderately Aggressive	Highly Aggressive
Compound Return (%)	11.1	12.4	13.5	14.5
Annual Standard Deviation (%)	7.9	11.1	14.5	18.0
Worst One-Year Return (%)	−4.5	−10.8	−17.5	−24.2
Worst Two-Year Cumulative Return (%)	−8.4	−19.6	−30.1	−39.9
Worst Three-Year Cumulative return(%)	7.6	2.2	−3.1	−9.9
Growth of a Dollar	$26.41	$37.27	$50.70	$66.49

Source: See sources and descriptions of data

An investor who chose the conservative portfolio achieved a very respectable 11.1 percent per annum compound rate of return and experienced a standard deviation of only 7.9 percent per annum. Also of great importance is that the worst one-year return was a loss of 4.5 percent, the worst two-year return was a loss of 8.4 percent, and there were no three-year periods when a loss was incurred. Finally, each dollar invested grew to $26.41.

Moving all the way to the right, an investor who chose the highly aggressive portfolio achieved an annual compound rate of return of 14.5 percent per annum, 3.4 percent per annum better than the performance of the conservative portfolio. The higher return, however, came at the expense of a greater standard deviation—18.0 percent per annum—over twice the standard deviation of the conservative portfolio. This outcome is not unexpected. Over the long term, greater risk should be accompanied by greater reward for accepting that risk. It is important to note that in addition to having to endure much greater volatility, the worst one-year loss for the highly aggressive portfolio was 19.7 percent greater and the worst cumulative two-year loss was 31.5 percent greater than that experienced by the conservative portfolio. In addition, while the conservative portfolio never experienced a loss over a three-year period, the highly aggressive portfolio lost almost 10 percent over the worst three-year period. The real compensation for enduring the "stomach acid" of those bad periods was that each dollar invested eventually grew to $66.49, over twice the result achieved by the conservative portfolio. As John Maynard Keynes said: "In the main, therefore, slumps are experiences to be lived through . . . with as much equanimity and patience as possible."[2]

The moderate and moderately aggressive portfolios also produced returns and standard deviations that were reflective of their levels of risk. How should the individual investor choose the portfolio that is right for him/her? Each investor should carefully consider the issues related to the three branches of the IPS decision tree—the willingness to take risk, the ability to take risk, and the need to take risk. We begin by examining the issues related to the willingness to take risk.

The Stomach Acid Test

Your ultimate success or failure will depend on your ability to ignore the worries of the world long enough to allow your investments to succeed. It isn't the head, but the stomach that determines [your] fate.　　—Peter Lynch, *Beating the Street*

How to Build a Model Portfolio

*If you want to see the greatest threat to your financial future,
go home and take a look in the mirror.*
— Jonathan Clements

The willingness to take risk is determined by taking the "stomach acid" test. This test involves asking the question, "Do you have the fortitude and discipline to stick with your predetermined investment strategy (asset allocation) when the going gets rough?" Successful investment management depends to a large degree on the ability of an individual to withstand the periods of stress and on his/her ability to overcome the severe emotional hurdles present during bear markets like the ones experienced in 1973–74 and 2000–02. In order to actually have achieved the superior returns of the more aggressive portfolios, you would not only have to endure the worst two years (1973–74) with a cumulative negative return of almost 40 percent, but you would also have needed the courage to buy more equities (except in the case of the all-equity portfolio) in order to rebalance at a time when the market incurred a major collapse and you were likely feeling lots of pain. An example follows.

Assume that an investor begins with $100,000 invested in the moderately aggressive portfolio. This means that the equity/fixed-income allocation is 80 percent/20 percent, or $80,000 invested in equities and $20,000 invested in fixed income. Assume that in the first year, equities drop in value by 40 percent, while the value of the fixed-income portfolio remains unchanged. Our investor's equity portfolio would have decreased by $32,000 ($80,000 × 40 percent). Our portfolio would now consist of $48,000 of equities and $20,000 of fixed income—a total value of the portfolio of $68,000. In order to maintain our 80 percent equity allocation, we need to increase our equity position to $54,400 ($68,000 × 80 percent). The result is that just when the market has collapsed, our investor will have to sell $6,400 of fixed-income assets and buy $6,400 of equities. Alternatively, if additional funds were available, our investor could purchase an additional $32,000 of equities, restoring the equity position to $80,000 and restoring the 80 percent/20 percent mix. It takes a lot of discipline and courage to buy in the face of a market collapse. But this is the only way an investor could have achieved the superior returns the moderately aggressive portfolio produced.

Since the aggressive portfolio produced the higher returns, we begin our stomach acid test here. The investor, keeping in mind Socrates's admonition—"Know thyself"—must look in the mirror and honestly answer the following question: Will I be able to sleep well if the performance of not only the single worst year experienced by this portfolio, a loss in excess of 24 percent, was repeated but would I have been able to sleep well after experiencing a second successive painful year that resulted in a cumulative loss of almost 40 percent? It is important to understand that if an investor overestimates their ability to withstand the pain of bear markets, he/she may panic and sell just when it is important to buy. Having sold out at the lows, the investor would almost certainly have been better off with a more conservative portfolio in the first place. In addition, this poor experience may cause the investor to avoid investing in the equity markets altogether in the future.

If the answer to our question is no, the investor should move to a less aggressive portfolio. The process should then be repeated until an acceptable level of risk is found. Keep in mind that these four portfolios are not the only ones that can be constructed. For example, if our hypothetical investor is not comfortable with the moderately aggressive portfolio but is willing to accept more risk than is inherent in the moderate portfolio, a 70 percent equity/30 percent fixed-income portfolio could be constructed.

The following table provides a guideline for investors to test their willingness to take risk.

How to Build a Model Portfolio

Willingness to Take Risk

Maximum Tolerable Loss (%)	Maximum Equity Exposure (%)
5	20
10	30
15	40
20	50
25	60
30	70
35	80
40	90
50	100

Keep in mind that the investor is making the choice between sleeping well and eating well. He/she cannot have it both ways. In other words, an investor choosing the conservative portfolio must be aware that historically the price for sleeping well (experiencing a standard deviation of about 8 percent) was leaving more than half of the potential investment dollars on the table ($26.41 versus $66.49).

While there is no one correct choice, it is important to understand the consequences of your choices. Robert Arnott put it this way: "If investors invest in a fashion that exceeds their own risk tolerance, so that when things go awry (as they inevitably will from time to time) they must abandon their strategy, they have done themselves a disservice by engaging in the strategy in the first place."[3] Let's now turn to the second branch of the IPS decision tree, the ability to take risk.

The Ability to Take Risk

An investor's ability to take risk is determined by three things: the investment horizon, the stability of their earned income, and the need for liquidity. Let's begin with the issue of the investment horizon. The longer the horizon, the greater the ability to wait out the almost inevitable bear markets. In addition, the longer the investment horizon, the more likely it is that equities will provide higher returns than fixed-income investments. The following table provides a guideline for this part of the ability to take risk test.

Ability to Take Risk

Investment Horizon	Maximum Equity Allocation (%)
0–3 Years	0
4 Years	10
5 Years	20
6 Years	30
7 Years	40
8 Years	50
9 Years	60
10 Years	70
11–14 Years	80
15–19 Years	90
20 Years or longer	100

An investor's ability to take risk is also impacted by the stability of their earned income. The greater the stability of earned income, the greater the ability to take the risks of equity ownership.

For example, a tenured professor has a greater ability to take risk than either a worker in a highly cyclical industry where layoffs are common or an entrepreneur who owns his/her own business.

The Liquidity Test

The need for liquidity is determined by the amount of near-term cash requirements as well as the potential for unanticipated calls on capital. The liquidity test begins by determining the amount of cash reserve one may need to meet unanticipated needs for cash such as medical bills, car or home repair, or even the loss of a job. Financial planners generally recommend a cash reserve of about six months of ordinary expenses. If our investor has expenses of $5,000 per month, a cash reserve of $30,000 should be built before making any equity or long-term fixed-income investments. Liquidity needs should only be invested in fixed-income securities with little to no investment risk, either maturity or credit (very short-term maturity and an investment rating of at least AA). The investor must then identify any known cash needs that must be met (e.g., the purchase of a car, a down payment on a home, or college tuition) as well as the anticipated time the expenditure will be made. The funds needed to provide for the expenditure should not be invested with an allocation that is greater than the one suggested in the above table. In addition, the maturity of the fixed-income component should not exceed the date when the expenditure is anticipated to occur.

To look at an example of how this table can be put to work, assume that our hypothetical investor has $250,000 available to invest and the following cash needs: four years of college tuition, room and board at $25,000 a year, beginning in year six; $30,000 for a new car in year three; and $30,000 for emergency reserves (six months × $5,000 per month in living expenses). The investor should hold $30,000 in short-term fixed-income investments (i.e., CDs or a money market account) for emergency expenses. The $30,000 required to buy the car should be held all in fixed-income assets because the time frame is only three years. However, instead of investing the funds in Treasury bills, the maturity could be extended to three years (if the extra maturity risk is offset by a greater yield) because the funds will not be needed until then. A good rule of thumb to consider is that if an extra year of maturity risk provides at least twenty basis points (0.2 percent) of incremental yield, then it is worth the risk to extend the maturity (but the maturity should never be longer than when the funds will be required). As an example, if the two-year treasury is yielding 2 percent, and the three-year treasury is yielding at least 2.20 percent, it would be worth considering accepting the incremental volatility risk to extend the maturity to the further date. If the yield is less than 2.20 percent, than the investor should choose the shorter maturity. The amount to be held in fixed-income investments to meet college expenses is calculated as follows:

Year 6	$25,000 × 70 percent = $17,500
Year 7	$25,000 × 60 percent = $15,000
Year 8	$25,000 × 50 percent = $12,500
Year 9	$25,000 × 40 percent = $10,000
Total	**$55,000**

(Note that for year six the maximum equity exposure recommended in the investment horizon table is 30 percent; thus the minimum allocation to fixed-income investments should be 70 percent). Note also that the maximum maturity for the $17,500 invested in fixed income to meet the funding need in year six should be six years.

The total allocated to fixed-income investments should be $60,000 for the car and an emergency reserve plus $55,000 for college tuition for a total of $115,000. Having $250,000 to invest, the asset allocation to equities should not exceed $135,000, or 54 percent—regardless of the outcome of the stomach acid test. In fact, if the stomach acid test produced a maximum acid level of equities below 54 percent, that lower number should be the upper limit. In other words, the equity asset allocation should always be the lower of the outcomes of the two tests.

As is the case with all the suggested risk-management tables and model portfolios, they are just guidelines. Investors willing to accept more risk might create an investment horizon risk table that instead of going out to twenty years only extends to ten years, with the equity allocation increasing about 15 percent each year beginning in year four. It's the discipline of the process, not the formula, that is important. However, I would certainly not recommend making any equity investments with cash needed within a three-year time frame.

In addition to ensuring that an investor has sufficient funds to meet all his/her known short-term expenses as well as an emergency reserve, the liquidity test provides another benefit. Since an investor will have set aside sufficient funds in a not-at-risk, liquid safety net, he/she should feel secure when the inevitable periods of poor market performance occur. With sufficient funds to cover expenses and a well-diversified portfolio, an investor improves the chances of having the discipline and courage to ride out the inevitable bad years. Difficult periods are built right into the investment strategy.

We now turn to the third and the most often overlooked branch of the IPS decision tree.

The Need to Take Risk

The third branch of the IPS decision tree is related to the investor's financial objectives or the need to take risk. The need to take risk is determined by the rate of return required to achieve the investor's financial objectives. Considering only the first two issues—the ability and willingness to take risk—while ignoring the need to take risk—is a serious and common mistake made by investors and advisors alike. The greater the rate of return needed to achieve one's financial objective, the more equity (and/or small and value) risk one needs to take. However, in considering the financial objective it is important to carefully consider what economists call the marginal utility of wealth—how much is any potential incremental wealth worth relative to the risk that must be accepted in order to achieve the greater *expected* return. While more money is always better than less, at some point most people achieve a lifestyle with which they are very comfortable. At that point, the taking on of incremental risk required to achieve a higher net worth is no longer acceptable to most people. The reason is that the potential damage of an unexpected negative outcome far exceeds the benefit that would be gained from incremental wealth. Thus each investor needs to decide at what level of wealth their unique utility of wealth curve starts flattening out—begins bending sharply to the right. Beyond this point there is little reason to take incremental risk in order to achieve a higher *expected* return. Many wealthy investors have experienced devastating losses that could easily have been avoided if they, or their advisors, considered this important issue. It is one of the great ironies of investing that the very people who can most afford to take risk (the very wealthy) have the lowest marginal utility of wealth and therefore the least need to take risk. The flip side of that coin, unfortunately, is that we find many 401(k) participants in their twenties and thirties, with high marginal utilities of wealth, who have very low (often even zero) allocations to equities.

It is important to note that the rate of return needed to meet your objective is influenced by many factors. Among these factors are: How high is the goal you set? The higher the goal, the greater the amount of risk that must be accepted. If the rate of return required to meet your goal is too high given your risk tolerance, you can choose to either accept the incremental risk or lower the goal (accepting, for example, the likelihood of a lower level lifestyle in retirement or a smaller estate to pass on to your heirs). Alternatively, you could choose to save more now, thus lowering your need to take risk. The price paid for being able to accept less risk is obviously a lower level of spending (lifestyle) today. More saving today (lower spending) provides the opportunity for either taking less risk (lower equity allocation) or the likelihood of a higher ending net worth. Less saving today has the opposite effect.

The expected rate of return on a portfolio is not only dependent on the equity to fixed-income allocation but also on the allocation to the specific asset classes within these broad categories. It is also dependent on the *current* level of both interest rates and stock prices (remember, high current valuations mean low future expected returns and vice versa). Thus it is not as easy (as it was in the cases of the ability and willingness to take risk) to provide a table with a guideline on the equity allocation needed to achieve a certain rate of return. Keeping this in mind, the following table provides a reasonable guideline (at the time I wrote this):

- It is based on the asset allocations used in the model portfolios—different allocations to the specific asset classes would result in different projections.

- It is based upon the use of passively managed funds.
- All the returns are pretax.
- The rate of return on a 100 percent fixed-income portfolio is based on the assumption that the investments will be in shorter term instruments (two- to three-year maturity)

Need to Take Risk

Financial Goal—Rate of Return Required (%)	Equity Allocation (%)
2.0	0
3.0	20
4.5	40
6.0	60
7.5	80
9.0	100

The Annual Checkup

The IPS should not be a static document; instead it should be a living one. The reason is that over time the assumptions made about the ability, willingness, and need to take risk will change. For example, the passage of time impacts the ability to take risk. Personal circumstances can change in dramatic fashion due to a death in the family, divorce, loss of a job, or an inheritance. Changes such as these can result in significant changes in the ability, willingness, and need to take risk. And even markets themselves can lead to a need for reassessing the asset-allocation decision. For example, the bull market of the late 1990s certainly reduced the need to take risk for those investors who had already accumulated significant assets. Thus a review of the IPS should have resulted in considering a lowering of the equity allocation.

If your personal circumstances change in dramatic fashion, then you should review your IPS as soon as possible. Otherwise, the IPS should be reviewed on an annual basis to ensure that the assumptions upon which the asset-allocation decisions were made still hold true. If the assumptions have changed, the IPS should be altered to reflect that change.

Now that you have seen how you can build a tailored portfolio and adapt it to your changing financial circumstances, I'll explain how to make the location decisions that relate to tax issues.

Allocating Assets Between Taxable and Tax-Advantaged Accounts

The only thing that hurts more than paying an income tax is not having to pay an income tax. —Lord Thomas R. Duwar

While the asset-allocation decision is the most important decision an investor makes, the asset-*location* decision is also an important one. While it does not impact the risk of a portfolio, it can have a substantial impact on the final wealth created through its impact on after-tax returns—the only kind we get to spend.

With the availability of tax-efficient passively managed/index funds, tax-managed passive asset-class/index funds and tax-efficient exchange-traded funds (ETFs), the winning strategy is to hold as much equity as possible in taxable accounts and hold taxable fixed-income investments and tax-inefficient real estate investment trusts (REITs) in tax-deferred accounts (e.g., IRA, 401(k),

403(b), profit sharing, etc.). This is likely to prove to be the winning strategy even with tax-inefficient actively managed equity funds. Since Roth accounts are not subject to taxation, the highest expected returning asset class should be located in that account.

The advantage of holding equities in a taxable account is based on:

- Tax-deferred accounts, such as IRAs, convert long-term capital gains on equities into ordinary income upon distribution. For most investors the ordinary income-tax rate is much higher.

- By holding equities in tax-deferred accounts, investors lose the potential for a "step-up in basis" (upon death) for tax purposes. The step-up may totally eliminate capital-gains taxes for the estate.

- Capital-gains taxes are due only when realized. Investors do have at least some ability to time the realization of gains. In addition, the advent of tax-managed funds and exchange-traded funds (ETFs) has greatly improved the tax efficiency of equity investing.

- When holding a diversified portfolio of equities and/or equity mutual funds in a taxable account, there may be opportunities to tax loss harvest, producing greater tax efficiency.

- If equities are held in a tax-deferred account, the investor loses the ability to donate appreciated shares to charity, thus avoiding capital-gains taxes altogether.

It is important that investors understand that the above analysis is based on *preference*—when they are going to hold both stocks and fixed-income investments and have a choice of location. Regardless of whether the account will hold stocks or fixed-income investments, investors should always prefer to first fund their deductible retirement account (i.e., IRA, 401(k), or 403(b)) or Roth IRA before investing any taxable dollars (except for creating an emergency fund). Because they are the most tax-efficient investment accounts, investors should take the maximum advantage of the ability under the law to fund them.

We need to cover two other points on asset location. First, foreign stock holdings often entail taxes on dividends being withheld at the source. Investors can, however, claim a foreign tax credit that can then be used as a credit against U.S. taxes. However, this credit does no good if the asset is not in a taxable account. How much of a problem is the loss of the credit? As of 2003, dividends from the average foreign stock are quite low—about 2.3 percent per annum. Since the tax withholding is 15 percent of that, the tax reduces annual returns by 0.35 percent.[4] Thus if there is a choice between holding similar United States and international asset classes in a taxable or tax-deferred account, the international asset should be held in the taxable account. It is important to remember that if the investment in international assets is a "fund of funds" (a fund that invests in other funds) then any foreign tax credit cannot be passed on to the investor by the fund of funds.

The exceptions to the strategy of preferring to hold equities in taxable accounts include:

- Investors with anticipated, or the potential for unanticipated, liquidity and/or cash-flow needs from their taxable holdings may want to consider holding some fixed-income investments (generally municipal bonds) in their taxable accounts. The need for fixed-income assets to be held in a taxable account can be determined by the outcome of the liquidity test. The holding of fixed-income assets in a taxable account may necessitate the need for holding some equity in a tax-deferred account.

- Investors needing to achieve a rate of return that requires them to hold a high equity allocation may need to hold some equities in a tax-deferred account. In this case the least tax-efficient equity holdings should first be allocated to the tax-deferred account. REITs are the least tax-efficient equity asset class and they should always be held in a tax-deferred account. Actively managed funds are also generally tax inefficient and thus generally (unless specifically tax managed) should be considered next in line when equities must be held in tax-deferred accounts. The next candidates for holding in tax-deferred accounts are passively managed small-cap and value funds (again unless tax managed), because they generally have higher turnover (and thus generally are less tax efficient) than large-cap and growth funds.

We need to cover one more point in regard to asset location. Balanced, or lifestyle, funds are very popular vehicles among individual investors. The use of these funds allows an individual investor to achieve some degree of diversification across asset classes while "keeping it simple"—simple because the investor needs to hold only one fund instead of several. While simplicity has its virtues, for those investors who have the ability to hold assets in both their taxable and tax-deferred accounts, these funds are not efficient from a tax perspective. Let's see why.

- Unless the fund is an all-equity fund, combining equities and fixed-income assets in one fund results in the investor holding one of the two asset classes in a tax-inefficient manner. If the fund is held in a taxable account, the investor is holding the fixed-income assets in a tax-inefficient location.

If the fund is held in a tax-deferred account, the equities are being held in a tax-inefficient location (losing the benefits of long-term capital-gains treatment, the ability to harvest losses, the ability to use the asset as a means of making a charitable contribution and avoid the capital-gains tax, and the potential for a step-up in basis upon death).

- If the fund is held in a taxable account, the investor loses the ability to harvest losses at the individual asset-class level.

- If the fund is in a tax-deferred account, then the investor loses the ability to use any foreign tax credits that are generated by the international equity holdings. Even in a taxable account, as a fund of funds, the investor loses the ability to utilize the foreign-tax credit.

- If the fund is held in a taxable account, the equities should be in funds that are tax managed. I am not aware of any lifestyle or balanced fund that tax manages the equity portion (which makes sense since the fund does not know the location in which it will be held).

Individually, these are all important negative features that impact the after-tax return of a lifestyle fund. Collectively, they are very damaging. The bottom line is that, in general, unless an investor is holding all of their investable assets in a tax-deferred account, lifestyle funds are best avoided (the exception might be for investors in the lowest tax bracket as they can hold tax-inefficient fixed-income assets in a taxable account). The more efficient investment strategy is to hold the individual assets in separate funds and in the most tax-efficient location.

CHAPTER 9

♦

Index Funds, Passive Asset-Class Funds, and ETFs

There are basically three types of investment vehicles available to implement a passive strategy—index funds, passive asset-class funds, and exchange-traded funds (ETFs). Since index funds are the most commonly used investment vehicles for individual (retail) investors who adopt passive investing as their investment strategy, we begin our discussion with them.

Index Funds

Index funds generally buy and hold all the securities within a particular index in a market cap—weighted fashion. Thus while an S&P 500 Index fund would own all five hundred stocks that comprise the index, it would not own an equal amount of each of the five hundred stocks. The largest holding might, for example, be 5 percent of the entire portfolio. There are many indices, and corresponding index funds, in which an individual can choose to invest, including large caps, small caps, value stocks, growth stocks, and real estate. There are also several index funds that replicate international and emerging-market indexes.

The benefits of indexing relative to active management are very clear.

- Relatively low costs.
- Relatively low turnover.
- Relatively greater tax efficiency.

The premier provider of index funds is clearly Vanguard. They have the broadest array of index funds and are generally the lowest cost provider. Fidelity, via its Spartan funds, is also an excellent choice for index funds.

Passive Asset-Class Funds

Index funds and passive asset-class funds are similar in the way that rectangles and squares are similar. All squares are rectangles, but not all rectangles are squares. Similarly, while all index funds are passively managed, not all passive asset-class funds are index funds. Let's see how passive asset-class investing is different from index investing.

Let's begin with a definition. An asset class is a group of securities that have similar risk characteristics. While index funds generally represent a specific asset class, we can define and thus create an asset-class fund for which there is no index. For example, the Bridgeway Ultra-Large 35 Fund buys and holds the largest thirty-five stocks. It is a passive asset-class fund (that does not use market-cap weighting, instead choosing to equal weight), but not an index fund, as there is no such index. What, if any advantages, do passive asset-class funds have?

Index funds seek to replicate the indices they are tracking and to minimize tracking error (have a different result than the index itself). The replication and minimization of tracking error, however, comes with costs, as we shall see. Passive asset-class funds, while investing only in securities within a specific asset class, have the advantage of not trying to replicate an index. Instead, they focus on achieving the greatest returns (and, if tax managed, the greatest after-tax returns) for a given level of risk (the risk of the asset class in which they are investing). This difference in objective allows passive asset-class funds to *maximize the advantages* of indexing and *minimize the disadvantages* of indexing. Let's look at some examples.

- Studies have found that initial public offerings (IPOs) make very poor investments. If a recent IPO were included in an index, an index fund would buy it. However, a passive asset-class fund could "screen out" IPOs by requiring that for any holding to be eligible for purchase it must meet a minimum listing requirement of perhaps one year.

- Very small-cap stocks delist from the exchanges at a rate that most investors would find astonishing. A passive asset-class fund might require tougher listing standards than the exchanges themselves require. By reducing delistings, returns can be improved.

- Index funds have forced turnover—they sell a stock when it leaves its index. Imagine the following scenario for a Russell 2000 Index fund. The fund buys and holds the stocks ranked 1001–3000 in the Russell 3000 Index. A stock is ranked 1001 at the start of the year. When the index is reconstituted at the end of the year, the stock is ranked 999. The fund now must sell the stock. One year later it is again ranked 1001. The fund must again buy the stock. In order to reduce this costly and nonproductive turnover, a passive asset-class fund might instead buy only the stocks with a ranking of greater than 1,000 and also create a *hold range* for stocks that with a ranking just below that figure. For example, they might continue to hold stocks (but not buy any more) as long as they were ranked between 800 and 1,000. If a stock's ranking moved to a figure of less than 800, only then would it be sold. Similarly, stocks can easily move from value to growth and back again. Not only do buy-and-hold ranges reduce costly turnover without impacting expected returns in any but a random manner, but they also improve tax efficiency.

- If the passive asset-class fund was a tax-managed fund, it might also only sell stocks that had long-term capital gains. If any short-term gains existed, the stock would be held until the gains became long term. An index fund, on the other hand, would sell the stock as soon as it left the index.

The asset class that presents the greatest opportunity for passive asset-class funds to improve upon the returns of index funds is small-cap stocks. Not only do small-cap stocks have large bid-offer spreads, but the low level of liquidity in these stocks also leads to large market-impact costs for active fund managers attempting to quickly get into, or out of, these stocks. Let's look at an example of how a passive asset-class fund, as long as it is willing to accept random tracking error, can benefit from the market-impact costs active managers incur.

XYZ is a small-cap stock with a market capitalization of about

$500 million. The stock only trades about one hundred thousand shares a day. The stock currently trades at 10 bid and 10 ¼ asked. Thus about $1 million of the company's shares change hands on a daily basis. Active fund ABC wishes to sell $5 million of the stock. It knows that if it begins a program to sell such a relatively large block of stock it will rapidly drive down the price against itself. It will also take at least several days to sell all of the stock. In the meantime, another stock the fund wishes to buy is expected (by the fund) to rise in value. In order to sell quickly (get out of the stock it currently owns and raise the funds to immediately buy the future expected outperformer before it rises in value) the active fund knows it must accept a discount. The anxious seller contacts market makers and requests them to find a buyer for the entire block. A passive fund is contacted to see if it is interested. The fund checks its portfolio of small-cap stocks. It finds that based on market-cap weighting it should, and currently does, own $5 million. However, it also has established a rule that randomly it can own up to twice that amount—so that it can exploit situations such as the one presented. Thus the fund can buy the whole block of the additional $5 million being offered and still be within its maximum tolerance of two times the appropriate market-cap weighting. The passive fund bids nine for the stock. Now obviously, with this type of discount it won't win every bid (the seller might not be willing to sell at that steep a discount and/or there might be competition for that block willing to bid at a somewhat higher price), but it will win some. This type of opportunistic block trading can turn the high trading costs of small-cap stocks into an advantage by not only reducing costs but also by creating the potential for negative trading costs. The reason is that the evidence is clear that the active funds that are selling, and having to absorb the market-impact costs, have no insight into the movement of stock prices. While the seller may believe the stock they are selling is overvalued, the historical evidence is that this is not the case. Thus, *on average,* the stock bought in a block trade at a discount will basically trade the next day at the same price (relative to the entire market) it traded at prior to the block trade.

All of the above are examples of how a passive asset-class fund might end up with a portfolio whose holdings are significantly different from the universe of initially eligible securities using market-cap weighting to determine the appropriate holdings. If the screens the fund chooses are based on solid academic evidence and commonsense rules, the end result should be superior returns and tracking error to a benchmark that is purely random.

The premier provider of passive asset-class funds is Dimensional Fund Advisors (DFA). Their funds are engineered to take advantage of all the aforementioned opportunities to add value. They also have passive asset-class funds for asset classes for which there are no index funds available yet are important for investors seeking to build globally diverse portfolios. Among the asset classes that make excellent diversifiers—as of this writing, there are no index funds replicating them—are the international asset classes of small, small value, and large value. DFA offers passive asset-class funds covering each of these. In addition, it offers not only a passively managed emerging-markets fund but also emerging-markets value and small-cap funds as well. DFA is also the only provider of passively managed funds that are also tax managed for the asset classes of small value, large value, and international large value. Finally, DFA adds value to its tax-managed funds in a manner that an index fund could not, by managing the amount of dividends the fund will receive, making the fund more tax efficient.

It is important to note that DFA's main business is the providing of passive asset-class funds to institutional investors. Their funds are not available to the general public. This is why most individual investors have never heard of them, despite the fact that they manage almost $50 billion of assets (about one-third of which is from individual investors) at the time of this writing. They must be purchased through a relatively small group of advisors that DFA approves based upon their commitment to both a passive investment strategy and to educating their clients on the benefits of such a strategy.

The only other current provider of passive asset-class funds is Bridgeway. The manager of the Bridgeway Fund family, John Montgomery, is highly regarded. Bridgeway offers a small number of domestic passive asset-class funds, focusing on both the very large-cap stocks and the smallest of the small-cap stocks.

Let's now turn to the third passive investment vehicle we can use, exchange-traded funds. What exactly are these vehicles and are they worthy of consideration?

Exchange-Traded Funds

Exchange-traded index securities, for all practical purposes, act like open-ended, no-load mutual funds. Like mutual funds, they can be created to represent virtually any index, asset class, or sector. Thus an exchange-traded fund (ETF) that represents the S&P 500 Index will look just like an S&P 500 Index fund. Because of their unique operating structure, however, ETFs offer the potential for greater tax efficiency, lower annual operating expenses, and more flexible trading characteristics.

Advantages of ETFs

- The unique structure and related redemption process of ETFs has allowed them to substantially reduce taxable distributions for individual investors, making them more tax efficient than similar index funds.

- Operating expense ratios that are very comparable to or even lower than a similar index fund.

- Because of tax and regulatory issues, most non-U.S. residents face restrictions on purchasing U.S. mutual funds. However, ETFs, because they trade as stocks, face no such problems.

Disadvantages

- Trading costs: Because ETFs trade like stocks, bid-offer spreads will be incurred when buying and selling.

- Brokerage commissions: When an investor purchases a no-load mutual fund directly from the fund sponsor, no fees are incurred. Once again, since ETFs are like stocks, brokerage commissions are always incurred. This becomes important when investing on a frequent basis and/or in very small amounts. Examples might be dollar-cost-averaging programs as well as in retirement and profit-sharing plans.

Summary

ETFs are appropriate investment vehicles for investors to consider as they seek to build a globally diversified portfolio. The leading providers of ETFs are Barclays Global Investors and State Street. Vanguard is also a participant in the ETF market, offering ETF versions of some of their index funds.

CHAPTER 10

◆

The Care and Maintenance
of the Portfolio

Everything should be made as simple as possible, but not simpler.
— Albert Einstein

My wife is a passionate gardener. She tends her garden with great care and discipline. Each season brings with it the need for certain tasks; if she does not accomplish these tasks, her garden might be filled with weeds, her plants destroyed by bugs, and her trees decayed by disease. The garden must undergo regular care and maintenance or it will not produce the desired result. The same regular maintenance must be performed on an investment portfolio or the investor will lose control over the most important determinant of risk and returns—the portfolio's asset allocation. One of the two most important items on the portfolio maintenance agenda is rebalancing. The other is tax management.

Rebalancing and Style Drift

Rebalancing a portfolio—the process of restoring a portfolio to its original asset allocations and risk profile—is integral to the winning investment strategy. We have already seen that it is important for every investor to choose the asset allocation that meets his/her ability, willingness, or need to take risk. Once the original investment allocations have been implemented, the process has only just begun. The reason that portfolio management via rebalancing is an ongoing process is that each asset class within the portfolio is likely to change in value by a different percentage over time. This performance variance will alter the amount of risk (and expected return) in the portfolio.

A simple example will illustrate this point. Assume an investor starting out with $100,000 to invest chooses an asset allocation of 80 percent equities ($80,000) and 20 percent fixed income ($20,000). If the value of the equity portion of the portfolio increases 40 percent while the fixed-income portion increases 5 percent, the investor would then have $112,000 in equities and $21,000 in fixed-income assets—a total portfolio worth $133,000. The difference in performance of the two asset classes causes the asset allocation to change from 80 percent/20 percent to 84 percent/16 percent. The portfolio now has different risk and return characteristics than the original portfolio; its expected return is greater, but so is its risk.

	Original Portfolio		New Portfolio	
Equity allocation	80%	$80,000	84%	$112,000
Fixed-income allocation	20%	$20,000	16%	$21,000
Total Portfolio	**100%**	**$100,000**	**100%**	**$133,000**

Two methods may be used to rebalance the portfolio and restore the desired 80/20 asset allocation. The first is to simply reallocate. A portfolio of $133,000 with an 80 percent/20 percent asset allocation would have $106,400 in equities and $26,600 in fixed-income assets. The investor would have to sell $5,600 of equities and buy an equal amount of fixed-income assets to restore the portfolio to the original level of risk. Unfortunately, this method of rebalancing may cause transaction fees to be incurred. In addition, unless the rebalancing occurs in a nontaxable account, taxes will be due on the capital gain realized on the sale of $5,600 of equities. Fortunately, the impact will not be great because we only sold a small portion of the equity portfolio. Taxes, however, should be avoided, or deferred, whenever possible because they reduce long-term returns. This is especially true of short-term capital gains because they are taxed at the generally higher ordinary income tax rate. Therefore, an investor must exercise judgment when weighing the benefits of rebalancing against the taxes generated. If taxes are not an issue, as with a tax-deferred account such as an IRA, there is no reason not to undertake regular rebalancing.

There is a more tax friendly way of rebalancing a portfolio. If an investor has generated additional investable funds, they can be used to add to the fixed-income portion of the portfolio so as to restore the original 80/20 allocation. With a current equity holding of $112,000, one would need a total portfolio of $140,000 ($112,000/ 80 percent = $140,000) to restore one's desired allocation. With one's portfolio currently valued at $133,000, one would need to purchase $7,000 of fixed-income assets to rebalance the portfolio. By adding new funds one avoids the taxable event; and because there are fewer trades, transaction costs are reduced. If there is insufficient new cash to fully accomplish the desired rebalancing, a combination of the two strategies can be used.

	End of Period Portfolio		Rebalanced Portfolio	
Equity Allocation	84%	$112,000	80%	$112,000
Fixed-Income Allocation	16%	$21,000	20%	$28,000
Total Portfolio	**100%**	**$133,000**	**100%**	**$140,000**

Style Drift

In addition to being a passionate gardener, my wife is an excellent cook. However, she always runs into problems when trying to get a recipe from her mom, who measures ingredients not by teaspoons or tablespoons but by "a little bit of this" or "a pinch of that." My wife does her best to interpret this folk wisdom, but her dishes never taste quite the same as my mother-in-law's. For example, if you deviate from a recipe by adding oregano when salt is called for, your result will drift away from what the original recipe produced. While the risks are usually low when you change a cooking recipe, changing an investment strategy can be a recipe for disaster. For example, when the manager of the actively managed domestic mutual fund you own decides to "ad lib" and buy some shares of Mexican companies, this manager is subjecting you to what is known as style drift. Instead of merely having a dish that tastes funny, you will own a portfolio that varies from the risk profile you expected and were willing to accept.

Rebalancing a portfolio restores the investor's original recipe: his/her desired risk profile. Without regularly rebalancing a portfolio, an investor will find that style drift has crept in. If the investor in our example had not rebalanced the portfolio, it would have drifted, unintentionally, toward a more aggressive style. We have seen how important it is to choose the portfolio allocation that is appropriate for each investor. Not only should you not allow market movements to change your asset allocation and undermine your chosen strategy, but you should not allow active portfolio managers to subject your portfolio to style drift.

The charters of most actively managed mutual funds give their portfolio managers great freedom to shift their allocations between asset classes at their discretion. Investors in such funds not only lose control of their asset-allocation decisions, but they also end up taking unintended risks by unknowingly investing in markets, or types of instruments, they wanted to avoid. Fidelity Magellan investors learned this lesson the hard way.

Over the years many investors have placed the equity portion of their portfolio in one of the world's largest mutual funds, Fidelity's Magellan. Unfortunately, in February 1996 Magellan's asset allocation was only 70 percent equity: 20 percent was in bonds, and 10 percent was in short-term marketable securities. Magellan's investment manager at the time, the highly regarded Jeffrey Vinik, was obviously making a big *bet* (with your money) that long-term bonds and short-term marketable securities would outperform the equity markets. How did his bet affect the investor's asset allocations? Again, assume that our investor with $100,000 to invest seeks an 80 percent equity/20 percent fixed-income allocation. She invests her entire $80,000 equity allocation in Fidelity Magellan. Due to the strategy deployed by Mr. Vinik, she actually had only $56,000 ($80,000 × 70 percent) invested in equities.

	Desired Allocation		Actual Allocation	
Equity Allocation	80%	$80,000	56%	$56,000
Fixed-Income Allocation	20%	$20,000	44%	$44,000
Total Portfolio	**100%**	**$100,000**	**100%**	**$100,000**

Our investor's equity allocation was subjected to style drift in that her exposure to the equity markets, at 56 percent, was less than the desired 80 percent. By placing funds with an active manager, she allowed someone else to modify her strategy. The key issue is not the outcome of Mr. Vinik's decision but the investor's loss of control of the asset-allocation process. Incidentally, the market subsequently soared to new highs, bonds fell in value, and Mr. Vinik moved on "to pursue other career alternatives." Notably, for the period February 1985 to June 1995, the composition of Fidelity's Magellan Fund "varied over time to such a degree that it would have been virtually impossible for investors to determine the asset classes in which they were investing, or the risks to which they were being exposed."[1]

The poor performance over the past few years of the industry's largest and arguably one of its most successful actively managed funds has created problems for advocates of active management. John Rekenthaler, the editor at Morningstar, admitted:

> I have argued for years that Magellan was not only wonderful for Fidelity, but also for active managers in the fund industry. Magellan's record argued that fund managers could outperform the market. But Magellan's trouble . . . is one more chip away at active management. If Magellan can be mortal, then all these funds are mortal, giving more credence to the

concept of investing in passive index funds which try to match market benchmarks such as the S&P 500 rather than beat them.[2]

If you think what happened to investors in Fidelity's Magellan Fund is an isolated incident, think again. The Strong Discovery Fund was a top performer from its inception in 1987 through 1995. However, through September 1996, while the S&P 500 Index was up 5 percent, investors in Strong Discovery experienced a loss of over 10 percent. The active manager of this fund managed to underperform the market by over 15 percent because he bet investor's money on a market downturn. Like Magellan's Vinik, he shifted fund assets from equities to the bond market. Unlike Vinik, he made a further bet on a market correction: by shorting the S&P 500 Index through the use of futures contracts, he was betting that he could buy back the contracts he had shorted at a lower price at a later date. (This sell high/buy low strategy is a reverse version of what investors probably thought he was being paid to do—buy low and sell high.) Unfortunately for the fund's investors, the market correction did not come. By midyear he threw in the towel on this strategy and he loaded up on equities, just as the market began a correction. The good news for him was that since his name is Richard Strong, he didn't have to worry about being fired. Unfortunately, there was no such good news for the investors in his fund. While they had relied on this fund for the equity portion of their portfolio, they instead ended up with a big bond position and a big derivative position (the S&P 500 Index futures contracts). In other words, like the investors in the Fidelity Magellan Fund, they lost control of the risks they were taking.[3]

You should also know that just one year earlier the Strong Discovery Fund had carried Morningstar's coveted five-star rating. So much for relying on ratings. Rating services like Morningstar and the trade publications that cover the financial markets have a perfect track record of predicting the past, but they have not demonstrated an ability to consistently predict the future. As a demonstration of their ability to predict the past, Morningstar subsequently downgraded the Strong Discovery Fund to two-star status.

Investors in passive asset-class funds are not subject to style drift because passive asset-class funds buy and hold assets within only their specific asset class. On the other hand, few active managers stick to their knitting. Domestic funds often hold foreign securities. Large-cap funds often hold mid- to small-cap stocks. Value funds hold growth stocks. And most active managers raise or lower their equity allocation based on their feel for the market. Now is an appropriate time to remember the lesson you learned about the three-factor model at the end of chapter 5. The three-factor model teaches that the vast majority of a portfolio's risk and returns are determined by the amount of exposure to each of the risk factors—equities, size, and value. And we have now seen evidence of how style-drifting active managers prevent investors from controlling this all-important determinant of returns.

Since the charters of actively managed mutual funds give their managers considerable latitude to create style drift, asset-class "name tags," like Morningstar's, are often of little value to investors. Only pure passively managed asset-class funds enable investors to achieve and maintain the asset allocation and risk exposure they desire.

Clearly, in addition to poor performance and tax inefficiency, active managers create unintended risks for investors and cause them to lose exposure to their desired risk factors. The obvious question is: Do actively managed mutual funds provide entertainment value that is significant enough to compensate for all of the negative attributes?

Rebalancing—Buy Low and Sell High

In addition to providing the all-important benefit of avoiding style drift, rebalancing can also add to portfolio returns. The rebalancing process is quite simple. It allows the investor to reduce the size of his position in the asset classes that performed relatively the best in the period (selling high) and increase the position in the asset classes that performed relatively the worst in the same period (buying low). Isn't it every investor's dream to buy low and sell high? Rebalancing over time will likely produce a bonus—the portfolio's annualized return will exceed the *weighted average* of the annualized returns of the component asset classes. And the more volatile the asset classes are within the portfolio, and the lower their correlations, the greater the effect of the rebalancing because you are buying at lower lows and selling at higher highs.

The rebalancing process is one of the reasons the model portfolios in our examples outperformed the market. The following analogy may help to clarify the situation. Asset classes do not go up or down in a straight line any more than .300 hitters get three hits in every ten at bats. A .300 batter who goes two for twenty (.100) will all of a sudden go thirteen for thirty (.433) and bat .300 for the entire period. Asset classes are like baseball players— just as there is no way to predict when a hitter will either go into a slump or go on a hot streak, we cannot predict when any particular asset class will be a winner or loser. The good news is that investors don't need that particular skill to be successful. Just as with baseball players, the longer the horizon, the more likely (albeit never certain) it is that the outcome will be as expected. The key to playing the winner's game, therefore, is to regularly rebalance and have faith that markets work in the long run.

It is important to recognize that whenever we rebalance by

buying and selling two asset classes with the same expected returns (i.e., U.S. large-cap stocks and international large-cap stocks) the risk and expected return of the portfolio remains unchanged. However, when we rebalance by selling a more risky asset class (with higher expected returns—e.g., equities) to buy a less risky asset class (with lower expected returns—e.g., U.S. government securities) we are lowering both the risk and the expected return of the portfolio. This is to emphasize that rebalancing is a *risk management tool* and not a tool designed to increase returns. Remember that the rebalancing bonus is defined as the amount by which the portfolio's annualized return will exceed the *weighted average* annualized return of the component asset classes.

Adding Discipline to the Process

Increased returns are not the only benefit of rebalancing; rebalancing also provides discipline to the investment process. Rebalancing provides investors with practice for resisting the temptation to second-guess their strategy during the inevitable difficult periods. The time to be a buyer (assuming you like to buy when prices are low) instead of a panicked seller is when an asset class is performing poorly. Rebalancing in good times, when markets are rising, enables you to develop the skills and the discipline to do it in tough times. It is easier for most investors to sell and take a profit than to buy when the market has just moved sharply lower.

At a minimum, rebalancing should be performed as part of the annual portfolio checkup. My own preference is to perform a portfolio "tune-up" on a quarterly basis. Rebalancing should also be done whenever new funds are available for investment. For example, when a mutual fund makes a year-end distribution, instead of automatically reinvesting the distribution in the same fund, the investor could redirect the distribution to other asset classes in order to accomplish as much rebalancing as possible. The use of new funds minimizes the number of transactions (only buys are needed, not sells) and thus may reduce transaction costs. It also minimizes the tax implications of rebalancing.

The 5/25 Percent Rule

Rebalancing may cause transaction fees to be incurred, and it may have tax implications. Therefore, it should only be done either when new funds are available for investment or when your asset allocation has shifted substantially out of alignment. I suggest using a 5/25 percent rule in an asset class's allocation before rebalancing would be implemented. That is, rebalancing should only occur if the change in an asset class's allocation is greater than either an absolute 5 percent or 25 percent of the original percentage allocation.

For example, let's assume an asset class was given an allocation of *10* percent. Applying the 5 percent rule, one would not rebalance unless that asset class's allocation had either risen to 15 percent (*10* percent +5 percent) or fallen to 5 percent (*10* percent −5 percent). Using the 25 percent rule one would, however, reallocate if it had risen or fallen by just 2.5 percent (*10* percent × 25 percent) to either 12.5 percent (*10* percent +2.5 percent) or 7.5 percent (*10* percent −2.5 percent). In this case the 25 percent figure was the governing factor. If one had a 50 percent asset-class allocation, the 5/25 percent rule would cause the 5 percent figure to be the governing factor since 5 percent is less than 25 percent of 50 percent, which is 12.5 percent. In other words, one rebalances if either the 5 percent or the 25 percent test indicates the need to do so.

The portfolio should undergo the 5/25 percent test on a quarterly basis, and the test should be applied at all three levels:

- at the broad level of equities and fixed income;
- at the level of domestic and international asset classes; and
- at the more narrowly defined individual asset-class level (such as emerging markets, real estate, small-cap, value, and so on).

For example, suppose one had six equity asset classes, each with an allocation of 10 percent, resulting in an equity allocation of 60 percent. If each equity class appreciated so that it then constituted 11 percent of the portfolio, no rebalancing would be required if one only looked at the individual asset-class level (the 5/25 percent rule was not triggered). However, looking at the broader equity-class level, one sees that rebalancing is required. With six equity asset classes each constituting 11 percent of the portfolio, the equity asset class as a whole is now at 66 percent. The equity allocation increasing from 60 percent to 66 percent would trigger the 5/25 percent rule. The reverse situation may occur where the broad asset classes remain within guidelines but the individual classes do not. Once again, just as with the model portfolios, the 5/25 percent test is just a guideline. You can create your own guideline for rebalancing for risk. The discipline that the process provides is far more important than the ratios used.

In summary, rebalancing offers many advantages and is an important part of the investment process.

- It should be performed regularly, using a disciplined approach, such as the 5/25 percent rule.

- It should be done whenever new investment dollars are available.
- It adds discipline to the investment process.
- By minimizing the effects of style drift, it maintains control of the most important determinant of the risks and returns of a portfolio—asset allocation.

Tax Management

While the winning strategy is to be a passive investor, passively managing the taxable portion of the portfolio without regard to taxes is a mistake. An investor can substantially improve the after-tax returns of a portfolio by actively tax managing the portfolio. Tax management involves the following.

- Choosing the most tax-efficient vehicles to implement your Investment Policy Statement (IPS).
- Harvesting losses throughout the year—whenever the value of tax deduction significantly exceeds the transactions cost of the trades required to harvest the loss—and immediately reinvesting the proceeds in a manner that avoids the wash sale rules that would cause the tax deduction to be disallowed. Portfolios should be checked on a quarterly basis to determine if there are opportunities to harvest losses. Waiting until the end of the year to perform tax-loss harvesting is an error because losses that might exist early in the year may no longer exist by the end of the year.
- Choosing the highest cost-basis purchases to sell first to

minimize gains and maximize losses. This involves keeping track of the cost basis of each share purchased.

• In general, never willingly realizing short-term gains. Not selling any shares until the holding period is sufficient to qualify for the lower long-term capital-gain rate. Note that if your equity allocation is well above target, you may wish to override this suggestion, weighing the risks of an "excessive" allocation to equities versus the potential tax savings.

• Trade around dividend dates. Shares of a fund should not be purchased just prior to the date of record for dividend payments to shareholders. Note that the ex-dividend date is not the same as the date of record. The ex-dividend date is the date after the record date when the dividend is "separated" from the fund. The fund then trades at a lower price, net of dividends. Depending on the size of the distribution that is expected, you should not consider buying within thirty to sixty days of the ex-dividend date.

There is another important tax strategy of which you should be aware. If you have held a fund for more than a year, you should always check to see what estimated distributions the fund plans to make during the year—specifically focusing on the amounts that will be ordinary income, short-term capital gains, and long-term capital gains. Most funds make distributions once a year, usually near the end of the year. However, some make them more frequently, and sometimes funds make special distributions. You can usually obtain this information from your fund prior to the record date. It is important to check to see if there are going to be large distributions that will be treated as either ordinary income or short-term gains. If this is true, then you might benefit from selling the fund before the ex-dividend date. By doing so, the increase in the net asset value will be treated as long-term capital gains, and taxes will be at the lower long-term rate. If the fund making the large payout is selling for less than your tax basis, you certainly should consider selling the fund prior to the distribution. Otherwise you will have to pay taxes on the distribution, despite having an unrealized loss on the fund—a tax hell for an investor if ever there were one.

Investors should coordinate any tax-planning activities with their CPA or tax attorney to ensure that any actions are beneficial to their overall situation and not just beneficial when viewed in isolation.

CHAPTER 11

$\blacklozenge$

Implementing the Winning Strategy

The beginning is the most important part of the work.
—Plato, *The Republic*

It is now time to put to work everything you know about MPT and passive asset-class investing. The implementation of this strategy begins with the creation of an investment policy statement. This chapter will focus on providing you with the information you need to develop your own investment policy statement, as well as the skills to implement that policy. We will also discuss the merits of using a financial advisor. For those investors not comfortable enough to go it alone, a checklist is provided to help you with selecting an advisor.

The Investment Policy Statement (IPS): Eleven Easy Steps Toward a Positive Investment Experience

I do not believe in a fate that falls on men however they act; but I do believe in a fate that falls on them unless they act.
—Gilbert K. Chesterton

Implementing the Winning Strategy

*Most battles are won or lost [in the preparation stage] long
before the first shot is fired.* —Napoleon

In the course of my career, I have operated several businesses,
served as a consultant to others, and even sat on the board of directors of public companies. From these experiences I learned that an
important ingredient of success is to put a business plan in place
before the start of operations. A business plan serves as a guidepost
and provides the discipline needed to adhere to a strategy over
time. As with any plan, a business plan must be reviewed on a
regular basis in order to adapt to changing market conditions.
Since serious investors should manage their assets as a business,
the development of a business plan, or, in this case, an investment
policy statement (IPS)—and an annual review of that statement—
is a critical step toward improving the likelihood of the success of
that plan. The IPS is thus the foundation of the investment plan,
outlining and prescribing a prudent and individualized investment
strategy.

Support for IPSs comes from Meir Statman, a behavioral finance professor at Santa Clara University. "Our psyches hold the
key to much of our investment behavior." He likens the situation to
antilock brakes. "When at high speed, the car in front of us stops
quickly, we instinctively hit the brake pedal hard and lock 'em up.
It doesn't matter that all the studies show that when the brakes lock,
we lose control." Statman suggests that investors need antilock
brakes for their investment portfolios as well.

Instinctively we react to investment situations in ways that
might have saved our lives fighting on distant battlefields
long ago. But, today they are counterproductive, like locking
up our brakes. When the market drops, our instinctive fear to

flight is so strong, even the most rational investors find themselves caving in, to their own demise. And market tops can often be called soon after the staunchest of bears throws in the towel and turns bullish.[1]

An IPS can act as an investor's antilock braking system. In short, your own IPS will provide you with the discipline to stick with your plan and will remove the emotion from the investment-decision process.

Before writing an IPS, you should thoroughly review your financial and personal status. The financial situation, job stability, investment horizon, tolerance for risk, and need for emergency reserves not only varies from investor to investor but changes over time for each individual. It is also very important to understand that the IPS should not be developed in isolation. Instead, it should be integrated into an overall financial plan, one that addresses investments, as well as such important issues as insurance and estate and tax planning. If an investor has charitable intentions, then this too should be integrated into the plan.

To properly develop a formal IPS, begin by listing all your financial assets and liabilities. Once this is complete, you should take the following steps:

Step 1. Take the liquidity test, ensuring that a cash reserve is created first. You should consider holding an amount equal to six month's normal spending in liquid assets such as a money market account or other forms of short-term fixed-income assets. Keep in mind that the less stable your earned income, the greater the need for emergency reserves.

Step 2. Continuing the liquidity test, constructing a ladder projecting your forecasted cash needs out to twenty years. Include such items as a down payment on a home, college tuition payments, and so on. Then apply the formula provided in chapter 8 for the liquidity test. This formula will give you the minimum amount that you should allocate to fixed-income assets.

Step 3. Take the stomach acid test, using the model portfolios from chapter 8. Make sure that you are willing and able to stick with your model portfolio through the inevitable bad days.

Step 4. Compare the results of the stomach acid test and the liquidity test and choose the one that has the higher (more conservative) fixed-income allocation.

Step 5. Compare the results of the need to take risk test with the outcomes of the prior steps. If the need to take risk test produces the lowest equity allocation, you should strongly consider this allocation. And remember the discussion on the marginal utility of wealth in chapter 8. While more money is always better than less, the question is are you willing to accept the incremental risks as the price for *likely* (not certain) greater wealth. A more difficult dilemma arises if the need to take risk is greater than the ability or willingness to do so. In this case you have to make choices such as:

- Lowering your financial goal and accepting a lesser lifestyle in retirement as the "price" for taking less risk.
- Increasing savings by lowering current consumption in order to reduce the need to take risk.
- Accepting the incremental risk because the marginal utility of wealth is great.

Two words of caution before you decide to take more risk. First, those who have more options can realistically accept more risk. Examples of options are the ability to work longer or to sell a second home or perhaps move to a lower cost community. If your options are limited, the more prudent approach is to either lower the goal or reduce current consumption in order to lower the need to take risk. Second, those with a knowledge of financial history know that things that have never happened before can, and do, happen—which is why one of my fifteen prudent rules of investing (see chapter 12) is to never treat the highly unlikely as impossible (nor the highly likely as certain). We need no more proof of this truth than to recall the events of September 11, 2001.

Setting Investment Objectives

Once these initial five steps are completed, you are ready to write the first part of your IPS: your investment strategy objectives. This part of the process is very important because it forces you to perform a sanity check on your asset-allocation decision. To illustrate, let me share the experience of Philip, a good friend.

Philip is an extremely nervous investor. His stomach acid test would probably produce an equity allocation that would asymptotically approach zero. He knows, however, that a very low equity allocation is apt to produce very little, if any, growth in the real value of his portfolio, which would be in direct conflict with his personal objective of retiring within ten to fifteen years. To attain his objective, Philip knows that he must take more risk. Having studied the model portfolios, he concludes that in order to retire within his desired time frame he must choose an equity allocation of at least 80 percent. The lower the equity allocation, the longer he would have to continue in the workforce. The results of the stomach acid test proved to be in direct conflict with his personal goals. Philip was counseled that there was no correct answer to his conundrum. He would have to choose which one of his objectives would have the greater priority, the need to sleep well or his desire for early retirement. Ultimately, Philip decided that his early retirement objective should take priority. He realized that this decision was apt to produce many sleepless nights and that his ability and willingness to stay the course might be sorely tested; accordingly, he set aside funds for a ten-year supply of extra-strength Maalox.

Philip's case perfectly illustrates why a written investment policy is necessary. Having written and signed his IPS, Philip had carefully thought through the process; he understood the risks and anticipated the inevitable bad days. He was now more likely to stick with his investment strategy than he otherwise would have been.

Step 6. Write down the goals that you have set for your investment portfolio. This will allow you to track, over time, the progress toward the goal, making appropriate adjustments along the way.

Step 7. Specifically list the percentage of assets you wish to allocate to equities and debt. This step is important, as it will provide discipline to the rebalancing process discussed in chapter 10. Then, within these two broad categories, establish the appropriate percentage allocations for each of the individual asset classes (such as small cap, value, U.S., international, emerging markets, and so on). Next list the ranges within which you will allow market movements to cause the designated allocation to drift before you will rebalance your portfolio. In chapter 10 a 5/25 percent guideline was provided as a suggestion.

The range you would be willing to tolerate at the broad asset-class level might be:

Equity:	Minimum 55%	Target 60%	Maximum 65%
Fixed Income:	Minimum 35%	Target 40%	Maximum 45%

The range which you would be willing to tolerate at the individual asset-class level might be:

Minimum 7.5%   Target 10%   Maximum 12.5%

Since rebalancing may generate capital-gains taxes, whenever possible rebalance with new investment dollars or do so using tax-advantaged accounts.

Step 8. Locate the most tax-efficient assets (generally equities) in your taxable accounts (to the extent possible) and the least tax efficient (generally fixed income and real estate) in your tax-advantaged accounts.

Step 9. Determine the investment style to be used. Hopefully you have been convinced that the prudent investment strategy is that all investments should be passively managed. If you seek excitement, however, you may decide to allocate a small percentage, perhaps 5 percent of your portfolio, to individual stocks or to actively managed funds (your entertainment portfolio). If you do include individual stocks in your portfolio, remember to include them in the asset allocation within which they fall (such as U.S. small cap).

Now you must establish procedures and controls to make sure your portfolio is being properly monitored and adapted, when necessary, to any changing personal situations. Establishing such controls and procedures is especially important if you have engaged an investment advisory firm to assist you in the investment process.

Step 10. A periodic schedule of events and reviews should be established:

Monthly: Review each monthly statement from the custodian holding your assets to be certain that it includes all current holdings and any transactions that occurred during the preceding month.

Quarterly: Review your portfolio thoroughly to see if either rebalancing or tax-loss harvesting is required. If you have engaged a financial advisor, he/she should be responsible for scheduling the meeting and setting the agenda and the objectives of that meeting. Prior to the meeting the advisor should prepare and send to you a report showing the current allocation so that you are both prepared to analyze your portfolio in depth. At this meeting there should also be a brief review of your IPS to determine whether it requires alteration.

Annually: There should be a thorough review of your portfolio, including rebalancing and tax management, especially if your investment time horizon has changed over the year. A change in investment time horizon will probably change the result of the liquidity test and may require that you alter your asset allocation. Because of certain events (e.g., divorce, loss of job, inheritance, a death in the family) it may also be necessary to change your established risk profile to one that is either more aggressive or more conservative. There should also be a thorough review of your IPS to determine whether any alterations need to be made, perhaps because unanticipated academic research has uncovered superior strategies. Finally, there should be an estate and tax-planning review to either make any required changes or to take advantage of emerging opportunities.

In addition, at the end of each year, investors should review their own personal performance, determining if they have adhered to their savings/withdrawal plan, and what, if any, role emotions played in their ability to stay the course. If they have not adhered to their plan, or they have allowed emotions to influence their actions, an adjustment will need to be made in their lifestyle or their objective will need to change. *Living with an error is a far greater mistake than making one in the first place.*

It is absolutely necessary for you to take control and fully implement your IPS. More than anything else, the implementation of your statement will determine the performance of your portfolio. Even if you engage a financial advisor, make sure that it is you who ultimately determines the contents of your IPS. Remember that it is your statement, not your advisor's. He/she should merely provide information and serve as devil's advocate, making sure that you have asked the right questions and have thought through the consequences of your answers. Your advisor may even make recommendations, it being understood that the consequences (risk and return implications) of those recommendations are fully explained. Since your ability and willingness to handle risk is best known to you, final investment decisions should never be delegated.

Step 11. You and your financial advisor, if one has been engaged, should sign the IPS. This action considerably heightens your commitment to carry out your investment plan. This is important because, as Johann Wolfgang von Goethe said: "To think is easy. To act is difficult. To act as one thinks is the most difficult of all." Finally, by having both parties sign the document, you minimize any confusion over objectives, policies, procedures, and appropriate investments. The dual signature also serves to protect each party in the event of a future disagreement.

Before concluding this discussion, I need to explain why a very important part, possibly even the most important part, of any investment strategy (and the IPS) is a commitment to save and invest as much as possible, as early in life as possible.

A Penny Saved, a Fortune Earned

Time and tide wait for no man. —Robert Frost

Archimedes, a famous Greek mathematician, believed that the most powerful force in the world was the lever. "Give me a lever long enough and a place to stand, and I will move the world." If Archimedes had understood the power of compound interest, he might have thought that compound interest is the most powerful force. Benjamin Franklin called it the "eighth wonder of the world."

When facing the choice between investing and consuming, investors need to have a good understanding of the power of compounding. Because of the power of compounding, investors should start saving and investing at as early an age as possible. This advice is at least as important as any provided in this book. The following is a dramatic example of why this is true.

Sally begins to save $5,000 a year at age twenty-five. She continues to save this amount for ten years, until age thirty-four, and then stops saving. Sam, on the other hand, does not start saving until age thirty-five. He then saves $5,000 a year for the next thirty years. Sally will have saved a total of $50,000 ($5,000 × 10). Sam will have saved a total of $150,000 ($5,000 × 30), or three times as much. Both investors placed their savings in investment accounts that generated the same 10 percent rate of return on their investment.

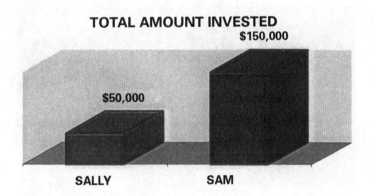

TOTAL AMOUNT INVESTED
$150,000
$50,000
SALLY   SAM

By age sixty-five, Sally will have generated a portfolio of about $1.4 million. Despite his having saved and invested three times as many dollars, Sam's portfolio will have grown to only about $820,000, 40 percent less than Sally's. At age seventy-five, the two portfolios will have grown to $3.6 million and $2.2 million, respectively.

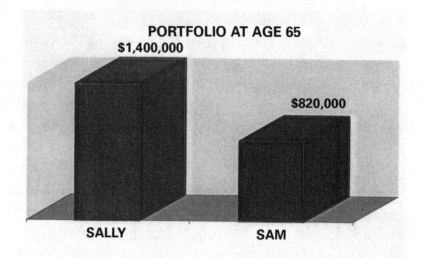

PORTFOLIO AT AGE 65

$1,400,000

$820,000

SALLY

SAM

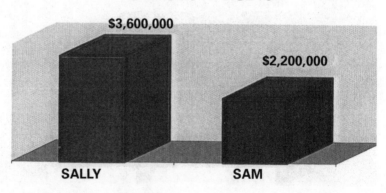

PORTFOLIO AT AGE 75

$3,600,000

$2,200,000

SALLY

SAM

Let's see what happens if an investor defers saving for an even longer period. Jane begins to save at age forty-five. Having waited until age forty-five to begin saving and investing, she must save $24,000 per annum for the next twenty years to achieve the same portfolio as Sally, who had saved only $5,000 per annum for ten years. John defers his savings program even longer and begins to

AMOUNT SAVED PER YEAR $87,000

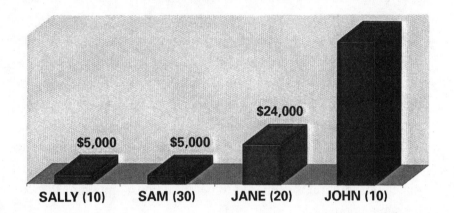

$5,000 — SALLY (10)
$5,000 — SAM (30)
$24,000 — JANE (20)
JOHN (10)

TOTAL AMOUNT INVESTED

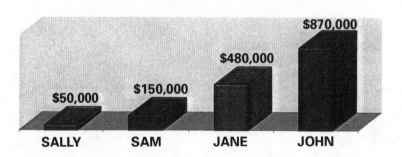

$50,000 — SALLY
$150,000 — SAM
$480,000 — JANE
$870,000 — JOHN

PORTFOLIO AT AGE 65

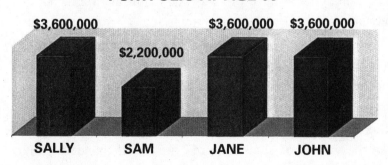

$3,600,000 — SALLY
$2,200,000 — SAM
$3,600,000 — JANE
$3,600,000 — JOHN

save at age fifty-five. He must save \$87,000 per year for the next ten years to achieve the same portfolio as Sally.

By deferring some consumption early in life, investors will be able to enjoy a far greater standard of living in their later years. In other words, investors should understand that the true price of an item purchased today is not what you paid for it. Instead it is the expected amount of foregone consumption one would likely be able to achieve at a later date had those same dollars been invested (while taking into account that, all other things being equal, immediate consumption is preferred to deferred consumption of the exact same goods).

The examples are clear evidence that an important part of the winning investment strategy is investing as early and as often as possible.

Selecting an Investment Advisor

If you don't know where you are going, you will probably end up somewhere else. —Laurence J. Peter

You now have the knowledge and tools to successfully implement the winner's strategy using passive asset-class investing. However, even though you have the necessary information to do so, you may not be comfortable enough to go it alone so you may decide to utilize the services of a financial advisor to help with the process. Even if you are comfortable enough with your knowledge of the financial markets to go it alone, there are a variety of reasons to hire a financial advisor.

Tennis players know that a pro can teach them the skills needed to make the variety of shots required for a well-rounded game.

The pro can also provide the winning strategy and the discipline to stick with that strategy. That is why even the top players in the world continue to have a coach. Investors can benefit from "coaching" in the same way a tennis player does. Just like the tennis pro, a good financial advisor will provide:

- The education necessary for the investor to play the game.
- The winning strategy.
- The discipline to stick with that strategy.

This last point is particularly important in light of the evidence provided by two studies. The first, Mark Carhart's study, the most comprehensive ever done on mutual-fund performance, found that since 1962 the average no-load fund outperformed the average load fund by 0.6 percent per annum. And that did not even take into account the commissions load-fund investors pay. The second study, by DALBAR, Inc., a Boston-based financial services firm, found that the actual returns earned by investors in no-load funds was 1.2 percent *less* than the return earned by investors in load funds. How could that possibly be? The answer is that the load investor, having paid a sales charge, was less likely to attempt market timing or to engage in performance chasing.[2]

Financial Advisory Firms Can Add Real Value

The following are ways that a good financial advisory firm can add value and questions you should ask when interviewing prospective firms.

- Do you provide ongoing access to the latest academic research on financial markets? It was not that long ago, for example, that the value effect was uncovered. How will that information be communicated to me?

- In what form and how often do you provide ongoing education? A good advisory firm will continue to educate its clients through conferences, seminars, and/or newsletters.

- Do you integrate an investment plan into a complete estate and tax plan? Tax strategies play an important part in determining the return on your portfolio as well as the preservation of the value of the estate you are able to pass on to your heirs. The advisory firm should be able to act as quarterback for your financial services team, which might include, among others, your accountant, attorney, and life insurance agent.

- How do you establish an investment policy? Will it incorporate my unique ability, willingness, and need to take risk?

- What is your process for developing an appropriate model portfolio and appropriate asset allocation? Do you perform the stomach acid, liquidity, and need to take risk tests; ensure that the appropriate "devil's advocate" questions are asked; and help select the specific investment vehicles?

- As appropriate, do you run Monte Carlo simulations to help analyze the odds of success of the strategy? Do you also assist in analyzing the output to help determine possible changes to the strategy based on the output?

- How often will you meet with me to discuss whether the investment policy remains appropriate over time and as personal circumstances change?

- Do you provide access to institutional-style, passive asset-class funds not available to the general public?

- What is your process for providing the discipline, during both good and bad times, to help me stick with the strategy? An investment advisor should be able to take the emotion out of the decision-making process.

- How do you determine the asset-location decision?

- Do you provide expertise over a broad range of financial issues, such as what type of mortgage to use when buying a home, the type and amount of life insurance that is appropriate, and whether a variable annuity is appropriate?

- Do you have the time and expertise to analyze new products as they are introduced to the market?

- Do you provide advice on funding future college expenses, understanding all the implications, including how it might impact the ability to obtain financial aid? Have you analyzed the various programs that are available (i.e., 529 plans, qualified tuition plans) so that you can advise me on which is the best choice?

- Will you track the performance of my portfolio and ensure that the rebalancing process is performed on a regular basis and in the most cost- and tax-efficient manner?

- How often do you check for tax-loss–harvesting opportunities?

- Do you provide regular reporting, at least on a quarterly basis, that clearly communicates the performance of both the overall portfolio and the individual investments?

- Do you provide for separate account management of either equity or fixed-income portfolios in accordance with an overall passive asset-class investment approach?

- Do you have the time to do all these things?

- Finally, how do you build trust, get to personally know me as a client, and establish rapport along with a high level of comfort?

The Checklist

If you hire an investment advisory firm, here is another checklist you will find useful.

- The investment philosophy of the advisory firm should be consistent with your own. Hopefully you have been convinced that winning investment strategy entails a commitment to diversified, global, passive asset-class investing, based on MPT. The advisory firm should require, and specifically sign off on, a jointly developed IPS.

- The investment advisory firm should not have conflicts of interests, such as earning commissions from the sale of investment products it recommends. Thus the firm should do business on a fee-only basis. This is the most likely way to ensure that your advisor's interests are aligned with your own.

- The firm should have a team with which you are comfortable. No one individual has all the knowledge and skills necessary to be able to assist over the entire spectrum of the categories listed above. My own experience is that I am a much more knowledgeable, and thus better, advisor because I work with a group of about twenty other knowledgeable advisors, each of whom makes the whole greater than the sum of the parts. A sole practitioner or a small firm can gain the benefits of a larger firm if it has a strategic relationship that allows it to access the greater resources of the larger firm.

- You should perform a careful due diligence on the firm and its principals. You should do a thorough reference check and make sure that both the firm and its individual members have the appropriate licenses. Most importantly, this due diligence should include a careful review of a document called the Form ADV that the advisory firm provides to prospective clients when they enter into an advisory agreement. This form is required by the Investment Advisors Act of 1940 and must be filed with the regulatory body with which a registered investment advisor (RIA) has registered [either the Security and Exchange Commission (SEC) or his/her state]. The ADV is basically a disclosure document that sets forth information about the RIA, including the investment strategy, fee schedules, conflicts of interest, regulatory incidents, and so on. All RIAs are required to furnish to new clients either a Form ADV or another document containing similar information in order to satisfy the "Brochure Rule" prescribed by the act.

- The firm should be able to demonstrate to you that it can add value in a way that *more than* justifies its fees.

There are two final recommendations. First, never give an advisor a general power of attorney without first seeking legal counsel. It is generally not necessary and can often lead to trouble. The custodian (the institution responsible for physically holding your assets and for keeping appropriate records) of your investment account should disburse funds to accounts that only you control. You should also receive confirmations of all transactions. A limited power of attorney, allowing the advisor to execute your instructions as well as to access your account information from the custodian, is sufficient.

Second, make sure that your assets are kept in custody by a financially strong institution with a good reputation for customer service. The custodian should be sufficiently insured to cover the value of your account.

An effective advisor can add value equal to many times his/her fee. For example, just by providing access to institutional-style passive asset-class funds an advisor can add expected returns in excess of the typical advisory fee, especially for higher net-worth individuals. In addition, the advisor can also help by simply preventing you from making some very poor investment decisions.

Sound financial advice is not expensive, especially when measured against the value an advisor can add. The typical investment advisory firm charges between 1 and 2 percent per annum, based on the amount of assets under management. For larger accounts (above $1 million) fees are generally between 0.5 and 1 percent per annum. For very large accounts (above $10 million) fees can be as low as 0.25 percent per annum or even lower. When comparing fees be sure you are comparing apples to apples as some firms only provide investment advice, while others provide a broader array of services, including estate and tax planning, within their fee structure. Finally, remember that while good advice may not be cheap, bad advice always costs you dearly, no matter how little you pay for it. In other words, sometimes you get (good advice) what you pay for, and sometimes you "pay for" (dearly) what you get (bad advice).

CHAPTER 12

◆

Summary

With all that is known about the poor results of active stock picking, why do so many investors still buy high-cost mutual funds and churn their portfolios? The answer is simple: because they are told to do so, every day, explicitly or implicitly, by the financial media and their advertisers.

—Gregory Baer and Gary Gensler,
The Great Mutual Fund Trap

You'll never get much of an argument against the low-cost indexing approach from us.

—*Morningstar Investor,* July 1997

For professional investors like myself, a sense of humor is essential. We are very aware that we are competing not only against the market averages but also against one another. It's an intense rivalry. We are each claiming that, "The stocks in my fund today will perform better than what you own in your fund." That implies we think we can predict the future, which is the occupation of charlatans. If you believe you or anyone else has a system that can predict the future of the stock market, the joke is on you.

—Ralph Wanger, *A Zebra in Lion Country*

We have now come to the end of the road. A brief summary and review of what Wall Street does not want you to know is appropriate.

- Markets are generally highly efficient.

- While it is not impossible to outperform an efficient market, the odds of doing so, even by professionals, are very low.

- Because past performance is not a reliable predictor of future performance, it has proven extremely difficult, if not impossible, to forecast which money managers and market gurus will be the lucky few.

- The question of whether or not markets are efficient is an interesting academic question. However, the real question facing investors is whether the prudent strategy is active or passive management. We saw clear evidence that even when market inefficiencies may exist, markets are not so inefficient that active managers are likely to overcome the costs of their efforts and the taxes generated by their trading activity.

- With institutions now controlling a market share approaching 90 percent of all trading, the competition among professionals is so tough that active management is highly likely to prove counterproductive. Since outperforming the market is a zero-sum game and most of the trading is done between institutional investors, there just are not enough victims for active managers to exploit.

- Efforts to time the market are also highly unlikely to prove productive because so much of the action occurs over very brief time frames.

- The use of active managers causes an investor to lose control of the asset-allocation decision, the single most important determinant of the expected return and risk of a portfolio. Active managers expose investors to style drift, which can have unanticipated and nasty consequences.

- Most of what is published by trade publications and the rating services and aired by so-called financial experts is really nothing more than investment pandering. To attach anything other than entertainment value to such reports can be dangerous to your economic health. These experts are all part of the loser's game hyped by Wall Street and the media because it is in their best interests, not yours.

Investors can easily play the winner's game, the investment strategy carrying the banner of a Nobel Prize and based on the EMH and MPT.

Fortunately, there is a sure way to win the loser's game of active management: Don't play! Rather than attempt to time the market or pick individual stocks, it is more productive to invest and stay invested. As Warren Buffett said: "We continue to make more money when snoring than when active." Mr. Buffett also said: "Most investors, both institutional and individual, will find that the best way to own common stocks is through an index fund that charges minimal fees. Those following this path are sure to beat the net results (after expenses and fees) delivered by the great majority of investment professionals."[1]

Economics professors Dwight Lee and James Verbrugge of the University of Georgia explain the power of the efficient markets theory in the following manner.

The efficient markets theory is practically alone among theories in that it becomes more powerful when people discover serious inconsistencies between it and the real world. If a clear efficient market anomaly is discovered, the behavior (or lack of behavior) that gives rise to it will tend to be eliminated by competition among investors for higher returns. . . . (For example) If stock prices are found to follow predictable seasonal patterns . . . this knowledge will elicit responses that have the effect of eliminating the very patterns that they were designed to exploit. . . . The implication is striking. The more empirical flaws that are discovered in the efficient markets theory the more robust the theory becomes. (In effect) Those who do the most to ensure that the efficient market theory remains fundamental to our understanding of financial economics are not its intellectual defenders, but those mounting the most serious empirical assault against it.[2]

The starting point for implementing the winning strategy is to buy passively managed funds as they are the surest way for investors to receive a market rate of return in a tax-efficient manner.

Markets compensate investors with expected returns commensurate with the degree of risk they take. By investing in asset classes that are higher risk, and therefore higher return, an investor can expect to outperform the market as a whole—while acknowledging that they are accepting greater risk. These higher risk, higher expected return asset classes are small-capitalization stocks, value stocks, and small-value stocks. An investor can reduce the overall risk of the portfolio by investing in a group of broad, global, diversified, passive asset-class funds. This strategy dampens volatility and creates a more efficient portfolio (greater return for similar risk). Using the stomach acid, liquidity, and the need to take risk tests, as well as the asset-allocation time horizon guideline, an investor can build a portfolio that is best tailored to his/her unique personal circumstances.

While investing in equities always entails risk, the longer the investment horizon, the more likely it is that equity investors will be rewarded for taking incremental risk—assuming they have the ability to remain disciplined during periods of economic crisis.

Summary

Disciplined investors think bear markets are really just periods when the market temporarily wears a big "for sale" sign. On July 8, 1932, the Dow Jones Industrial Average (DJIA) recorded an intra-day low of 40. Seventy-one years later it had grown over 225 times, and that doesn't include dividends. As author Nick Murray says: "Success is purely a function of two things: 1) recognition of the inevitability of major market declines; and 2) emotional/behavioral preparation to regard such declines as non-events."[3]

Once you build a suitable portfolio and appropriately place assets in the most tax-efficient location, there is a need for regular checkups, especially if your personal situation has altered your ability, willingness, or need to take risk. The maintenance should include rebalancing your portfolio in order to prevent market movements from shifting your risk profile through style drift. Disciplined rebalancing maintains the portfolio's risk profile and is likely to provide a rebalancing bonus by buying low and selling high. Regular maintenance also involves managing the tax situation and checking to see if losses can be harvested in a cost-effective manner.

A formal investment policy statement should be drawn up to serve as a guide for you and your investment advisor (if you have engaged one). In searching for an investment advisor who can add value, during the interview you should use the checklist provided. Finally, investors who have portfolios with large unrealized gains need not be trapped into inaction by their desire, correct as it may be, to defer taxes (see appendix A).

Clearly, it is very difficult to beat the market. As technology and the ability to process information continue their rapid progress, it will only become more difficult to do so. With so many practitioners trying, some will inevitably succeed. But investors should not rely on the past performance of those who have previously beaten the market because past success has historically been a very poor predictor of future success.

If you do manage to find an active manager who has beaten the market, check to see if he/she has done so on an after-tax basis. Then check his/her asset allocation. If an active manager has managed to beat the market, it is highly probable he/she invested in the high-return asset classes of small-cap, value, or small-value stocks. The following study backs up this assertion.

A study of some nine hundred funds (either growth funds or growth and income funds) from 1988 to 1994 found that the returns posted by managers with degrees from universities whose entering students have high SAT scores—such as the Ivy League colleges—beat competitors from lower ranked schools by more than a full percentage point. Younger managers and M.B.A. holders also out-performed their older and non-M.B.A. rivals.

The reason behind the superior performance was both simple and predictable. The researchers found that "high SAT" managers and those with M.B.A.s tended to invest in high-risk, high-return stocks! Sound familiar? You don't need an M.B.A. and you don't have to pay an active money manager large fees to generate supe-rior returns. All you really need is a faith that markets work—that risks and returns are highly correlated.[4]

Investors also need to beware of studies that claim that active managers do beat their benchmarks. It is highly likely that these studies have been "polluted" by what is called survivorship bias; that is, unsuccessful funds usually are made to disappear before their performance becomes embarrassing. In the most comprehen-sive study ever done on mutual funds, covering the period 1962–93, Mark Carhart found that by 1993 fully one-third of all funds in his sample had disappeared. This shows how important survivorship bias is.[5] Another study found that: "In 1996 alone 242 (5 percent) of the 4,555 stock funds tracked by Lipper Analytical

Services, Inc. were merged or liquidated. Such disappearances caused Lipper's fund-performance averages, like wine and cheese, to improve with age. In 1986 Lipper reported that 568 stock funds delivered an average 1986 return of 13.4 percent. By 1997 Lipper put the average 1986 return at 14.7 percent."[6] The reason for the improvement is that 134 (24 percent) of the original 568 funds were made to disappear. For example, if a provider of a family of funds has two small-cap funds and one is performing poorly, the provider will merge the poorly performing one into the stronger one, simply making the poor performance disappear. One study found that "over the fifteen-year period ending December, 1992, the annual return of all equity mutual funds was 15.6 percent per annum. When you include all the funds that failed to survive the entire period the annual return dropped to 14.8 percent. The cumulative difference in returns was 781 percent versus 689 percent."[7]

Thanks to an unfortunate decision by the SEC, investors now have to contend with more fairy tales when analyzing mutual-fund performance. Until now investors had only to contend with the aforementioned problem of survivorship bias. The SEC has given permission to mutual funds to report the preinception performance of "incubator funds" in their historical performance figures. This ruling gives the industry carte blanche to create dozens of funds, seed them with their own capital, and then take public only the few that rack up good performance records. The same fund manager could be given three funds to manage and then take public only the one "winner." The two "losers" would simply disappear, as if they had never existed. Thus the "winner" is allowed to report the returns achieved during the incubation period, but reporting is not required for the two "losers." Another problem is that these incubator funds will have reduced operating expenses, including no advertising expenses and probably lower management fees, further distorting reality.

This unfortunate ruling provides the Wall Street establishment with ammunition to keep alive the myth that active managers add value. Unfortunately for uninformed investors, the story is unlikely to have a fairy tale's happy ending.

In fairness to the popular press, they do occasionally acknowledge the advantages of passively managed funds. Tyler Mathisen, the executive editor of *Money,* writes: "Bogle [of the Vanguard group of funds, the largest provider of retail index funds] wins: Index funds should be the core of most portfolios today."[8] And columnist Susan Lee for *Worth* writes: "The index fund is a truly awesome invention. A cheap S&P 500 or a Wilshire 5000 Index fund ought to constitute at least half of your portfolio."[9] The only problem with these statements is that neither magazine will give passive management a wholehearted endorsement. If passively managed funds (e.g., index funds) are so good, why shouldn't they be the only ones an investor should use? These magazines withhold such wholehearted endorsement for two reasons. First, if the magazine's readers believed in passive management, who would buy magazines touting which stocks and mutual funds to buy? Second, these magazines carry a great amount of advertising from actively managed mutual funds. They do not want to lose valuable advertising revenue. You must remember whose interests they have at heart.

I have attempted to explain the concepts of modern portfolio theory (MPT) in a way that every reader can understand. John Bogle did all of us a great service by breaking down this complex body of work into two obvious facts:

1. Since all investors collectively own the entire stock market, if passive investors—holding all stocks, forever—can match the gross return of the stock market [because the

whole must equal the sum of the parts], active investors, as a group, can do no better. They too must match the gross return of the stock market.

2. Since the management fees and transaction costs incurred by passive investors are substantially lower than those incurred by active investors, and both provide equal gross returns, then passive investors must earn higher net returns.[10]

In addition to Bogle's insights, remember that passive managers are more tax efficient due to their lower turnover. As a result, passive investors as a group earn higher after-tax returns than active investors.

As Bogle stated: "As the logicians would say, QED. So it is demonstrated."[11]

My fondest wish is that you have found this book not only educational but practical as well. Information is worth very little if you do not know how to use it. I have tried to provide you with much of the information you need to improve your investment results and give you the tools with which to accomplish that objective. I also tried to make it an enjoyable experience. I know the hard work that goes into writing a book. (How anyone did so prior to the advent of personal computers and word-processing software is beyond me.) Nevertheless, I hope you had as much fun reading it as I had writing it. Debunking legends can be lots of fun.

Before concluding, the following "Fifteen Rules of Prudent Investing" are offered. Keep them in mind as you travel on your investment journey—they will protect you from making some of the most common investment mistakes even professional investors make.

1. Do not take more risk than you have the ability, willingness, or need to take.

2. A well-thought-out business plan is the necessary condition for successful investing; the sufficient condition is having the discipline to stay the course.

3. Never treat the highly improbable as impossible or the highly likely as certain.

4. The only thing worse than having to pay taxes is not having to pay them.

5. The safest port in a sea of uncertainty is diversification.

6. Diversification is always working; sometimes you like the results and sometimes you don't.

7. Identifying a mispriced security is the necessary condition for outperforming the market; the sufficient condition is being able to exploit any mispricing after the expenses of the effort.

8. Equity investing is a positive-sum game; expenses make *outperforming* the market a negative-sum game.

9. Owning individual stocks and sector funds is speculating not investing.

10. Before acting on seemingly valuable information, ask yourself why you believe that information is not already incorporated into prices.

11. The four most dangerous investment words are "This Time It's Different."

12. Never work with a commission-based advisor—there is a misalignment of interests.

13. Never invest in any security of which you do not fully understand the nature of all of the risks, avoiding new or

"interesting" investment products—products designed to be sold, not bought.

14. The market can remain irrational longer than you can remain solvent.

15. Good advice does not have to be expensive; but bad advice always costs you dearly—no matter how little you pay for it.

A fitting conclusion to this book is the comments of two noted financial experts. At an economic forecasting conference, Steve Forbes quoted his grandfather, who founded the magazine eighty years before: "You make more money selling the advice than following it."[12] Finally, Jonathan Clements of the *Wall Street Journal* offered this advice: "Ignore market timers, Wall Street strategists, technical analysts, and bozo journalists who make market predictions. Admit to your therapist that you can't beat the market."[13]

You have now been introduced to MPT and its associated investment strategies. I know of no better way to describe my hopes for your relationship with this powerful knowledge than to recall what Humphrey Bogart said to Claude Rains in the last scene from *Casablanca* as they faded into the mist: "I think this is the beginning of a beautiful friendship."

The MPT Challenge

When my firm meets with a potential client, we often conclude our presentation with the following challenge.

"Take our presentation to your current advisor, whomever they might be. If they can show you even one good reason, backed by any credible academic study, that you should not utilize the strategies described in our presentation for at least the core (vast majority) of your investment portfolio, we will walk away from your business."

To date, no one has beaten the MPT challenge.

Appendices

APPENDIX A

◆

How to Analyze the Hold or Sell Decision— Trapped by a Low Tax Basis?

The greatest of all gifts is the power to estimate things at their true worth.
                                                    —La Rochefoucauld

You are convinced that passive asset-class investing is the way to invest the core, if not all, of your portfolio. Unfortunately, you are currently invested in actively managed funds. The only thing preventing you from selling these funds and investing the proceeds in a passively managed portfolio is that your current portfolio has a low tax basis, and you do not want to pay the capital-gains tax. You prefer to continue to defer the tax on the unrealized capital gain. What to do? (Of course, if your funds are in a tax-advantaged account, like an IRA, this is not an issue.)

The first thing you should do is check to see if you really have a tax problem. Many investors forget to add reinvested distributions (on which taxes have already been paid) into their cost basis. Once you have done so, the gain may not be as large as you thought. If you still have a big gain, you should investigate whether or not it is still advantageous to sell your actively managed funds, pay the requisite taxes now, and reinvest the proceeds into a passively managed asset-class portfolio. Use the following example as a guide.

Assume that you have a portfolio of actively managed funds with a current value of $200,000 and a tax basis of $150,000. If we assume a total state (5 percent) and federal (15 percent) capital-gains tax of 20 percent, you would pay a tax of $10,000 ($50,000 × 20 percent), leaving you with only $190,000 to reinvest. We have seen that the average actively managed fund underperforms its benchmark by close to 2 percent per annum. Let's assume that your fund is better than average and will only underperform by 1 percent per annum on a pretax basis. Since after-tax returns are the only ones that matter, assume that your funds will underperform a passive alternative by a further 1 percent per annum due to tax inefficiency. That brings us to a total expected underperformance of 2 percent per annum. With the availability of tax-managed funds, which improve on the tax efficiency of index and passive asset-class funds, we can now raise our underperformance estimate to perhaps as much as 3 percent per annum.

If we assume that the fund you are currently holding is a large growth fund and you are contemplating building a more diversified by asset class portfolio (similar to the ones in the model portfolios), we need to make one further adjustment. Because the more diversified portfolio has a higher expected return (it has greater exposure to the risk factors of size and value) the expected underperformance of your current holding should be raised. Let's assume another 1 percent. This brings the total expected underperformance to about 4 percent.

One can now estimate how long it will take to recoup the lost tax dollars. We take the $190,000 available for investment and multiply it by the 4 percent expected improvement in returns; the annual benefit is $7,600. Dividing this figure into $10,000, we arrive at a break-even point of just over one year! Even if we cut our estimate savings to just 1 percent annum, the annual benefit would be $1,900, resulting in a break-even point of about five years—which would still be a very high return on your "investment" (if you think of paying the tax and switching to a passive strategy as an investment in higher future expected returns). Given the other benefits provided by the passive asset-class strategy, including gaining control over the asset-allocation decision, this decision should be easy. The conclusion: Given the dramatic lowering of the capital-gains tax in 2003, you may not be as trapped as you think.

APPENDIX B

◆

Monte Carlo Simulations

Since we know we live in a world with cloudy crystal balls and all we can do is estimate returns, it is best not to treat a portfolio's estimated return as a certain return. It is better to consider the possible dispersion of likely returns, and then estimate the odds of successfully achieving the financial goal. The goal is generally, though not always, defined as achieving and maintaining an acceptable lifestyle—not running out of money while still alive. Said another way, the goal generally is not to retire with as much wealth as possible but is instead to be as sure as possible that you do not retire poor and run the risk of running out of assets while still alive. The task is best accomplished through the use of a Monte Carlo simulator—a computer simulation with a built-in random process, allowing one to see the probabilities of different possible outcomes of an investment strategy. The computer program will produce numerous random iterations (usually at least one thousand and often many thousands), letting one see the odds of meeting a goal. Since thousands of iterations are run, one has to think in terms of probability rather that one outcome.

In simple terms, your investment life is divided into an accumulation phase when you're working and making contributions, and a distribution phase that begins when you retire and lasts as long as you live. The inputs into the Monte Carlo simulation are the investment assumptions (expected returns, standard deviations, and correlations), future deposits into the investment account, the desired annual withdrawal amount, and the number of years the account must last. The output is summarized by assigning probabilities to the various investment outcomes. For example, in looking at the final wealth at a target age (that should be at least as long as life expectancy), the following probabilities might be shown:

- You have a 50 percent probability of having more than $1 million at age ninety, and
- You have a 20 percent probability of having $0 at age ninety.

Because the cost of "losing" is so great, most investors should concentrate on the downside risk of outliving their portfolio. There are two uncertainties one faces in forecasting returns. First, future returns may approximate the expected returns, but the year-to-year returns can vary dramatically. Low or negative returns in the early years of retirement, combined with the impact of withdrawals from the portfolio, can have a devastating impact on the ability of an investor to achieve his/her goals. Second, the annualized returns over the time period may be less than the expected returns. A Monte Carlo simulation incorporates these uncertainties by selecting a return each year that is drawn from a distribution that encompasses the expected average annual return and expected volatility of the portfolio.

The ultimate goal is to make sure that the investor is comfortable with the projected likelihood of success—the odds that he/she will be able to withdraw sufficient funds from the portfolio each year and achieve his/her financial goal. The goal might be to maintain a desired lifestyle and not run out of money while still alive. Or it might be to leave a certain size estate to heirs. Each investor is different in how they perceive the probabilities and final wealth figures. For some individuals, odds of success of 80 percent might be sufficient, while for others 95 percent would be required to allow them to sleep at night. Investors with flexibility (e.g., the ability to delay retirement and work longer, the willingness and ability to live a lesser lifestyle, or the ability to sell assets such as a second home) can logically accept lower odds of success than those without options.

Because there are often trade-offs that must be made between the lifestyle desired and the odds of success, the output of a Monte Carlo simulation provides us with a very important tool. The process allows for the examination of the pros and cons of various alternative strategies in an unemotional manner. For example, after examining the output, an investor might decide that he/she is taking more risk than needed to achieve his/her goals. This is an easy situation to deal with as it simply involves either lowering the equity allocation and/or lowering the exposure to risky asset classes. Or perhaps he/she is not taking enough risk to provide acceptable odds of success. If this is the case, then the decisions are much tougher ones. For example, he/she must decide to: take more risk than he/she would otherwise like to take, lower the goal, save more thus lowering current lifestyle, or live with the estimated risk of failure.

An important benefit of a Monte Carlo simulation is that it allows for an analysis of how marginal changes in inputs impact the odds of achieving the financial goal. For example, let's assume that the input results in an 80 percent chance of success. The program allows one to see the impact on those odds of increasing (or decreasing) savings by $X a month. If that change increased (decreased) the odds of success to 85 (75) percent, the investor might decide that it would be worthwhile reducing (increasing) current consumption to improve (lower) the odds of success by that amount. On the other hand, if it only raised (lowered) the odds of success to 81 (79) percent, a different conclusion might be drawn.

The output also allows for the analysis of how changes in the asset allocation impact the odds of success. If increasing the equity allocation from 70 to 80 percent increased the odds of success from 80 to 90 percent, an investor might decide that it was worth the extra risk of more equity ownership (and the extra stomach acid it was likely to produce along the way). Alternatively, if it only increased the odds of success to 81 percent, a different decision might be made. Analysis can be easily done for changes in withdrawal rates as well (impact on future lifestyle). For example, if a 4 percent withdrawal rate produced a 95 percent chance of success, and a 5 percent withdrawal rate lowered the odds of success to 90 percent, an investor might choose to raise the withdrawal rate, accepting a somewhat lower likelihood of success in return for greater consumption. However, if that decision is made and the risks do show up, the investor must be prepared to accept a lower lifestyle in the future.

Another use of the simulation program is to look at how delaying retirement by X years impacts various issues, such as the need to save, the withdrawal rate, or the equity allocation required. The same analysis can be done for taking retirement at an earlier age. This allows investors to determine if an extra (less) year of working is worth the greater (lesser) lifestyle that can be expected now and/or in the future or how an extra (less) year of work impacts the need to take risk. For example, each extra (less) year of work might: allow for a reduced (increased) need to save of $X per year, or allow for a Y percent increase (decrease) in the withdrawal rate, or allow for a reduction (increase) in the equity allocation of Z percent.

There are many software programs available that provide the ability to do Monte Carlo simulations. As you can see, the process is very complex. It is, however, an extremely valuable tool. A good financial advisor with experience using these models can add significant value to the process.

APPENDIX C

◆

Even with a Clear Crystal Ball

One of the most remarkable and revealing stories on relying on trade publications for advice is the following tale. The story also provides valuable insight into the skills of active managers and their ability to beat a passive strategy. Each year *BusinessWeek* and *Forbes* publish their "Best Buy" list of U.S. mutual funds. Their recommendations are broken down into major asset classes, including U.S. small cap, U.S. small-cap value, U.S. large cap, and U.S. large-cap value. A portfolio can be constructed with an equal weighting of 25 percent for each of these asset classes and an equal weighting of the recommended funds within each asset class. Using the Morningstar database, a comparison can then be made between the performance of these active managers with the performance of an equivalent portfolio of passively managed asset-class funds for the period January 1992–December 1996. Presumably the funds that made their respective Best Buy lists had produced superior performance.

In other words, if you went back in time to January 1992 and had a crystal ball that allowed you to see the 1997 "Best Buy" lists, you could create a portfolio of the Best Buy funds. To compare the performance of the crystal ball's Best Buy portfolio with

Appendix C

Business Week & Forbes Best Buys
vs.
Passive Asset-Class Strategy

Five-Year Annualized Returns
January 1992–December 1996

Business Week (BW) "Best Performers" *Forbes* (F) "Best Buys" vs. DFA or Simulated Index		
Small Cap		**Average Return of "Best Buy" Funds**
Acorn Fund (BW, F)	17.6%	
Baron Asset Fund (BW, F)	20.0%	
Managers Special Equity (BW)	17.4%	
DFA 9–10	**19.5%**	18.33%
Small-Cap Value		
Fidelity Low-Priced Stock (BW)	20.8%	
Franklin Balance Sheet Investment (BW)	18.9%	
Linder Growth Funds—Investor (F)	14.3%	
Skyline Fund—Special Equities (F)	20.6%	
DFA Small Value Fund*	**20.8%**	18.65%
*CRSP Small Value Index from 1/92 to 3/93		
Large-Cap Value		
Babson Value Fund (BW, F)	18.6%	
Dodge & Cox Stock Fund (F)	17.6%	
Fidelity Destiny I (BW)	19.8%	
Fidelity Equity—Income Fund (BW, F)	17.4%	
Oppenheimer Quest Opportunity A (BW)	18.5%	

Safeco Income Fund (F)	14.9%	
Vanguard Windsor II (F)	16.7%	
DFA Large Value Fund**	**20.8%**	17.64%
**CRSP Large Value Index from 1/92 to 3/93		
Large-Cap Growth		
Columbia Growth Fund (F)	15.1%	
Dreyfus Appreciation Fund (BW, F)	13.6%	
Fidelity Growth Company (F)	14.1%	
Harbor Capital Appreciation (F)	13.5%	
Phoenix Growth A (BW)	10.5%	
Vanguard U.S. Growth Portfolio (BW, F)	12.9%	
DFA Large CO Fund	**14.9%**	13.28%
Total Return **Passive Managed Portfolio** **vs.** **Actively Managed "Best Buy"** **Portfolio**	**19.0%**	**17.00%**

Source: *BusinessWeek* (2/3/97)
   Forbes (2/10/97)

a passive asset-class strategy, DFA's passive asset-class funds were used for the periods that they were available, and the Center for Research in Security Prices (CRSP) asset-class indices were used for the remaining periods.

The actively managed portfolio produced an annualized return of 17 percent. Not a bad performance, except for the fact that it underperformed the passively managed portfolio by a full 2 percent per annum. Even with the benefit of a crystal ball, the Best Buy funds underperformed a passively managed strategy. In addition to producing 2 percent per annum better returns, the passive strategy was also superior from a risk-adjusted perspective. The Best Buy funds generated only about 90 percent of the returns of the passive strategy while, on average, they incurred greater volatility than the passive asset-class funds. Simply put, the Best Buy portfolio produced lower returns and greater risk than did an apples-to-apples passive asset-class portfolio.

If a crystal ball that enabled you to see *BusinessWeek* and *Forbes* issues five years before they were printed did not help you create a portfolio that outperformed a similar passively managed portfolio, are you willing to risk your investment dollars without a crystal ball?

APPENDIX D

◆

The IPO Myth

One of the recurring themes of this book is that it is in Wall Street's interests to keep alive the myth that active management adds value. Another important myth that needs exposing is that initial public offerings (IPOs) make great investments. Wall Street firms generate great fee income from these transactions. Investors seem to love them as they desperately search for the next Microsoft. Let's look at the reality of actual performance. A study covering the period 1970–90 examined the returns from a strategy of buying every IPO at the end of the first day's closing price and then holding each investment for five years. The return provided by this strategy would have been just 5 percent, or 7 percent per annum less than a benchmark of an investment in companies with the same market capitalization as each IPO had on its first day of trading.[1]

University of Florida finance professor Jay Ritter looked at 1,006 IPOs that raised at least $20 million from 1988 to 1993. He found that the median IPO underperformed the Russell 3000 by 30 percent in the three years after going public. He also found that 46 percent of IPOs produced negative returns.[2]

Another study examining the performance of IPOs issued in

1993 and how they performed through mid-October 1998 found that the average IPO had returned just one-third as much as the S&P 500 Index. Amazingly, over one-half were trading below their offering price, and one-third were down over 50 percent![3]

And finally, a study covering the period 1988–95 and 1,232 IPOs found very similarly disappointing results, with 25 percent of all offerings actually closing the first day of trading below their offering price.[4] This study also found that the IPOs defined as "extra hot," meaning they rose 60 percent or more on the first day of trading, were the very worst performers going forward—over the next year they underperformed the market by 2 to 3 percent *per month*.[5]

In the face of this poor performance, why do investors continue to chase the latest IPO? I believe there are two explanations.

- Unless an investor happens to read scholarly publications such as the *Journal of Finance,* he/she is unlikely to be aware of the facts. It is simply not in Wall Street's interest for investors to be informed.

- Even when informed, investors often act in what appear to be irrational ways—another example of "the triumph of hope over experience." Investors seem to be willing to accept the high probability of low returns in exchange for the small chance of a home run or, possibly even more important, a great story to tell at the next cocktail party.

APPENDIX E

◆

News Flash: Top Performance Is a Poor Indicator of Future Performance

This was the headline of a report released by Smith Barney (now Citigroup) Consulting Group. Issuing this report comes under the definition of chutzpah, the Yiddish word for "nerve." For those who need an explanation of this term, my favorite is that the definition of chutzpah is when a child who has killed his parents throws himself on the mercy of the court as an orphan.

Smith Barney is one of the largest providers of retail mutual funds. On the one hand, they spend large amounts of dollars advertising the past performance records of their top-performing funds and tout their Morningstar ratings of four and five stars. Presumably, investors will be tempted into buying these funds based upon their prior performance and the expectation that their superior performance will continue into the future. On the other hand, they publish a study the very first words of which are: "One of the most common investor mistakes is choosing an investment management firm or mutual fund based on recent top performance." As evidence that investors choose the top past performers, they cited a survey of how more than thirty-three hundred mutual fund investors performed at Columbia University's Graduate School of Business. On a scale of 1 (lowest) to 5 (highest), survey respondents gave past performance a score of 4.62, far outdistancing other criteria such as fees (2.28) and investment style (1.68). They also cited a study by the Financial Research Corp, which found that 75 percent of net new cash flowing into mutual funds was invested in Morningstar's four- and five-star funds.

To test the hypothesis that by purchasing shares of the recent top-performing funds individual investors were following a winning strategy, Smith Barney studied seventy-two equity managers with at least ten-year track records. The managers studied covered the full spectrum of investment styles from large cap to small cap, from value to growth, and from domestic to international. The study's conclusion: "For all the periods studied top performing managers were more likely to drop to the bottom of performance comparisons in subsequent periods than to repeat their peer-beating performances." In fact, "The investment returns of top quintile managers tended to plunge precipitously while the returns of bottom quintile managers tended to rise dramatically."[1]

Continuing to advertise past performance, knowing that past performance is a very poor predictor of future performance, certainly sounds like chutzpah to me.

APPENDIX F

◆

What If Everyone Indexed?

Perhaps the question that I am most often asked about the EMH is: What would happen if everyone indexed? First, we are a long way from that happening, even at the current pace of change. It is estimated that institutions probably now have in the neighborhood of 40 percent of their assets committed to passive strategies. By comparison, individuals still have about 85 percent of their total mutual fund assets in actively managed funds.[1] Second, there will always be some trading activity from the exercise of stock options, estates, mergers and acquisitions, etc. In addition, even if individuals stopped trading stocks, companies would still be active in buying other companies. With that in mind let's deal with the issue of the likelihood of active managers either gaining or losing an advantage as the trend toward passive management marches on.

Let's first address the issue of information efficiency. With less active management there will be fewer professionals researching and recommending securities. Active management proponents would argue that it would therefore be easier to gain a competitive advantage. This is the same argument they currently make about those "inefficient" small cap and "really inefficient" emerging markets. Unfortunately for active managers, as we have seen, their underperformance against their proper benchmarks has been just as great, if not more so, in these asset classes than it has been in the large-cap arena. One of the reasons, and perhaps the main reason, is that in these "inefficient" asset classes the costs of trading, both in terms of bid-offer spreads and market impacts, are much greater than they are in the large-cap asset class. Less efficient markets are typically characterized by lower trading volumes. The lower trading activity results in less liquidity and greater trading costs.

As more investors move to passive strategies, it is logical to conclude that trading activity would decline. Yet while we have seen a shift to passive management by both individuals and institutions, trading volumes continue to set new records. The only conclusion to draw is that the remaining active participants are becoming more active—increasing their turnover. However, if as investors shifted to passive management trading activity actually fell, liquidity would decline and trading costs would rise. The increase in trading costs would raise the already substantial hurdle that active managers have to overcome in order to outperform. Based on the evidence we have from the "inefficient" small cap and emerging markets, it seems highly likely that any information advantage gained by a lessening of competition for information would be more than offset by an increase in trading costs. Remember, for active management to be the winning strategy it is a necessary, but not sufficient, condition that the markets are informationally inefficient. The other condition is that the costs of implementing an active strategy must be small enough that market inefficiencies can be exploited, after expenses.

There is another interesting conclusion that can be drawn about the trend toward passive investing. Remember that for active managers to win, they must exploit the mistakes of others. (To date, the evidence is that they have not been able to find enough victims to exploit.) I ask you to now consider the following. If active investors begin to switch to passive strategies, it seems likely that those abandoning active management are investors who have had a poor experience with active investing. The reason this seems logical is that it is not likely that an individual would abandon a winning strategy. The only other logical explanation I can come up with is that an individual simply recognized that he/she was lucky. That conclusion would be inconsistent with behavioral studies that all show that individuals tend to take credit for their success as skill based and attribute failures to bad luck. In either case it seems logical to conclude that the remaining players are likely to be the ones with the most "skill" (at least they believe the superior results were due to skill and not random good luck). Therefore we can conclude that as the "less skilled" investors abandon active strategies, the remaining competition, on average, is likely to get tougher and tougher.

While it is highly unlikely that everyone will abandon active strategies (hope does spring eternal), I see nothing in the trend to passive investing that gives reason for optimism among the believers in active management. In fact just the opposite appears to be true.

APPENDIX G

◆

Investment Implications
of the Tax Act of 2003

The tax act of 2003 provided much good news for investors. The following are implications of the act of which investors should be aware.

- The lowering of rates, both income and long-term capital gains, reduces the tax penalty created by the relatively high turnover of active investors (both mutual funds and individual stocks). However, it *raises* the penalty for active investors *relative* to passive investors. The reason is that the *spread* between ordinary income tax rates (the rates at which realized short-term capital gains are taxed) and long-term capital-gain rates widened. For high tax bracket investors the income-tax rates were reduced by less than the 5 percent by which long-term capital-gain rates were lowered (from 20 to 15 percent).
- The widening of the spread between ordinary income and long-term capital-gain rates increases the benefits, and thus the value, of the tax-management strategy of never intentionally realizing short-term capital gains.

- The lowering of the capital-gain rates, and the widening of the gap between the tax on ordinary income and the tax on capital gains, increases the importance of the *asset-location* decision. To the maximum extent possible, tax-efficient equities should be located in taxable accounts, and tax-inefficient fixed income should be located in tax-deferred accounts (the exception being tax-inefficient REITs, which should be held either in a tax-deferred account, a nontaxable account like a Roth, or inside of a low-cost variable annuity). Holding equities in tax-deferred accounts converts long-term capital gains into ordinary income. Among the other disadvantages of holding equities in tax-deferred accounts are: inability to harvest losses, loss of ability to donate appreciated shares to charity during your life (avoiding the tax on the gain), loss of the foreign tax credit on international assets, and loss of the potential for stepped-up basis upon death.

- The lowering of the capital-gains tax rate, along with the lowering of the tax on dividends, further reduces the already almost non-existent advantage of using variable annuities for the purpose of providing a tax shelter for equities. The one exception is for REITs.

- The lowering of the tax on dividends makes dividend-paying common stocks more attractive. Value stocks tend to have higher dividend yields (partly because of their distressed price), thus the penalty for holding them in taxable accounts has been reduced.

- With the reduction in the tax on dividends, some preferred stocks become more attractive for taxable accounts (remember that the market rapidly adjusts prices to account for new information). The offset is that the greater demand for them in taxable accounts lowers their yield, making them less attractive for tax-deferred accounts (which is generally where you want to hold fixed-income assets). Also note that most preferred stocks will not be eligible for the "preferred" treatment of lower tax rates as they are considered debt, not equity. Investors should be very careful to investigate the tax implications before purchasing a preferred stock.

• The lowering of ordinary income-tax rates reduces the value of the tax benefit provided by mortgage debt. This should be taken into consideration when deciding on how to finance a home purchase, as well as when considering the potential for prepaying a mortgage.

Hopefully the above analysis is of value. However, as always, it is recommended that you consult your tax advisor.

APPENDIX H

◆

Commodities: A Diversification and Hedging Tool

Commodities, also known as real (or hard) assets, are an interesting asset class from a portfolio perspective. The historical evidence demonstrates that the Goldman Sachs Commodities Index (GSCI), representing a broad cross section of principal raw and semifinished goods used by producers and consumers, has characteristics that are important to investors. The GSCI, in part because it is heavily weighted to oil and natural gas, has exhibited low correlation with both U.S. and international equities, while also exhibiting low correlation with bonds. In addition, the asset class has provided attractive returns over a reasonably long time frame. Thus commodities appear to be worthy of consideration for inclusion in a globally diversified portfolio. Let's first examine the historical evidence. Then we will consider the issue of implementation, keeping in mind that strategies don't have costs, but implementation does.

Correlation with Stocks and Bonds

As we would expect, commodity prices are positively correlated with inflation. Because bonds provide nominal returns (other than inflation-indexed bonds), they are negatively correlated with inflation. Thus in periods of high inflation, they perform very poorly. In addition, despite the conventional wisdom that equities provide a hedge against inflation, equities have a slightly negative correlation with inflation, especially *unexpected* inflation. Thus commodities not only hedge unexpected inflation, but also diversify some of the risks of owning both stocks and bonds. The following table illustrates this point.

Annual Correlation with GSCI 1970–2003[1]

Inflation	0.29
S&P 500	−0.23
EAFE	−0.21
T-Bonds	−0.39

The GSCI

The GSCI is world-production weighted; the quantity of each commodity in the index is determined by the average quantity of production in the last five years of available data. Currently, the GSCI contains twenty-six commodities from all commodity sectors: six energy products, nine metals, and eleven agricultural products. As of October 24, 2003, the weightings for the GSCI were:[2]

- Energy: 64.8 percent (of which natural gas was about 11 percent and oil-related commodities 54 percent).

- Industrial metals: 6.8 percent (of which aluminum is about 3 percent, copper about 2 percent, and the remainder consists of lead, nickel, and zinc).

- Precious metals: 2.5 percent (of which gold is about 2.1 percent and silver the remainder).

- Agriculture: 18.1 percent (of which wheat is about 5 percent, corn about 4.5 percent, soybeans 2.5 percent, cotton and sugar each about 2 percent, with coffee, coca, and orange juice each representing 0.7 percent or less).

- Livestock: 7.8 percent (of which cattle is about 5 percent and hogs about 2.5 percent).

Just as the weightings of an equity index change as individual stock prices change, so does the percent of the index represented by each component change as individual commodity prices change.

It is important to note the very heavy weighting of energy-related commodities. This heavy weighting contributes to the negative correlation of the index to both stocks and bonds. The United States has experienced more than one unexpected upward shock to energy prices. The upward shocks lead to unexpected increases in inflation (a negative for both stocks and bonds) and also act as a tax on consumers, depressing economic activity (another negative for stocks).

Gaining Exposure to Commodities

Exposure can be gained through a passive portfolio of long positions in futures contracts that are traded on the Chicago Mercantile

Exchange. However, unlike a passive equity portfolio, a passive futures portfolio requires regular transactions for the simple reason that futures contracts expire. Thus contracts must be continually "rolled over" to the next maturity. Because futures contracts require collateral (typically in the form of U.S. Treasury bills), the return on an investment in commodities is not simply the change in price of the futures contract. Specifically, the total return (TR) on the collateralized futures position is equal to the spot return plus two additional components: the interest from the financial collateral plus the futures' "roll yield."

Spot return: Represents the basic up-and-down movements in the price of the underlying commodities. The spot return of the GSCI-TR (Total Return Index) is the production-weighted spot return of the twenty-six underlying commodity futures.

Roll return: Represents the cost or benefit of rolling the futures positions forward each month. Whether this is positive or negative for an individual commodity depends on whether the price for the contract being rolled into is lower (backwardation) or higher (contango) than the contract being rolled out of. The primary purpose of the commodity futures markets is to provide an efficient and effective mechanism to manage price risk of the producers and consumers of commodities. Buying or selling futures contracts establishes a price level now for commodities items to be delivered later, thus eliminating price risk. *Normal* backwardation is the result of business owners seeking to hedge price risk. Speculators (who have no intention of making or taking delivery, but instead seek to profit from a change in the price) demand a premium in order to accept that risk. That premium is in the form of lower futures prices. For example, if the GSCI rolls from January crude oil at $15.00 to February crude oil at $14.75, that represents a roll return of +1.67 percent ($0.25/$15.00) for crude oil for that month—a result of selling the January contract and buying (at a lower price) the February contract.

Collateral return: This represents the interest earned on a cash position equal to 100 percent of the dollar face value of the underlying futures contracts. The GSCI-TR imputes a three-month Treasury bill return to this cash position.

The following table covers the period from 1970 to 2003:[3]

	Compound Total Return (%)	Annual Standard Deviation (%)
GSCI	11.9	24.5
S&P 500	11.3	17.5
EAFE	10.8	22.7
Treasury Bonds	9.2	11.8
Treasury Bills	6.3	2.8
Inflation	4.8	3.2

Note that the GSCI provided equity-like returns with equity-like volatility. Thus this is a risky asset class. However, because of the negative correlation with both bonds and stocks, including an allocation to the GSCI in a portfolio would have increased returns and reduced volatility.[4]

It is important to note that the returns of the GSCI are not only related to inflation, but to changes in the rate of inflation. This can be observed by examining the results of the period 1980–89.[5] Inflation, as measured by the Consumer Price Indexes (CPI), declined from 13.3 percent in 1979 to 4.6 percent in 1989 (and hit a low of just 1.1 percent in 1986).

	Compound Annual Total Return (%)	Annual Standard Deviation (%)
GSCI	10.7	16.8
S&P 500	17.6	12.7
EAFE	22.0	23.4
Treasury Bonds	12.6	15.1
Inflation	5.1	3.2

During this period of declining inflation, the GSCI not only underperformed stocks, but underperformed bonds as well. In addition, during this period the volatility of the asset class was still quite high. However, we should not confuse strategy and outcome. Gaining benefits in periods of unexpected high and/or rising inflation means we should expect the reverse in periods of unexpected low and/or falling inflation. This is what diversification is all about. For the thirty-four-year period 1970–2003, there were only two years (1981 and 2001) when the GSCI-TR and either the S&P 500 or the EAFE Index produced negative returns. It is also worth noting that during the severe bear market of 1973–74, the GSCI-TR returned 75 percent and 40 percent, respectively.[6] This is a very important point given that most investors are highly risk averse. Thus the average risk-averse investor should have a preference to hold assets that tend to perform well when other assets in their portfolio are performing poorly.

As is the case with any risky asset class, investors considering commodities must be very patient and disciplined investors willing to accept very high volatility. The reason is that a risky asset class can provide very poor returns for a very long time. For example, for the ten-year period ending 1999, the *real* return to the GSCI-TR was just 0.9 percent. This compares to a *real* return of 14.8 percent for the S&P 500. For the twenty-year period ending

1999, the comparable *real* returns were 3.1 and 13.3 percent, re-spectively. However, for the thirty-year period ending 1999, the real returns were a much closer 6.3 and 8.2 percent, respectively.[7] Thus it appears that risk-averse investors, seeking a hedge against the risks of owning stocks and bonds, should consider an alloca-tion to commodities.

There is another reason to consider commodities—they provide a hedge against "event risk." Equities have significant exposure to event risk. Unexpected events like wars, disruption to oil supplies, political instability, or even a colder than normal winter, can drive up energy prices, acting like a tax on consumption and negatively impacting the economy and stock prices. Similarly, droughts, floods, and crop freezes can all reduce the supply of agricultural products, and strikes and labor unrest can drive up the prices of precious and industrial metals. These various events are also un-correlated to each other, providing an important diversification benefit if one has invested in a broad commodity index.[8]

Most shocks to commodities are negatively correlated with fi-nancial assets because they tend to suddenly reduce supply rather than increase it. Supply shocks not only lead to inflation (which is negatively correlated with stocks) but also to higher costs of pro-duction inputs (putting pressure on profits). Because commodity shocks tend to favor supply disruptions rather than sudden in-creases in supply, commodities tend to provide positive returns at the same time financial markets are providing negative returns. Thus the more investors are sensitive to event risk the more they should consider holding commodities as a hedge against that type of risk. Therefore, while many investors think of commodities as "too risky," the more risk averse an investor, at least to event risk, the more they should consider including an allocation to com-modities. And the more sensitive they are, the greater should be the allocation.

A Risk-Reduction Tool

The benefit of using commodities, as a risk-reduction tool, can be demonstrated by examining their returns during years when either stocks and/or bonds had negative returns. For period 1970–2003 there were nine years when long-term bonds had negative returns, producing an average loss of 3.2 percent. In all nine years commodities produced positive returns, averaging 29.5 percent. For the same period, the S&P 500 Index had eight years of negative returns, producing an average loss of 12.5 percent. In six of the eight years commodities provided positive returns, with the average return for all eight years being 22.6 percent.

Years of Negative Returns of Long-Term
Government Bonds (1970–2003)

Year	Return of Long-Term Government Bonds (%)	Return of GSCI Index (%)
1973	−1.1	75.0
1977	−0.7	10.4
1978	−1.2	31.6
1979	−1.2	33.8
1980	−4.0	11.1
1987	−2.7	23.8
1994	−7.8	5.3
1996	−0.9	33.9
1999	−9.0	40.9
Average Return	**−3.2**	**+29.5**

**Years of Negative Returns of the
S&P 500 Index (1970–2003)**

Year	Return of S&P 500 Index (%)	Return of GSCI Index (%)
1973	−14.7	75.0
1974	−26.5	39.5
1977	−7.2	10.4
1981	−4.9	−23.0
1990	−3.2	29.1
2000	−9.1	49.8
2001	−11.9	−31.9
2002	−22.1	32.1
Average Return	**−12.5**	**+22.6**

Implementation

From a strategic standpoint, it appears that an allocation to commodities would be a prudent strategy. However, there are many issues that must be considered when implementing a strategy. One obvious consideration is the tax implications. Since all gains will result from interest income and the trading of futures contracts, all gains will be short term. Thus this asset class would only be appropriate for a tax-deferred or nontaxable account (e.g., Roth). The next consideration is that a fund manager must be hired to implement the strategy. Currently there are only two mutual funds that are available to the general public that focus on this asset class. The Oppenheimer Real Asset Fund attempts to mimic (not replicate) the GSCI. The PIMCO Commodity Real Return Strategy Fund attempts to replicate the Dow Jones–AIG Commodities Index.

There is an important difference between the GSCI and the Dow Jones–AIG Indices. The GSCI is a production-weighted index. As a result it is heavily weighted to oil and natural gas. This heavy weighting toward energy, as we discussed, provides important diversification benefits. The Dow Jones–AIG Index is a broad-based index of future contracts on twenty physical commodities. However, no related group of commodities (i.e., energy, precious metals, livestock, or grain) can make up more than 33 percent of the index, and no single commodity can constitute more than 15 percent or less than 2 percent of the index. The weightings are based on liquidity (2/3) and to a lesser degree production (1/3). These constraints lead to broader diversification. The 2002 weightings were: petroleum, 24 percent; grains, 20 percent; industrial metals, 16 percent; precious metals, 10 percent; soft commodities (coffee, cotton, cocoa, and sugar), 10 percent; livestock, 9 percent; and vegetable oils, 2 percent. This index produces similar correlations to stocks and bonds to those of the GSCI. For the period 1991–2003, the annual correlations of the Dow Jones–AIG Index with the S&P 500 Index and long-term U.S. Treasury bonds were approximately −0.21 and −0.14, respectively. The negative correlations provide evidence that the Dow–AIG Index should make for a good diversifier. In addition, for the period 1991–2003, the Dow Jones–AIG Index provided higher returns with less volatility relative to the GSCI. Another benefit of the Dow Jones–AIG Index relative to the GSCI Index is the potential for a "rebalancing bonus" within the index due to its construction methodology and the low correlation between different commodities.

When it comes to implementation, there are several problems with each fund. Let's begin with the Oppenheimer fund. The Class A shares of the fund have a very high expense ratio of 1.68 percent. If that was not bad enough, the fund also carries a 5.75 percent load. (An institutional version is available through financial advisors. Its expense ratio is a still high 1.06 percent.) In addition, the funds that are used as collateral for the futures contracts can be invested in instruments that entail both prepayment (mortgage-backed securities) and credit risk. In addition, the fund is actively managed, allowing the manager discretion in terms of weighting exposure to the various commodities within the GSCI. For the first six full years of its existence (1998–2003) the fund provided a compound annualized return of 2.64 percent, producing a total return of 16.93 percent. (This is compared to annualized and total returns of 6.65 percent and 47.14 percent for the GSCI Index.) In terms of correlation, the fund's correlation with long-term Treasury bonds was 0, and its correlation with the S&P 500 Index was −0.19.

The PIMCO fund, which began operations in the fall of 2002, is a bit more investor friendly, with an expense ratio of 1.24 percent. Fortunately, a lower cost (0.74 percent) institutional version is available through investment advisors. Another positive is that the fund invests much of its collateral in inflation-protected securities. This strategy is consistent with one of the reasons (inflation hedge) for including exposure to commodities in a portfolio. However, it should be noted that, like the Oppenheimer Fund, it has the discretion to take on credit risk (i.e., invest in junk bonds) and prepayment risk (i.e., invest in mortgage-backed securities). The fund also has the ability to take on currency risk as well through investments in nondollar-denominated assets.

Conclusion

An allocation to commodities via the use of a "real return" fund using an indexed-commodity approach, along with investing collateral in short-term or inflation-protected securities of the highest credit quality, has intuitive appeal. The attractions are the low correlation to both bonds and stocks and the inflation hedge that neither stocks nor bonds offer. The greater the risk of inflation to the financial health of an investor, the more this asset class should be given consideration for inclusion in a portfolio. However, as was noted, investors in this asset class must be highly disciplined and patient investors. Not only can the returns be very low for long periods, but returns are also highly volatile. For example, the returns of the Oppenheimer Real Asset Fund (A shares) for the six years 1998–2003 were –45, 37, 44, –31, 27, and 23 percent, respectively. It is important to note, however, that the high volatility combined with the low correlation with both stocks and bonds will provide a rebalancing bonus to investors that have the discipline to stay the course.

One last point needs to be considered. Investors seeking the diversification and inflation-protection benefits that commodities can provide must be prepared to accept the psychological risk known as tracking error. Adding commodities to a portfolio will virtually ensure that the portfolio's returns do not track those of the equity markets. This is, however, not a problem unique to commodities. It is true of most asset classes. The low correlation of commodities to equities, however, increases the risk of tracking-error regret. Thus only educated and disciplined investors should consider including commodities in their portfolio.

The bottom line is that the asset class does have appeal for disciplined long-term investors seeking a hedge against inflation and the risks of stocks and bonds. While there currently exists no implementation vehicle that meets all the appropriate policy criteria (i.e., passive, low cost, investment of collateral in only instruments of the highest credit quality, no currency risk, and no prepayment risk) on balance the PIMCO fund is worth considering, and it is the clear current preference.

APPENDIX I

◆

Recommended Investment Vehicles and Sample Portfolios

Note that funds with an asterisk are tax managed (TM) and therefore are strongly recommended for taxable accounts. Two asterisks mean the fund is appropriate for only nontaxable accounts. The funds/securities listed are not based on historical returns, but rather each meets the criteria of a passive, low-cost alternative that can be useful in representing a particular asset class in a portfolio.

Domestic Equities	International Equities
Large Cap	**Large Cap**
Bridgeway Ultra-Large 35*	DFA Large Cap International
DFA Large Cap	Fidelity Spartan International
Dreyfus Basic S&P 500	Vanguard Developed Markets
Fidelity Spartan 500	Vanguard European
SSgA S&P 500	Vanguard Pacific
USAA 500	Vanguard TM International*
Vanguard 500 Index	Vanguard Total International
DFA Enhanced Large**	iShares MSCI EAFE
iShares S&P 500 Index	iShares S&P Europe 350 Index

Vanguard Total Stock Market

Vanguard Total Stock Market VIPERs

Fidelity Spartan Total Market

iShares Russell 1000

iShares Russell 3000

DFA TM US Equity

iShares S&PTOPIX 150 (Japan)

iShares MSCI Pacific ex-Japan

Large-Cap Value

DFA Large Cap Value

DFA TM Marketwide Value*

Vanguard Value

iShares S&P 400 Value

iShares Russell 3000 Value

streetTRACKS DJ Large Value

Large-Cap Value

DFA International Value

DFA TM International Value*

Small Cap

Bridgeway Ultra-Small Company*

DFA Small Cap

DFA TM Small Cap*

DFA Micro Cap

Vanguard SmallCap

Vanguard TM SmallCap*

iShares S&P 600

Small Cap

DFA International Small Company

Small-Cap Value

DFA Small Cap Value

DFA TM Small Cap Value*

Vanguard SmallCap Value

iShares S&P 600 Value

StreetTRACKS DJ Small Value

Small-Cap Value

DFA International Small Cap Value

Real Estate

DFA Real Estate**

Vanguard REIT**

streetTRACKS Wilshire REIT**

TIAA Real Estate Account***

Precious Metals Equity

Vanguard Precious Metals
  and Mining

Commodities

PIMCO Commodity Real
  Return Strategy

Fixed Income: Taxable

DFA Two-Year Global

DFA Global Bond

iShares 1–3 Year Treasury Bond Index

iShares 7–10 Year Treasury
  Bond Index

TIAA-CREF Fixed-Income Annuities

Vanguard Short-Term Treasury

Vanguard Short-Term Bond Index

Vanguard Intermediate-Term Index

Vanguard Inflation-Protected
  Securities**

iShares Lehman TIPS**

I bonds

Emerging Markets

DFA Emerging Markets

DFA Emerging Markets Small Cap

DFA Emerging Markets Value

Vanguard Emerging Markets

iShares MSCI Emerging Markets Index

Fixed Income: Tax-Exempt

DFA Short-Term Municipal Bond
  Portfolio

Vanguard Limited-Term Tax-Exempt

Vanguard Intermediate-Term
  Tax-Exempt

***Note that the TIAA Real Estate Account is only available to qualified investors, and may not be available in all states (most notably California).

Investors need to be aware that the DFA funds are only available through approved financial advisors. There are several hundred such advisors around the country.

The following are sample portfolios for investors using either DFA funds or Vanguard funds in combination with iShares as appropriate. It is important to note that these are only samples in the sense that they are good *starting points* to consider. How much you allocate to each asset class is a personal decision the implications of which should be thoroughly considered prior to implementation.

Sample Portfolios Using DFA Funds and Vanguard Funds/iShares

Tax-Deferred Account: DFA

Asset Class	Target Allocation (%)
DFA Enhanced Large	14
DFA US Large Value	14
DFA US Micro Cap	14
DFA US Small Value	14
DFA Real Estate	14
Total U.S.	**70**
DFA Int'l Large Value	7.5
DFA Int'l Small	7.5
DFA Int'l Small Value	7.5
DFA Emerging Markets	3.75
DFA Emerging Markets Value	3.75
Total Int'l	**30**

Appendix I

Taxable Account: DFA

Asset Class	Target Allocation (%)
DFA Large Company	17.5
DFA Tax-Managed US Marketwide Value	17.5
DFA Tax-Managed US Small	17.5
DFA Tax-Managed US Small Value	17.5
Total U.S.	**70**
DFA Tax-Managed Int'l Large Value	7.5
DFA Int'l Small	7.5
DFA Int'l Small Value	7.5
DFA Emerging Markets	3.75
DFA Emerging Markets Value	3.75
Total Int'l	**30**

Tax-Deferred Account: Vanguard

Asset Class	Target Allocation (%)
Vanguard S&P 500	14
Vanguard Windsor	14
Vanguard SmallCap	14
Vanguard Small Value	14
Vanguard Real Estate	14
Total U.S.	**70**
Vanguard Europe	10
Vanguard Pacific	10
Vanguard Emerging Markets	10
Total Int'l	**30 Percent**

Taxable Account: Vanguard/iShares

Asset Class	Target Allocation (%)
Vanguard 500 Index or iShares 500	17.5
iShares 400V	17.5
Vanguard Tax-Managed US Small or iShares 600	17.5
iShares 600V	17.5
Total U.S.	**70**
Vanguard Tax-Managed International	20
Vanguard Emerging Markets	10
Total Int'l	**30**

Sources and Descriptions of Data for Model and Control Portfolios

One of the benefits of passive asset-class management is the ability to simulate portfolio performance (because with no attempt at security selection or at market timing we basically know what assets were contained within a specific asset class). Wherever possible live data was used. When live data was not available, simulated data was used. Where no data series was available, as in the case of the emerging markets asset class prior to 1987, other data series were substituted with as close a match as possible. Once again I would like to thank DFA. The sections of this book that use control and model portfolios to demonstrate the power of modern portfolio theory (MPT) and the importance of an individual's tolerance for risk in making asset-allocation decisions would not have been possible without the permissions of the following people and organizations. I would like to thank them for their cooperation.

1. U.S. Large Cap—1973–December 1990 S&P 500 Index. January 1991–2003 DFA US Large Company Portfolio net of all fees.

2. Lehman Government/Credit Bond Index–Lehman Brothers.

3. MSCI EAFE Index—Morgan Stanley Capital International.

4. US Small Cap—1973–March 1992 © CRSP, University of Chicago. Used with permission. All rights reserved. April 1992–March 2001 DFA US 6–10 Small Company Portfolio net of all fees. April 2001–2003 DFA US Small Cap Portfolio net of all fees.

5. U.S. Small Value—1973–March 1993 Fama/French US Small Value (excluding Utilities) Simulated Portfolio. April 1993–March 2001 DFA 6–10 Value Portfolio net of all fees. April 2001–DFA US Small Cap Value Portfolio net of all fees.

6. U.S. Large Value—1973–March 1993 Fama/French US Large Value (excluding Utilities) Simulated Portfolio. April 1993–2003 DFA US Large Cap Value Portfolio net of all fees.

7. Real Estate—1973–74 50 percent: US Small Cap as defined above. Used with permission. All rights reserved, and 50 percent US Small Value as defined above. 1975–December 1992 Prof. Donald Keim, Wharton School, excludes health-care REITS. January 1993–2003 DFA Real Estate Portfolio net of all fees.

8. International Value—1973–1974 50 percent EAFE Index and 50 percent international small. 1975–March 1993

Fama/French. April 1993–June 1993 MSCI EAFE Index (substituted due to lack of data); July 1993–February 1994 DFA International High Book-to-Market and Value Portfolios; March 1994–2003 DFA International Value Portfolio net of all fees.

9. International Small—Various sources were used including: Nomura Securities Investment Trust Management Company, Ltd., Tokyo, for the Japanese small company stocks (smaller half of first section, Tokyo Stock Exchange); Prof. Elroy Dimson and Prof. Paul Marsh of the London Business School for the U.K. small-company stocks (Hoare Govett Smaller Companies Index); DFA's Japan, Continental, United Kingdom, and Pacific Rim small-company portfolios; and DFA's International Small Company Portfolio.

- Nineteen seventy-three–March 1986 50 percent: smaller half of Tokyo Stock Exchange, and 50 percent Hoare Govett Smaller Companies Index.

- April 1986–June 1988 50 percent: DFA Japan, and 50 percent DFA United Kingdom Small Company Portfolios net of all fees.

- July 1988–September 1989 50 percent: 50 percent DFA Japan, 30 percent DFA Continental, and 20 percent DFA United Kingdom Small Company Portfolios net of all fees.

- October 1989–March 1990 40 percent: DFA Japan, 30 percent DFA Continental, 20 percent DFA United Kingdom, and 10 percent Pacific Rim Small Company Portfolios net of all fees.

- April 1990–1992 40 percent: DFA Japan, 35 percent DFA Continental, 15 percent DFA United Kingdom, and 10 percent DFA Pacific Rim Small Company Portfolios net of all fees.

- Nineteen ninety-three–September 1996 35 percent: DFA Japan, 35 percent DFA Continental, 15 percent DFA United Kingdom, and 15 percent DFA Pacific Rim Small Company Portfolios net of all fees.

- October 1996–2003 DFA International Small Company Portfolio net of all fees

10. Emerging Markets—Countries currently include Argentina, Brazil, Chile, Hungary, Indonesia, Israel, Malaysia, Mexico, Philippines, Poland, South Korea, Taiwan, Thailand, and Turkey. Nineteen seventy-three–74: International small as above, 1975–86 50 percent, international large value, and 50 percent: international small as above. Nineteen eighty-seven–February 1993 MSCI Emerging Markets Index (equally weighted). March 1993–May 1994 DFA Emerging Markets Closed-End Portfolio net of all fees. June 1994–2003 DFA Emerging Markets Portfolio net of all fees.

11. Two-year fixed income—DFA: Nineteen seventy-three–February 1996 simulated using U.S. government instruments with maximum maturity of two years; March 1996–2003 DFA Two-Year Global Fixed Income Portfolio.

Notes

Foreword

1. *Wall Street Journal,* December 24, 1998.

Introduction

1. *Wall Street Journal,* January 28, 1997.
2. *Wall Street Journal,* October 4, 1999.
3. Standard & Poor's, Annual Survey of S&P Indexed Products as of December 2002.
4. Ron Kozlowski, "Indexed Assets Pass $3 Trillion Mark for First Time," *Pensions & Investments* (March 22, 2004).
5. Nassim Nicholas Taleb, *Fooled by Randomness.*

Chapter 1: Why Individual Investors Play the Loser's Game

1. Roger G. Ibbotson and Paul D. Kaplan, "Does Asset Allocation Policy Explain 40%, 90%, or 100% of Performance?" *Financial Analysts Journal* (January/February 2000).
2. ABC News' *20/20,* November 27, 1992.
3. *New York Times,* March 30, 1997.
4. Ibid.
5. Ibid.
6. Quoted in Peter Bernstein, *Against the Gods.*
7. *San Francisco Chronicle,* November 24, 1996.

Chapter 2: Active Portfolio Management Is a Loser's Game

1. Brad Barber and Terrance Odean, "Trading Is Hazardous to Your Wealth: The Common Stock Investment Performance of Individual Investors," *Journal of Finance* (April 2000).

2. Brad Barber and Terrance Odean, "Do Investors Trade Too Much?" *American Economic Review* (December 1999).

3. Brad Barber and Terrance Odean, "Boys Will Be Boys: Gender, Overconfidence and Common Stock Investment," *Quarterly Journal of Economics* (February 2001).

4. Brad Barber and Terrance Odean, "Too Many Cooks Spoil the Profit: The Performance of Investment Clubs," *Financial Analysts Journal* (January/February 2000).

5. www.dfaus.com.

6. *Fortune* (March 15, 1999).

7. *Fortune* (October 11, 1999).

8. "Why Top Performance Is a Poor Indicator of Future Performance," Smith Barney Consulting Group, 1997.

9. Charles Ellis, *Winning the Loser's Game: Timeless Strategies for Successful Investing*, p. 6.

10. Quoted in Dean LeBaron and Romesh Vaitilingam, *The Ultimate Investor*, p. 200.

11. *New York Times* News Service, 1997.

12. *Wall Street Journal,* January 3, 2002.

13. Jonathan Clements, *25 Myths You've Got to Avoid If You Want to Manage Your Money Right,* p. 86.

14. *Newsweek* (August 7, 1995).

15. *Barron's* Online (June 2, 1997).

16. Rick Ferri, *Serious Money.*

17. *BusinessWeek* (June 9, 2003).

18. *Journal of Finance* (June 1995).

19. *American Association of Individual Investors Journal* (September 1996).

20. W. Scott Simon, *Index Mutual Funds.*

21. *BusinessWeek* (March 9, 1998).

22. Christopher R. Blake and Matthew R. Morey, "Morningstar Ratings

and Mutual Fund Performance," *Journal of Financial and Quantitative Analysis* (September 2000).

23. John Bogle, "The Stock Market Universe—Stars, Comets, and the Sun," speech before the Financial Analysts of Philadelphia, February 15, 2001.
24. *New York Times,* May 19, 2002.
25. *Fortune* (July 8, 2002).
26. *Investment Advisor* (September 1994).
27. *Kiplinger's Personal Finance* magazine (February 1997).
28. *Wall Street Journal,* April 5, 1996.
29. *BusinessWeek* (June 16, 1997).
30. *Wall Street Journal,* July 3, 1997.
31. John Merrill, *Beyond Stocks.*
32. Ibid.
33. Burton Malkiel, *A Random Walk Down Wall Street,* p. 179.
34. Andrew Smithers and Stephen Wright, *Valuing Wall Street.*
35. FutureMetrics and Dimensional Fund Advisors.
36. *Financial Analysts Journal* (July/August 1996).
37. Charles Ellis, *Investment Policy: How to Win the Loser's Game,* p. 24.
38. *St. Louis Post-Dispatch,* July 6, 1997.
39. Peter Bernstein, *Against the Gods.*
40. Standard and Poor's Indices vs. Active Funds Scorecard, Fourth Quarter 2002.
41. *Fortune* (February 17, 1997).
42. John Bogle, *John Bogle on Investing,* p. 89.
43. *Fortune* (February 17, 1997).
44. John Bogle, *John Bogle on Investing,* p. 89.
45. Lipper Analytical Services.
46. Standard and Poor's Indices vs. Active Funds Scorecard, Fourth Quarter 2002.
47. Ibid.
48. Richard E. Evans and Burton G. Malkiel, *The Index Fund Solution.*
49. *BusinessWeek* (February 22, 1999).

50. Edited by Peter Bernstein, *The Portable MBA in Investing.*
51. Burton Malkiel, *A Random Walk Down Wall Street.*
52. *SmartMoney* (June 1997).
53. Ibid.
54. Edited by Peter Bernstein, *The Portable MBA in Investing.*
55. *Financial Advisor* (March 2001).
56. Introduction to the Restatement, pp. 5–6.
57. Ron Kozlowski, "Indexed Assets Pass $3 Trillion Mark for First Time," *Pensions & Investments* (March 22, 2004).
58. *Institutional Investor* (May 1997).
59. Morningstar.com.

Chapter 3: Efficient Markets I—Information and Costs

1. *Wall Street Journal,* July 14, 1997.
2. Peter Bernstein, *Against the Gods.*
3. *Journal of Applied Economics* (Spring 1996).
4. *Financial Management* (Spring 1996).
5. Michael Buckle, Andrew Clare, Owain ap Gwilym, and Stephen Thomas, "The Transaction-by-Transaction of Interest Rate and Equity Index Futures to Macroeconomic Announcements," *Journal of Derivatives* (Winter 1998).
6. *Fortune* (March 17, 1997).
7. *Journal of Portfolio Management* (Fall 1974).
8. Edited by Peter Bernstein, *The Portable MBA in Investing.*
9. *Investment Policy,* Charles Ellis.
10. *BusinessWeek* (March 9, 1998).
11. John Merrill, *Beyond Stocks.*
12. Richard Thaler, *The Winner's Curse.*
13. John Merrill, *Beyond Stocks.*
14. *Wall Street Journal,* January 2, 1997.
15. *Wall Street Journal,* January 30, 1997.
16. *Worth* (September, 1995).
17. *Fortune* (December 23, 1996).
18. *Wall Street Journal,* March 17, 1997.
19. *Fortune* (May 12, 1997).
20. *St. Louis Post-Dispatch,* October 4, 1997.

21. Nick Murray, *The Excellent Investment Advisor.*
22. Mark Carhart, "On Persistence in Mutual Fund Performance," *Journal of Finance* (March 1997).
23. Russ Wermers, "Mutual Fund Performance: An Empirical Decomposition into Stock-Picking Talent, Style, Transaction Costs, and Expenses," *Journal of Finance* (August 2000).
24. Standard and Poor's Indices vs. Active Funds Scorecard, Fourth Quarter 2002.
25. David Booth, "The Value Added of Active Management: International Single Country Funds," January 1997.
26. "Efficient Markets: Fund Managers as Fruit Flies," *Investors Chronicle,* March 22, 1996.
27. *Wall Street Journal,* December 30, 1996.
28. *Journal of Finance* (March 1959).
29. Burton Malkiel, *A Random Walk Down Wall Street.*
30. William Sherden, *The Fortune Sellers.*
31. Yo, "Bond Index Funds Wield Better Yields," *InvestmentNews,* January 25, 1999.
32. Kevin Stephenson, "Just How Bad Are Economists at Predicting Interest Rates?" *Journal of Investing* (Summer 1997).
33. John Bogle, *Bogle on Mutual Funds.*
34. William Reichenstein, "Bond Fund Returns and Expenses: A Study of Bond Market Efficiency," *Journal of Investing* (Winter 1999).
35. Dale L. Domian and William Reichenstein, "Predicting Municipal Bond Fund Returns," *Journal of Investing* (Fall 2002).
36. Bridge/Dimensional Fund Advisors.
37. *New York Times,* July 11, 1999.
38. *St. Louis Post-Dispatch,* August 12, 1997.
39. Robert D. Arnott, Andrew L. Berkin, and Jia Ye, "How Well Have Taxable Investors Been Served in the 1980s and 1990s?" *Journal of Portfolio Management* (Summer 2000).
40. *Barron's* (June 15, 1998).
41. Money.cnn.com, February 1999.
42. *Wall Street Journal,* December 22, 1998.

Chapter 4: Efficient Markets II—Risk

1. Nai-fu Chen and Feng Zhang, "Risk and Return of Value Stocks," *The Journal of Business* (October 1998).
2. *Journal of Applied Corporate Finance* (Summer 1993).
3. Bala Arshanapalli, "The Dimensions of International Equity Style," *Journal of Investing* (Spring 1998).
4. Christopher R. Blake, Edwin J. Elton, and Martin Gruber, "The Performance of Bond Mutual Funds," *The Journal of Business* (July 1993).
5. Dimensional Fund Advisors.
6. David Plecha, Dimensional Fund Advisors, "Fixed Income Investing," working paper, July 2001.

Chapter 5: The Five-Factor Model

1. Dimensional Fund Advisors.
2. *Fortune* (April 3, 1995).

Chapter 6: Volatility, Return, and Risk

1. Dimensional Fund Advisors.

Chapter 7: Six Steps to a Diversified Portfolio

1. *Wall Street Journal,* June 17, 1997.

Chapter 8: How to Build a Model Portfolio

1. David Laster, "Measuring Gains from International Equity Diversification: The Bootstrap Approach," *Journal of Investing* (Fall 1998).
2. John Merrill, *Beyond Stocks.*
3. Edited by Peter Bernstein, *The Portable MBA in Investing.*
4. Susan E. K. Christoffersen, Christopher C. Geczy, David K. Musto, and Adam V. Reed, "The Limits to Dividend Arbitrage: Implications for Cross-Border Investment." Draft (May 2003). (http://knowledge.wharton.upenn.edu/index.cfm)

Chapter 10: The Care and Maintenance of the Portfolio
1. *Financial Planning* (February 1997).
2. *Wall Street Journal,* October 8, 1996.
3. *BusinessWeek* (September 16, 1996).

Chapter 11: Implementing the Winning Strategy
1. *Fee Advisor* (September/October 1996).
2. John Merrill, *Beyond Stocks.*

Chapter 12: Summary
1. 1997 annual letter to shareholders of Berkshire Hathaway.
2. Dwight Lee and James Verbrugge, "The Efficient Market Theory Thrives on Criticism," *Journal of Applied Corporate Finance* (Spring 1996).
3. Nick Murray, *The Excellent Investment Advisor.*
4. *BusinessWeek* (March 10, 1997).
5. *Journal of Finance* (March 1997).
6. *Wall Street Journal,* April 4, 1997.
7. John Bogle, *Bogle on Mutual Funds.*
8. *Money* (August 1995).
9. *Worth* (February 1996).
10. John Bogle, *Bogle on Mutual Funds.*
11. Ibid.
12. *St. Louis Post-Dispatch,* October 4, 1997.
13. *Wall Street Journal,* December 31, 1996.

Appendix D: The IPO Myth
1. *Journal of Finance* (March 1995).
2. *Wall Street Journal,* February 24, 1999.
3. *Fortune* (November 23, 1998).
4. *Journal of Finance* (June 1999).
5. *Wall Street Journal,* February 24, 1999.

Appendix E: News Flash: Top Performance Is a Poor Indicator of Future Performance

1. "Why Top Performance Is a Poor Indicator of Future Performance," Smith Barney Consulting Group, 1997.

Appendix F: What If Everyone Indexed?

1. Investment Company Institute.

Appendix H: Commodities: A Diversification and Hedging Tool

1. Dimensional Fund Advisors.
2. www.gs.com/gsci.
3. Dimensional Fund Advisors.
4. Paul D. Kaplan and Scott L. Lummer, "GSCI Collateralized Futures As a Hedging and Diversification Tool for Institutional Portfolios: An Update," *Journal of Investing* (Winter 1998).
5. Dimensional Fund Advisors.
6. Dimensional Fund Advisors.
7. Christopher A. Moth and John Kirk, "Real Return Fund: The Case for a Real Asset Class," Institute for Fiduciary Education, July 1, 2000.
8. Mark J. P. Anson, *Handbook of Alternative Assets,* p. 203.

Glossary

Active management The attempt to uncover securities the market has either under- or overvalued; also the attempt to time investment decisions in order to be more heavily invested when the market is rising and less so when the market is falling.

Alpha A measure of performance against a benchmark. *Positive alpha* represents outperformance; *negative alpha* represents underperformance.

Arbitrage The process by which investors exploit the price difference between two exactly alike securities by simultaneously buying one at a lower price and selling the other at a higher price (thereby avoiding risk). This action locks in a risk-free profit for the arbitrageur (person engaging in the arbitrage) and, in an efficient market, eventually brings the prices back into equilibrium.

Asset allocation The process of determining what percentage of assets should be dedicated to which specific asset classes. Also the outcome of that process.

Asset class A group of assets with similar risk and reward characteristics. Cash, debt instruments, real estate, and equities are examples of asset classes. Within a general asset class, such as equities, there are more specific classes such as large-cap stocks and small-cap stocks, and domestic and international stocks.

Barra Indices The Barra Indices divide the three major S&P Indices (400 for mid cap, 500 for large cap, and 600 for small cap) into growth and value subindices. The top 50 percent of the market capitalization of stocks as ranked by BtM are considered value stocks and the bottom 50 percent are considered growth stocks. This creates both value and growth indices for all three S&P Indices.

Basis point One one-hundredth of 1 percent, or 0.0001.

Benchmark An appropriate standard against which investments can be judged. Actively managed large-cap growth funds should be judged against a large-cap growth index, such as the S&P 500, while small-cap managers should be judged against a small-cap index, such as the Russell 2000.

Bid-offer spread The bid is the price at which you can sell a security, and the offer is the price you must pay to buy a security. The spread is the difference between the two prices.

Book-to-market value (BtM) The ratio of the book value per share to the market price per share, or book value divided by market capitalization.

Book value An accounting term for the equity of a company. Equity is equal to assets less liabilities; it is often expressed in pershare terms. Book value per share is equal to equity divided by the number of shares.

Call An option contract that gives the holder the right, but not the obligation, to buy a security at a predetermined price on a specific date *(European call)* or during a specific period *(American call)*.

Churning Excessive trading in a client's account by a broker seeking to maximize commissions, regardless of the client's best interests. Churning is illegal.

Closet index fund   An actively managed fund whose holdings closely resemble the holdings of an index fund.

Coefficient of correlation   A statistical parameter that quantifies how closely related the price movement of different securities or asset classes is; the higher the coefficient, the more prices tend to move in the same direction.

Compensated risk   Risk that cannot be diversified away (e.g., the risk of owning stocks). The market rewards investors for accepting compensated risk with a risk premium (greater *expected* return) commensurate with the amount of risk accepted.

Concave investing   Specifically the opposite of convex investing. Investors follow a strategy of purchasing yesterday's underperformers (buying low) and selling yesterday's outperformers (selling high).

Convex investing   The tendency for individual investors to buy yesterday's top-performing stocks and mutual funds (buying high) and sell yesterday's underperformers (selling low).

Constant maturity   An interest-rate benchmark based on the yield of a synthetic security of appropriate maturity as interpolated from the Treasury yield curve. For example, the five-year constant-maturity Treasury rate is an average yield on U.S. Treasury securities adjusted to a constant maturity of five years, as made available by the Federal Reserve Board. The return of the constant maturity five-year Treasury assumes a strategy consisting of purchasing a five-year bond and then holding it for one year and then selling it replacing it with a new bond with a five-year maturity.

CPI   Consumer price index. A measure of price inflation.

Correlation   In mathematics, correlation is the measure of the linear relationship between two variables. Values can range from +1.00 (perfect correlation) to −1.00 (perfect negative correlation). An example of a strong positive correlation would be stocks of two oil companies. A strong negative correlation might exist between an oil company (that benefits from rising oil prices) and an airline company (that would benefit from a fall in oil prices).

CRSP Center for Research in Security Prices at the University of Chicago, a financial research center at the University of Chicago Graduate School of Business. CRSP creates and maintains premier historical U.S. databases for stocks (NASDAQ, AMEX, NYSE), indices, bonds, and mutual funds. These databases are used by leaders in academic and corporate communities for financial, economic, and accounting research.

Data mining A technique for building predictive models of the real world by discerning patterns in masses of historical data.

Diamond An exchange-traded fund that replicates the Dow Jones Industrial Average.

Distressed stocks Stocks with high BtM and/or low P/E ratios. Distressed stocks are generally considered to be value stocks.

DJIA Dow Jones Industrial Average. An index of thirty of the largest U.S. stocks.

Duration The approximate change in the value of a fixed-income security that will result from a 1 percent change in interest rates. Duration is stated in years. For example, a five-year duration means the bond will decrease in value by approximately 5 percent if interest rates rise 1 percent and increase in value by approximately 5 percent if interest rates fall 1 percent. Unlike maturity, duration takes into account interest payments that occur throughout the life of the bond. The longer the duration, the more volatile the instrument.

EAFE Index The Europe, Australasia, and Far East Index, similar to the S&P 500 Index in that it consists of the stocks of the large companies from the EAFE countries. The stocks within the index are weighted by market capitalization.

Efficient market A state in which trading systems fail to produce returns in excess of the market's overall rate of return because everything currently knowable about a company is already incorporated into the stock price. The next piece of available information will be random as to whether it will be better or worse than the market expects. An efficient market is also one in which the trading costs are low.

Emerging markets The capital markets of less developed countries that are beginning to develop characteristics of developed countries, such as higher per capita income. Countries typically included in this category would be Brazil, Mexico, Thailand, and Korea.

Efficient Markets Hypothesis (EMH) A hypothesis that markets are efficient. (See efficient market.)

Exchange-traded fund (ETF) For practical purposes these act like open-ended, no-load mutual funds. Like mutual funds, they can be created to represent virtually any index or asset class. ETFs represent a cross between an exchange-listed stock and an open-ended, no-load mutual fund. Like stocks (but unlike mutual funds), they trade throughout the day.

Ex-ante Before the fact.

Expense ratio The operating expenses of a fund expressed as a percentage of total assets. These expenses are subtracted from the investment performance of a fund in order to determine the net return to shareholders.

Ex-post After the fact.

Five percent/25 percent rule Numerical formula used to determine the need to rebalance a portfolio.

Fundamental security analysis The attempt to uncover mispriced securities by focusing on predicting future earnings.

Futures contract An agreement to purchase or sell a specific collection of securities or a physical commodity at a specified price and time in the future. For example, an S&P 500 futures contract represents ownership interest in the S&P 500 Index at a specified price for delivery on a specific date on a particular exchange.

Growth stock   A stock trading, relative to the overall market, at a high P/E ratio (or at a relatively low BtM ratio) because the market anticipates rapid earnings growth relative to the overall market.

Hedge fund   A fund that generally has the ability to invest in a wide variety of asset classes. These funds often use leverage in an attempt to increase returns.

I bond   A bond that provides both a fixed rate of return and an inflation-protection component. The principal value of the bond increases by the total of the fixed rate and the inflation component. The income is deferred for federal and state and local income-tax purposes until the bond is sold or it matures.

Index fund   A passively managed fund that seeks to replicate the performance of a particular index (e.g., the Wilshire 5000, the S&P 500, or the Russell 2000) by buying all the securities in that index in direct proportion to their weight by market capitalization within that index and holding them.

Initial public offering (IPO)   The first offering of a company's stock to the public.

Institutional fund   A mutual fund that is not available to individual investors. Typical clients are insurance companies, trust companies, pension and profit-sharing plans, and endowment funds.

Institutional-style fund   A mutual fund that is available to individual investors, under certain conditions, such as through registered investment advisors. These advisors require their clients to commit to the same type of disciplined, long-term, buy-and-hold strategy that is typical of institutional investors.

Investment graffiti Advice on market or securities values that is designed to titillate, stimulate, and excite you into action but has no basis in reality.

Investment pornography Extreme examples of investment graffiti.

Leverage The use of debt to increase the amount of assets that can be acquired, for example, to buy stock. Leverage increases the riskiness of a portfolio.

Loser's game A game in which, while it is not impossible to win, the odds of winning are so low that it does not pay to play.

Market capitalization The market price per share times the number of shares.

Market-cap weighting The percentage holding of individual stocks determined by their percentage of market capitalization relative to the total market capitalization of all stocks within an index or other benchmark. An index fund's holdings are market-cap weighted, not equally weighted.

Micro-cap The smallest stocks by market capitalization: The ninth and tenth CRSP deciles. Other definitions used are the smallest 5 percent of stocks by market capitalization and stocks with a market capitalization of less than about $200 million.

Modern Portfolio Theory (MPT) A body of academic work founded on the following concepts. First, markets are too efficient to allow returns in excess of the market's overall rate of return to be achieved consistently through trading systems. Active management is therefore counterproductive. Second, asset classes can be expected to achieve, over sustained periods, returns that are commensurate with their level of risk. Riskier asset classes, such as small companies and value companies, will produce higher returns as compensation for their higher risk. Third, diversification across asset classes can increase returns and reduce risk. For any given level of risk, a portfolio can be constructed that will produce the highest expected return. Finally, there is no one right portfolio for every investor. Each investor must choose an asset allocation that results in a portfolio with an acceptable level of risk.

Mortgage-backed security (MBS) A financial instrument representing an interest in a pool of mortgage loans (either commercial or residential).

MPT Modern Portfolio Theory.

NAIC National Association of Investment Clubs.

NASD The National Association of Securities Dealers.

NASDQ or **NASDAQ** The National Association of Securities Dealers (Automated) Quotations. A computerized marketplace in which securities are traded, frequently called the "over-the-counter market."

NASDAQ-100 Index The one-hundred largest capitalization stocks listed on NASDAQ.

NAV Net asset value.

Negative Convexity If its duration decreases when interest rates fall, a security exhibits negative convexity.

No-load A mutual fund that does not impose any charge for purchases or sales.

Nominal returns Returns that have not been adjusted for the impact of inflation.

NYSE New York Stock Exchange.

Out of sample Data from a study covering different time periods or different geographic regions from those of the original study.

P/E ratio The ratio of stock price to earnings. Stocks with high P/E ratios are considered growth stocks; stocks with low P/E ratios are considered value stocks.

Passive asset-class funds Funds that buy and hold all (or a large sample of) securities within a particular asset class. The weighting of each security within the fund is typically equal to its weighting, by market capitalization, within the asset class. Each security is then typically held until it no longer fits the definition of the asset class to which the fund is seeking exposure. For example, a small company might grow into a large company and then no longer fit within the small company asset class. Fund managers may also use common sense and research to implement screens to eliminate certain securities from consideration (in an attempt to improve risk-adjusted returns). To be considered a passive fund, however, those screens cannot be based on any technical or fundamental security analysis. Examples of passive screens would be: minimum market capitalization, minimum number of years of operating history, and minimum number of market makers in the company stock.

Passive management A buy-and-hold investment strategy, specifically contrary to active management. Characteristics of the passive-management approach include: lower portfolio turnover, lower operating expenses and transactions costs, greater tax efficiency, fully invested at all times, no style drift, and a long-term perspective.

Positive convexity If its duration increases when interest rates fall, a security exhibits positive convexity.

Prudent Investor Rule A doctrine imbedded within the American legal code stating that a person responsible for the management of someone else's assets must manage those assets in a manner appropriate to the financial circumstance and tolerance for risk of the beneficiary.

Put An option contract that gives the holder the right, but not the obligation, to sell a security at a predetermined price on a specific date *(European put)* or during a specific period *(American put)*.

Qubes (QQQ) An exchange-traded fund that tracks the NASDAQ-100 Index.

Real returns Returns that reflect purchasing power as they are adjusted for the impact of inflation.

Rebalancing The process of restoring a portfolio to its original asset allocation. Rebalancing can be accomplished either through adding newly investable funds or by selling portions of the best-performing asset classes and using the proceeds to purchase additional amounts of the underperforming asset classes.

Registered investment advisor A designation representing that a financial consultant's firm is registered with the appropriate national (SEC) or state regulators and that the RIA representatives for that firm have passed the required exams.

REIT Real Estate Investment Trust. A trust that invests in real estate.

Risk premium The higher *expected,* not guaranteed, return for accepting the possibility of a negative outcome.

Russell 1000 The largest one thousand companies within the Russell 3000 Index.

Russell 2000 The smallest two thousand of the largest three thousand stocks within the Russell 3000 Index. Generally used as a benchmark for small-cap stocks.

Retail funds Mutual funds that are sold to the general public, as opposed to institutional investors.

ROA Return on assets.

S&P 400 Index A market-cap-weighted index of four hundred mid-cap stocks.

S&P 500 Index A market-cap-weighted index of five hundred of the largest U.S. stocks designed to cover a broad and representative sampling of industries.

S&P 600 Index A market-cap-weighted index of six hundred small-cap stocks.

SEC   Securities and Exchange Commission.

Sector Fund   A fund that restricts its investments to a single industry or sector of the economy (e.g., health care, technology).

Serial correlation   The correlation of a variable with itself over successive time intervals. Also known as autocorrelation.

Sharpe Ratio   A measure of the annual average return earned above the average rate of return earned on riskless one-month U.S. Treasury bills relative to the risk taken, with risk being defined as standard deviation of returns. Example: The return earned on an asset was 10 percent. The rate of one-month Treasury bills was 4 percent. The standard deviation was 20 percent. The Sharpe Ratio would be equal to 10 percent minus 4 percent (6 percent) divided by 20 percent, or 0.3.

Short selling   Borrowing a security for the purpose of immediately selling it, with the expectation that the investor will be able to buy the security back at a later date at a lower price.

Spiders (SPDR)   Exchange-traded funds that replicate the various S&P Indices.

Standard deviation   A measure of volatility or risk. For example, given a portfolio with a 12 percent annualized return and an 11 percent standard deviation, an investor can expect that in thirteen out of twenty annual periods (about two-thirds of the time) the return on that portfolio will fall within one standard deviation, or between 1 percent (12 percent − 11 percent) and 23 percent (12 percent + 11 percent). The remaining one-third of the time an investor should expect that the annual return will fall outside the 1 percent–23 percent range. Two standard deviations (11 percent × 2) would account for 95 percent (19 out of 20) of the periods. The range of expected returns would be between −10 percent (12 percent − 22 percent) and 34 percent (12 percent + 22 percent). The greater the standard deviation, the greater the volatility of a portfolio. Standard deviation can be measured for varying time periods, e.g., you can have a monthly standard deviation or an annualized standard deviation measuring the volatility for a given time frame.

Style drift   The moving away from the original asset allocation of a portfolio, either by the purchase of securities outside the particular asset class a fund represents or by not rebalancing to adjust for significant differences in performance of the various asset classes within a portfolio.

Survivorship bias   Funds that perform poorly close because of redemptions by investors or they are merged out of existence by their sponsor. If care is not taken to include the performance data of all funds that existed during an analysis period (whether or not the funds disappeared), results can be skewed to appear better than the reality.

Tactical Asset Allocation (TAA)   Attempt to outperform a benchmark by actively shifting the portfolio's exposure to various asset classes (the portfolio's asset allocation).

Three-Factor Model   Differences in stock returns are best explained by company size (market capitalization) and price (book-to-market [BtM] ratio) characteristics. Taken together, research has shown that the three factors on average explain more than 96 percent of the performance of diversified stock portfolios.

TIPS   Treasury Inflation-Protected Security. A bond that receives a fixed stated rate of return, but also increases its principal by the changes in the Consumer Price Index. Its fixed-interest payment is calculated on the inflated principal, which is eventually repaid at maturity.

Tracking error   The amount by which the performance of a fund differs from the appropriate index or benchmark. More generally, when referring to a whole portfolio, the amount by which the performance of the portfolio differs from a widely accepted benchmark, such as the S&P 500 Index or the Wilshire 5000 Index.

Turnover The trading activity of a fund as it sells securities from a portfolio and replaces them with new ones. Assume that a fund began the year with a portfolio of $100 million in various securities. If the fund sold $50 million of the original securities and replaced them with $50 million of new securities, it would have a turnover rate of 50 percent.

Uncompensated risk Risk that can be diversified away (e.g., the risk of owning a single stock or sector of the market). Since the risk can be diversified away, investors are not rewarded with a risk premium (higher expected return) for accepting this type of risk.

Value stocks Companies that have relatively low P/E ratios or relatively high BtM ratios. These are considered the opposite of growth stocks.

Variable annuity An investment product with an insurance component. Taxes are deferred until funds are withdrawn.

WEBS World Equity Benchmark Securities are exchange-traded funds that track various foreign country indices such as the United Kingdom, German, and French equivalents of the S&P 500 Index.

Winner's game A game in which the odds of winning are reasonably high and the prize of winning is commensurate with the risk of playing.

Recommended Reading

One of the reasons I decided to write this book is that I found no comprehensive book that explained to the average investor how markets work, why they work the way they do, and how to make them work for you. I tried to accomplish these objectives and to provide some very specific guidance on ways you can implement what you have learned. I hope I have succeeded.

In my research I have come across several books that I believe should be read by every investor. They are all written in a way that can provide value to every reader. These books are:

- Gary Belsky and Thomas Gilovich, *Why Smart People Make Big Money Mistakes.*
- Peter Bernstein, *Capital Ideas* and *Against the Gods.*
- William Bernstein, *The Intelligent Asset Allocator* and *The Four Pillars of Investing.*
- John Bogle, *Common Sense on Mutual Funds.*
- Charles Ellis, *Winning the Loser's Game.*
- Martin Fridson, *Investment Illusions.*
- Howard Kurtz, *The Fortune Tellers.*

Recommended Reading

- Burton G. Malkiel, *A Random Walk Down Wall Street.*
- Ron Ross, *The Unbeatable Market.*
- Bill Schultheis, *The Coffeehouse Investor.*
- Jeremy Siegel, *Stocks for the Long Run.*
- William Sharpe, *Portfolio Theory and Capital Markets.*
- Hersh Shefrin, *Beyond Greed and Fear.*
- William Sherden, *The Fortune Sellers.*
- W. Scott Simon, *Index Mutual Funds* and *The Prudent Investor Act.*
- Nassim Nicholas Taleb, *Fooled by Randomness.*
- Bruce J. Temkin, Don Phillips, and Deborah Thomas, *The Terrible Truth About Investing.*
- Ben Warwick, *Searching for Alpha.*

I would like to note that I owe a special thanks to Charles Ellis. His book provided the link between understanding the winner and loser games of tennis and the winner and loser games in the world of investing.

For those interested in learning about the history of financial follies there are three excellent books. The first is Charles Mackay's *Extraordinary Popular Delusions and the Madness of Crowds* (1841). His book is as relevant today as it was when it was first published more than 160 years ago. The others are *Devil Take the Hindmost,* by Edward Chancellor, and *Irrational Exuberance,* by Robert Shiller.

Acknowledgments

No book is ever the work of one individual. This book is no exception. I thank my partners at Buckingham Asset Management and BAM Advisor Services: Susan Shackelford-Davis, Paul Forman, Steve Funk, Bob Gellman, Ed Goldberg, Joe Hempen, Mont Levy, Irv Rothenberg, Bert Schweizer III, and Stuart Zimmerman, for their support and encouragement. I would also like to thank Wendy Cook, Rick Hill, Jared Kizer, Laura Latragna, Vladimir Masek, and Steve Nothum for their contributions. Vladimir, thank you very much for your valuable insights and editorial suggestions. Steve and Jared, thanks for the help on fact checking and statistical analysis. Any errors are certainly mine.

A special note of thanks goes to my good friend Larry Goldfarb, who not only provided editorial assistance but also contributed greatly to the organization and structure of the original edition of this book.

The greatest contribution was made by my agent, Sam Fleischman, who, through his suggestions on structuring and his editing work, added tremendously to the quality of the book. Any shortcomings are mine. I cannot imagine a better relationship between author and agent.

Acknowledgments

Many other people made valuable contributions. I would be remiss if I did not give a special note of thanks to Dana Stephens for all the technical computer support he provided. Without him there would never have been a manuscript.

I thank the people at DFA. They provided the source for much of the material and anecdotes in the book. A special thanks to Weston Wellington of DFA. I have learned much from him. He seems to always be able to explain difficult concepts in an easy and often humorous way. Weston was the source of much of the humor in the book. I would also like to thank Bo Cornell of DFA for his assistance.

I especially thank the love of my life, my wife, Mona. She showed tremendous patience in reading and rereading the numerous drafts. If the book manages to make clear difficult concepts, she deserves the credit. I would also like to thank her for her tremendous support and understanding for the lost weekends and the many nights that I sat at the computer well into the early morning hours. She has always provided whatever support was needed, and then some—walking through life with her has truly been a gracious experience.

Finally, I thank my mother for always believing in me, for always supporting me, and for being the best mother anyone could ask for.

Index

Index

Index

Index

Index

Index

Index

Index

Index